The
FADE OUT

IMAGE COMICS, INC.
Robert Kirkman - Chief Operating Officer
Erik Larsen - Chief Financial Officer
Todd McFarlane - President
Marc Silvestri - Chief Executive Officer
Jim Valentino - Vice-President
Eric Stephenson - Publisher
Ron Richards - Director of Business Development
Jennifer de Guzman - Director of Trade Book Sales
Kat Salazar - Director of PR & Marketing
Corey Murphy - Director of Retail Sales
Jeremy Sullivan - Director of Digital Sales
Emilio Bautista - Sales Assistant
Branwyn Bigglestone - Senior Accounts Manager
Emily Miller - Accounts Manager
Jessica Ambriz - Administrative Assistant
Tyler Shainline - Events Coordinator
David Brothers - Content Manager
Jonathan Chan - Production Manager
Drew Gill - Art Director
Meredith Wallace - Print Manager
Addison Duke - Production Artist
Vincent Kukua - Production Artist
Tricia Ramos - Production Assistant
IMAGECOMICS.COM

MEDIA INQUIRIES SHOULD BE DIRECTED TO UTA - Agents Julien Thuan and Geoff Morley

THE FADE OUT: ACT ONE. First printing. February 2015. Contains material originally published in magazine form as THE FADE OUT #1-4.

ISBN: 978-1-63215-171-1

 Publication design by Sean Phillips

The
FADE OUT

Ed Brubaker
Sean Phillips
Colors by
Elizabeth Breitweiser

Act One

Cast Of Characters

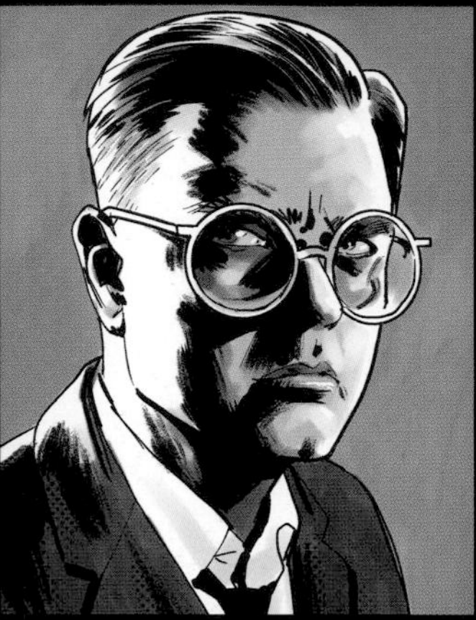

CHARLIE PARISH
Screenwriter

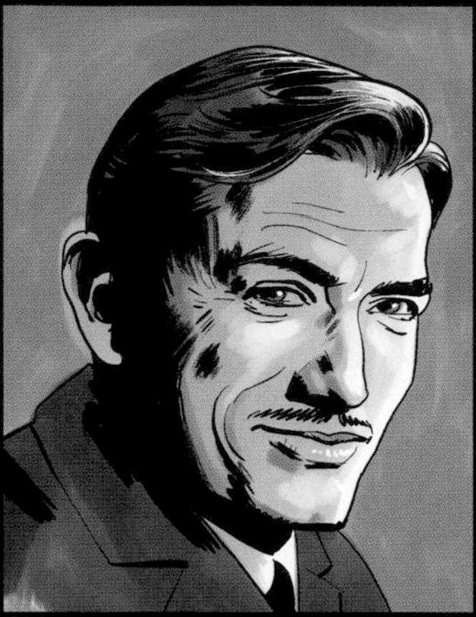

EARL RATH
Dashing Leading Man

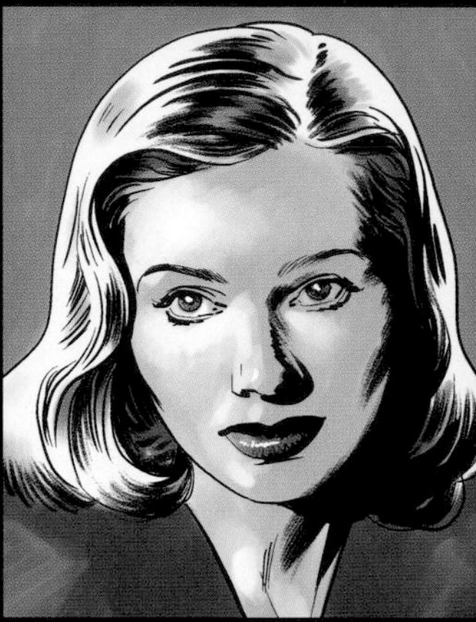

VALERIA SOMMERS
Up-and-coming Starlet

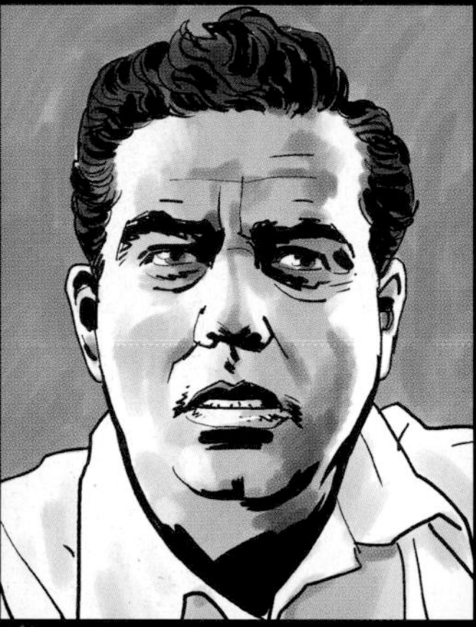

GIL MASON
Ex-Screenwriter

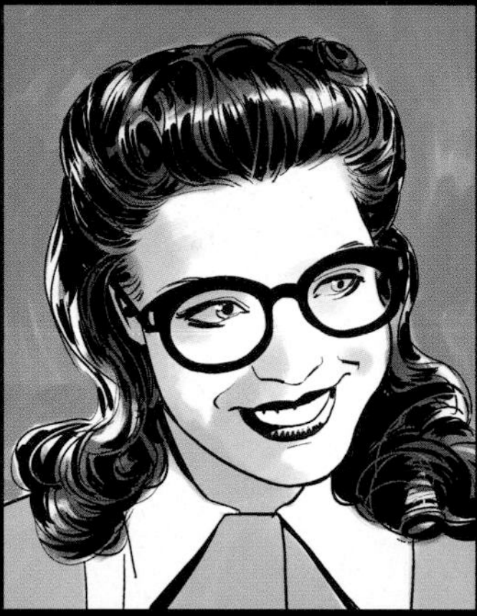

DOTTIE QUINN
Studio Publicity Girl

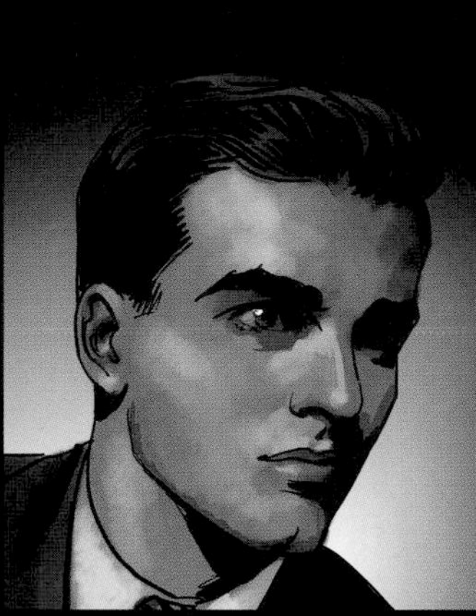

TYLER GRAVES
Hollywood Heart-throb

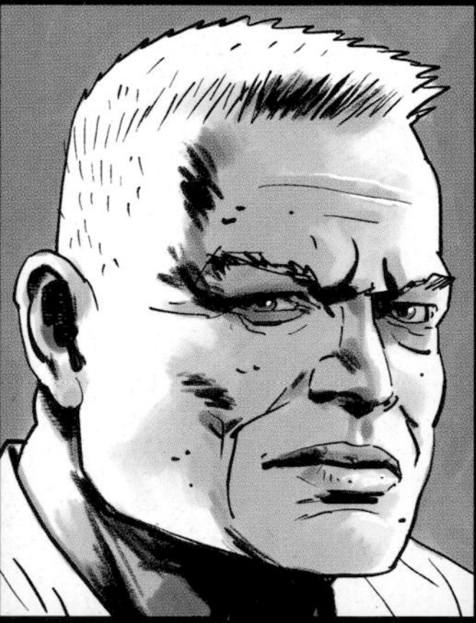

PHIL BRODSKY
Studio Security

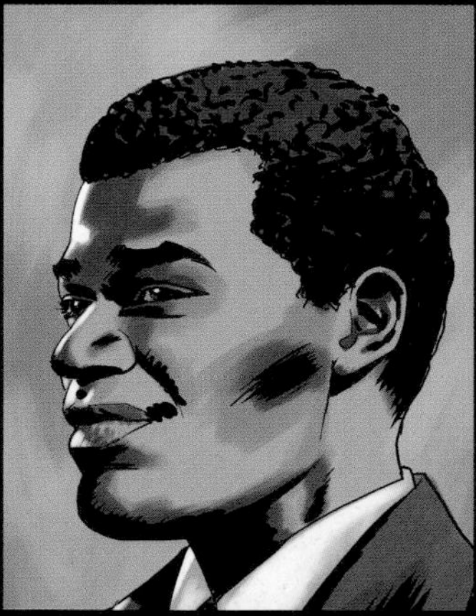

JACK "FLAPJACK" JONES
One-time Child Actor

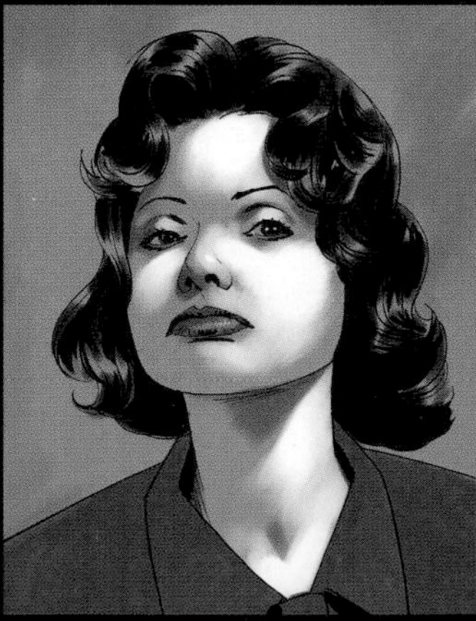

MELBA MASON
Unhappily Married

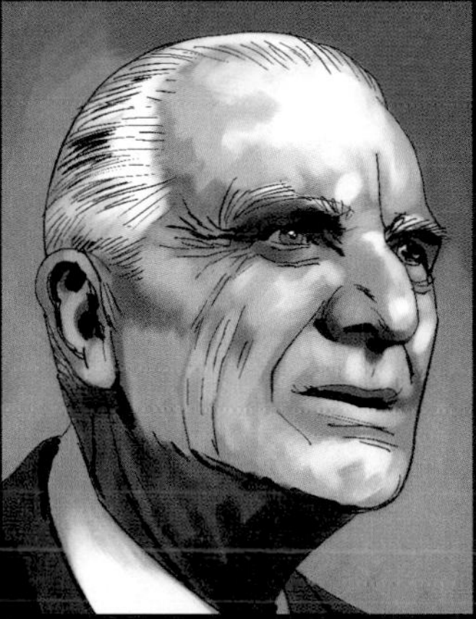

VICTOR THURSBY
Co-Founder of Victory Street Pictures

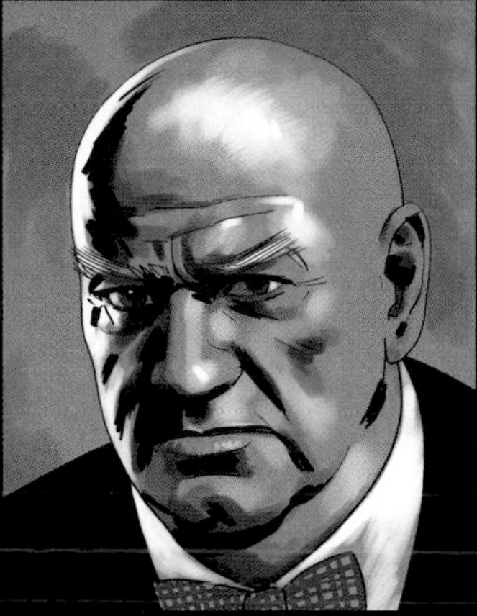

FRANZ SCHMITT
German Expatriate Director

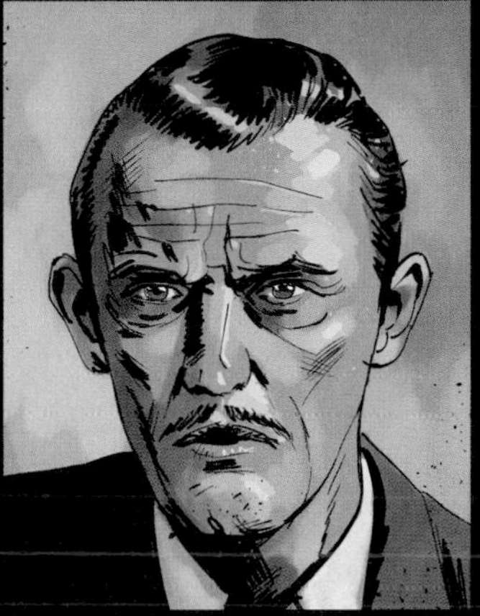

TOM GREAVEY
Middle-Aged Talent Agent

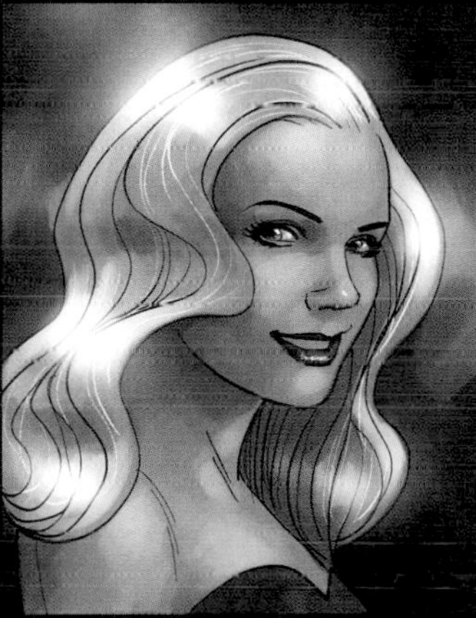

MAYA SILVER
The Replacement Blonde

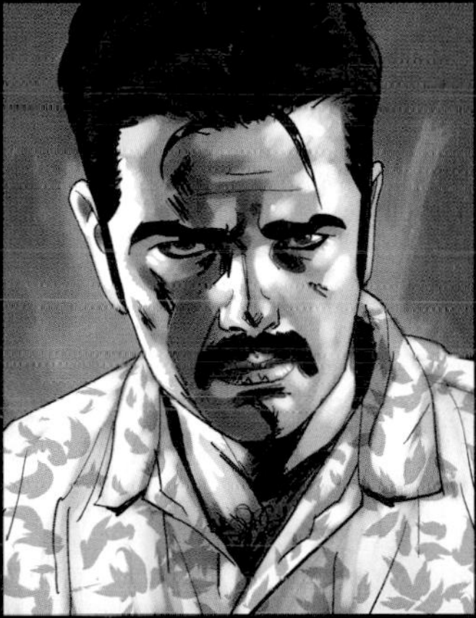

ARMANDO LOPEZ
Big Band Trumpet Player

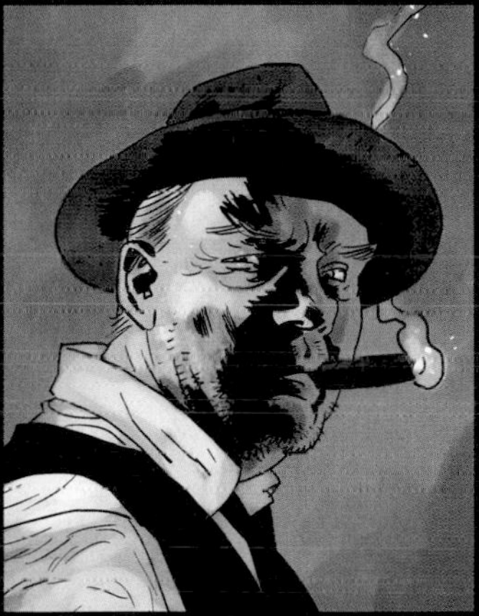

STEVIE TURNER
Photographer to the Stars

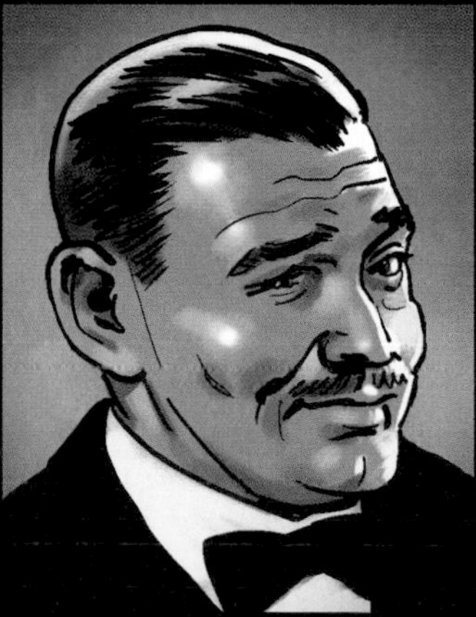

CLARK GABLE
"Frankly, my dear... I don't give a damn."

The Wild Party

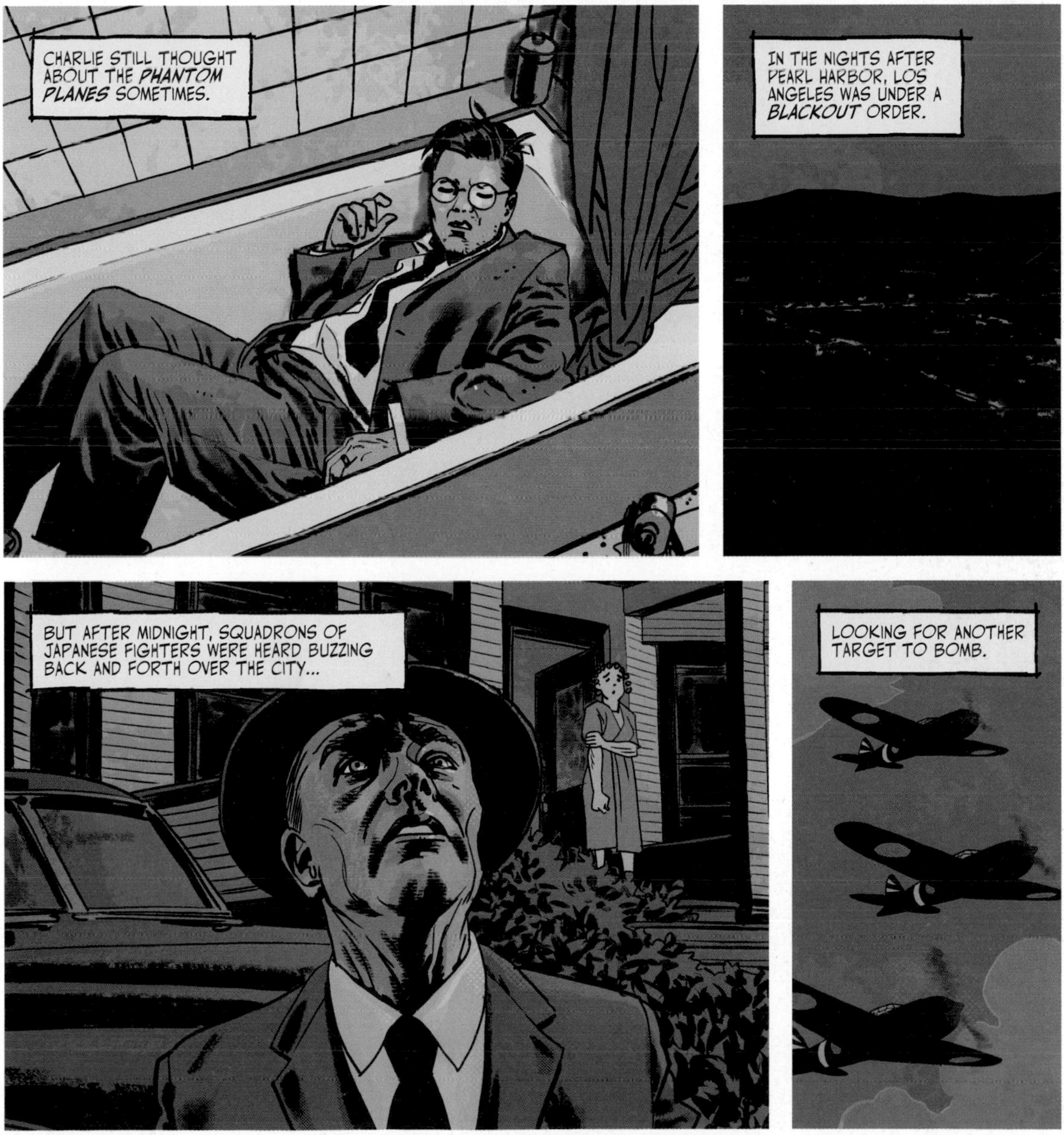
CHARLIE STILL THOUGHT ABOUT THE *PHANTOM PLANES* SOMETIMES.
IN THE NIGHTS AFTER PEARL HARBOR, LOS ANGELES WAS UNDER A *BLACKOUT* ORDER.
BUT AFTER MIDNIGHT, SQUADRONS OF JAPANESE FIGHTERS WERE HEARD BUZZING BACK AND FORTH OVER THE CITY...
LOOKING FOR ANOTHER TARGET TO BOMB.

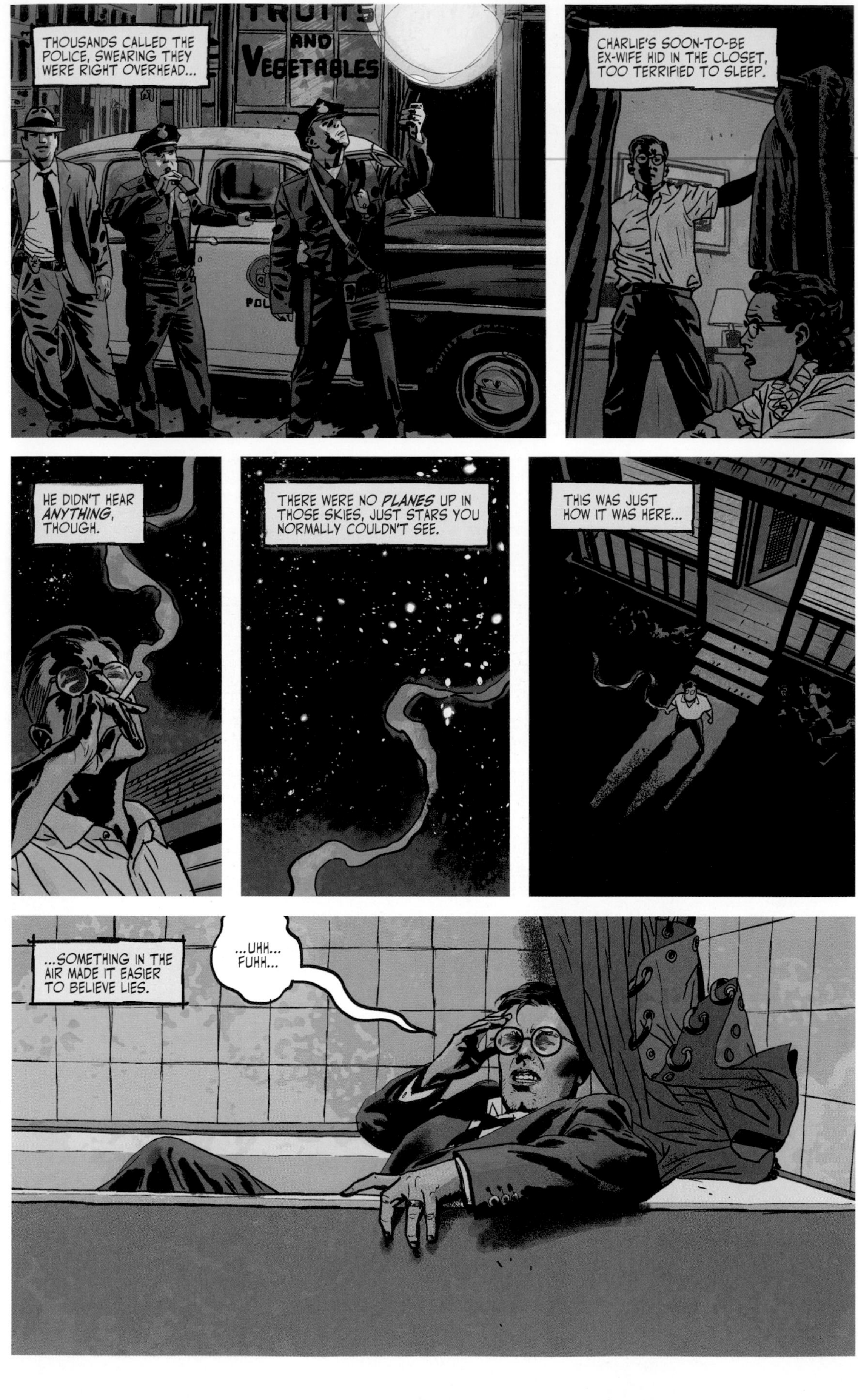
THOUSANDS CALLED THE POLICE, SWEARING THEY WERE RIGHT OVERHEAD...
FRUITS AND VEGETABLES
CHARLIE'S SOON-TO-BE EX-WIFE HID IN THE CLOSET, TOO TERRIFIED TO SLEEP.
HE DIDN'T HEAR *ANYTHING*, THOUGH.
THERE WERE NO *PLANES* UP IN THOSE SKIES, JUST STARS YOU NORMALLY COULDN'T SEE.
THIS WAS JUST HOW IT WAS HERE...
...SOMETHING IN THE AIR MADE IT EASIER TO BELIEVE LIES.
...UHH... FUHH...

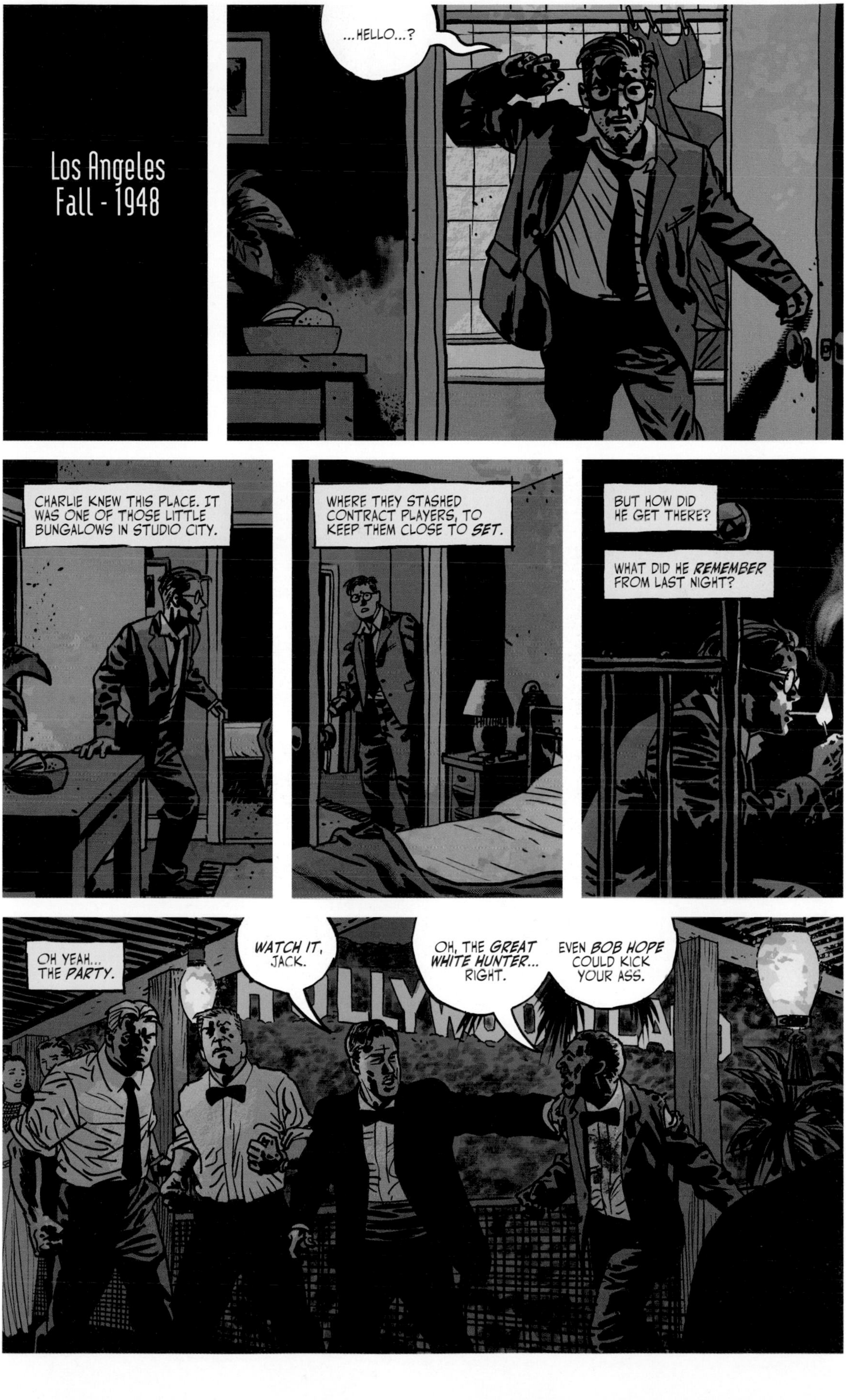
Los Angeles
Fall - 1948
...HELLO...?
CHARLIE KNEW THIS PLACE. IT WAS ONE OF THOSE LITTLE BUNGALOWS IN STUDIO CITY.
WHERE THEY STASHED CONTRACT PLAYERS, TO KEEP THEM CLOSE TO SET.
BUT HOW DID HE GET THERE?
WHAT DID HE REMEMBER FROM LAST NIGHT?
OH YEAH... THE PARTY.
WATCH IT, JACK.
OH, THE GREAT WHITE HUNTER... RIGHT.
EVEN BOB HOPE COULD KICK YOUR ASS.

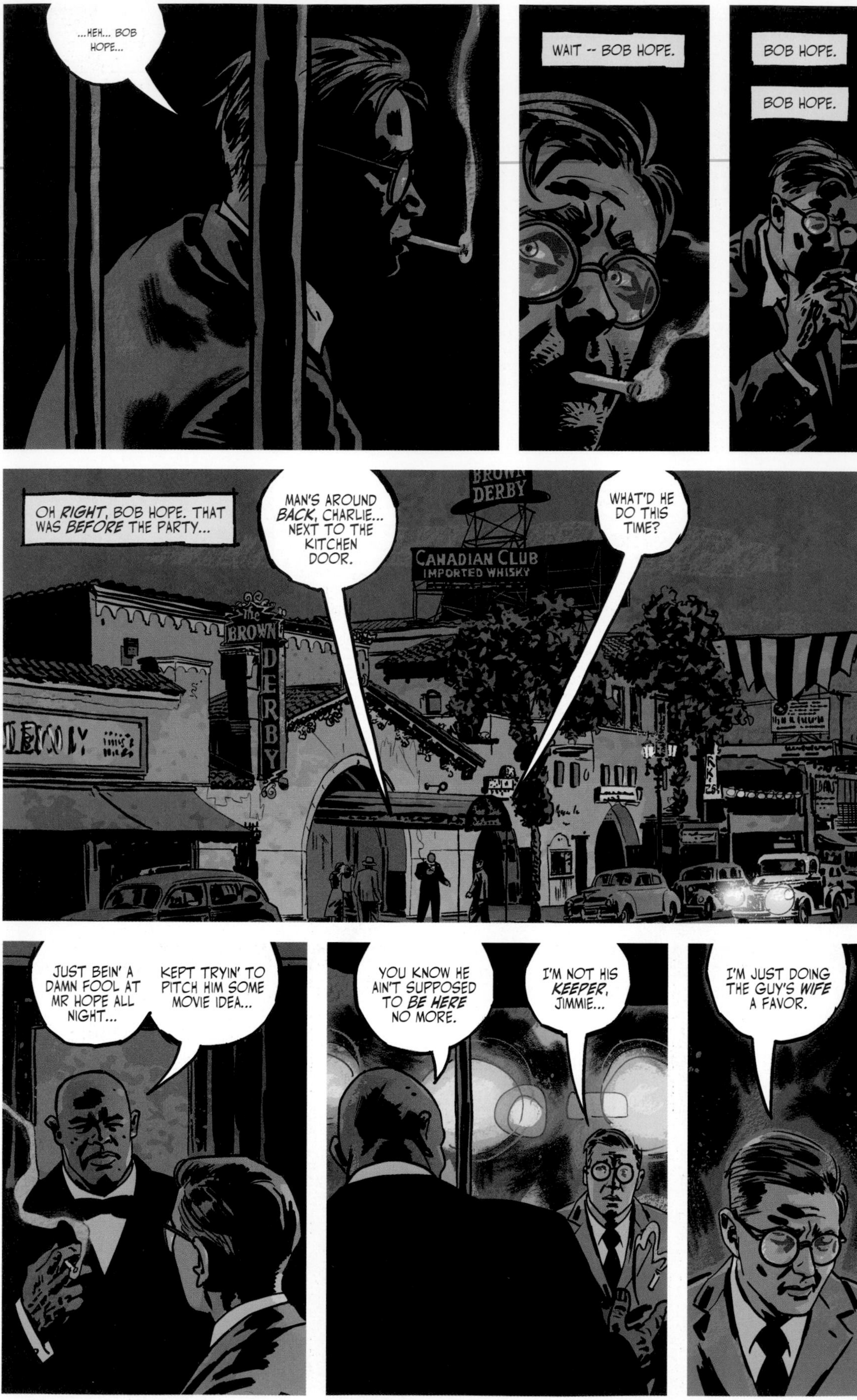
...HEH... BOB HOPE...
WAIT -- BOB HOPE.
BOB HOPE.
BOB HOPE.
OH RIGHT, BOB HOPE. THAT WAS BEFORE THE PARTY...
MAN'S AROUND BACK, CHARLIE... NEXT TO THE KITCHEN DOOR.
BROWN DERBY
CANADIAN CLUB IMPORTED WHISKY
The BROWN DERBY
WHAT'D HE DO THIS TIME?
JUST BEIN' A DAMN FOOL AT MR HOPE ALL NIGHT...
KEPT TRYIN' TO PITCH HIM SOME MOVIE IDEA...
YOU KNOW HE AIN'T SUPPOSED TO BE HERE NO MORE.
I'M NOT HIS KEEPER, JIMMIE...
I'M JUST DOING THE GUY'S WIFE A FAVOR.

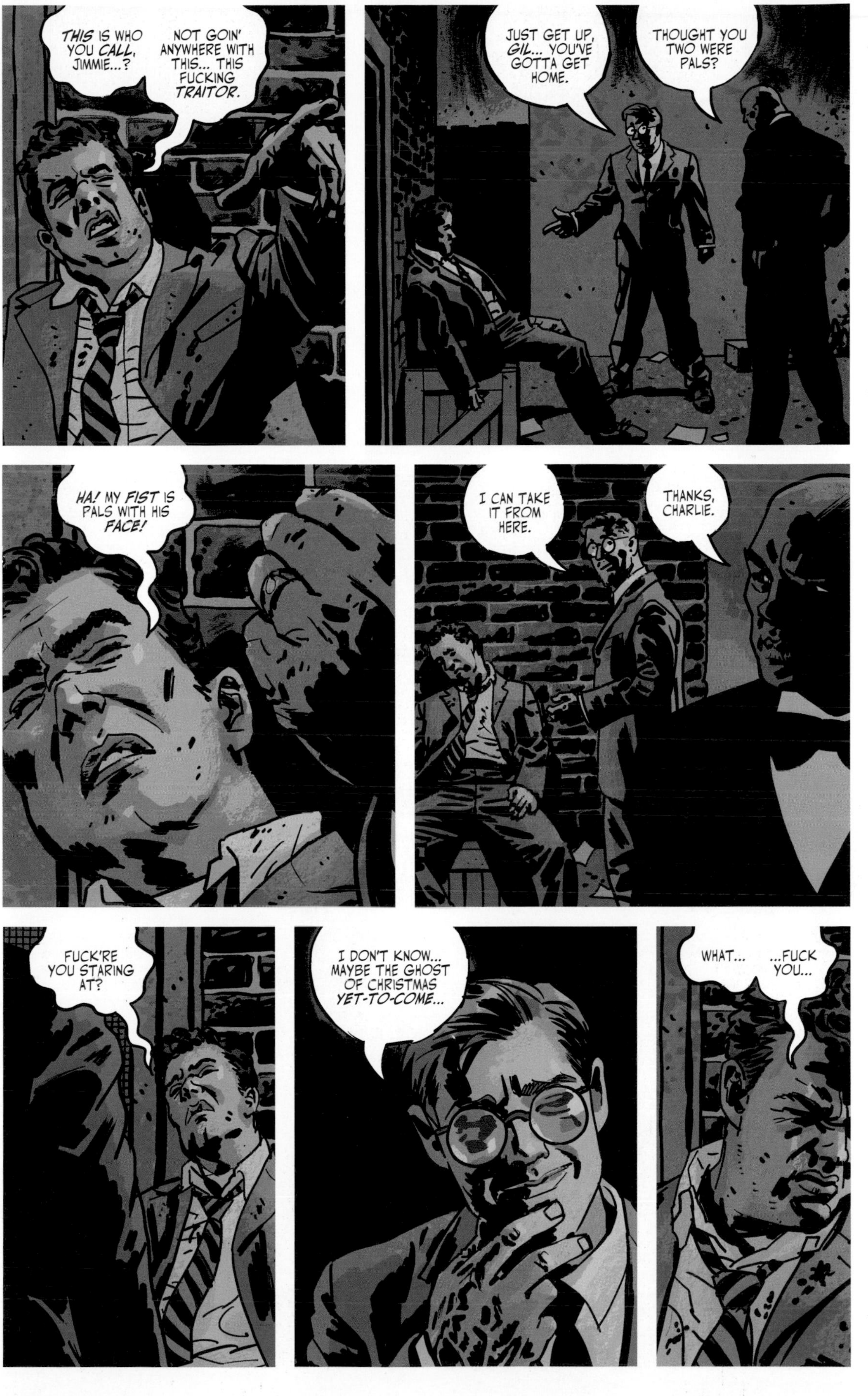
THIS IS WHO YOU CALL, JIMMIE...?
NOT GOIN' ANYWHERE WITH THIS... THIS FUCKING TRAITOR.
JUST GET UP, GIL... YOU'VE GOTTA GET HOME.
THOUGHT YOU TWO WERE PALS?
HA! MY FIST IS PALS WITH HIS FACE!
I CAN TAKE IT FROM HERE.
THANKS, CHARLIE.
FUCK'RE YOU STARING AT?
I DON'T KNOW... MAYBE THE GHOST OF CHRISTMAS YET-TO-COME...
WHAT...
...FUCK YOU...

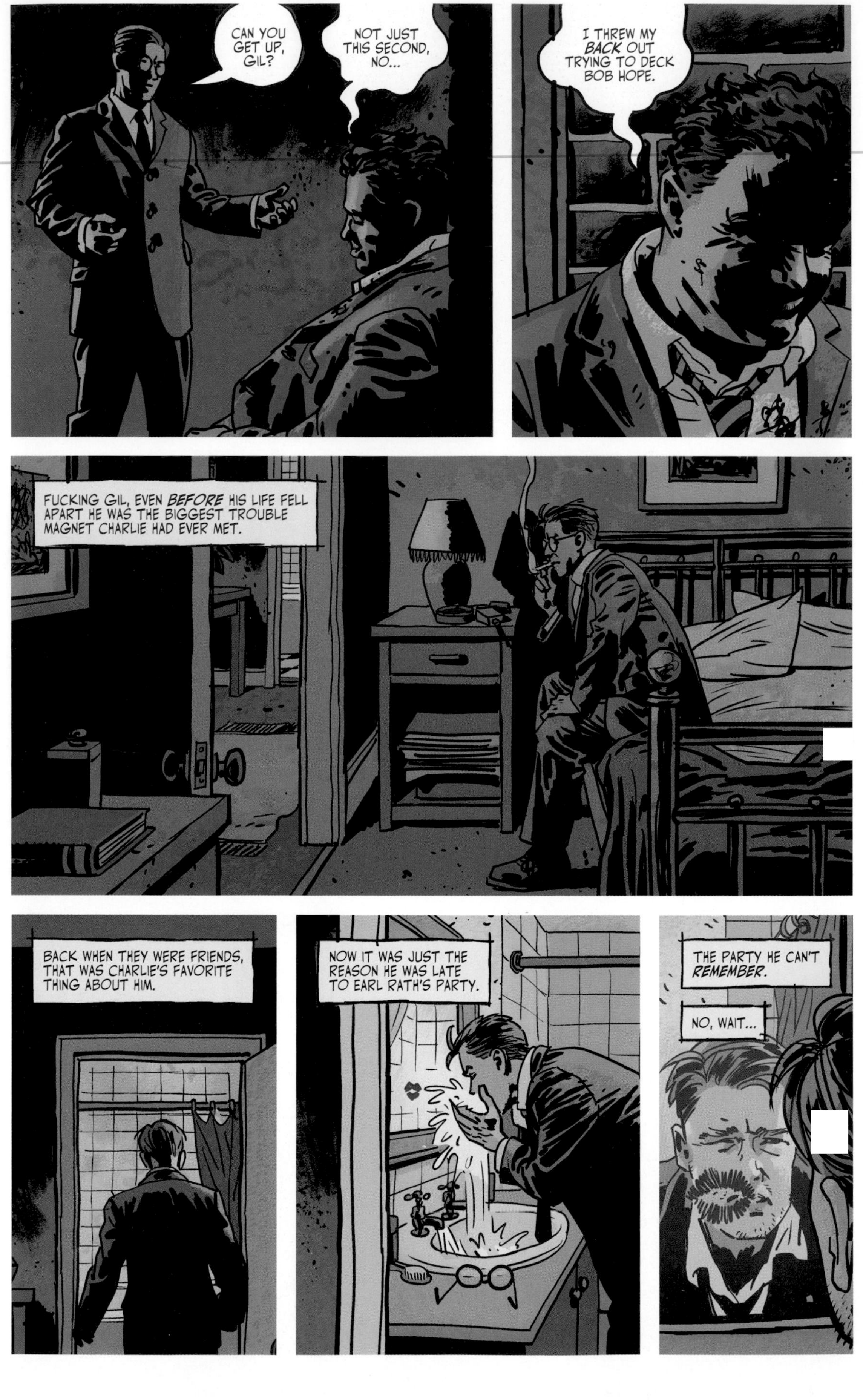
CAN YOU GET UP, GIL?
NOT JUST THIS SECOND, NO...
I THREW MY *BACK* OUT TRYING TO DECK BOB HOPE.
FUCKING GIL, EVEN *BEFORE* HIS LIFE FELL APART HE WAS THE BIGGEST TROUBLE MAGNET CHARLIE HAD EVER MET.
BACK WHEN THEY WERE FRIENDS, THAT WAS CHARLIE'S FAVORITE THING ABOUT HIM.
NOW IT WAS JUST THE REASON HE WAS LATE TO EARL RATH'S PARTY.
THE PARTY HE CAN'T *REMEMBER*.
NO, WAIT...

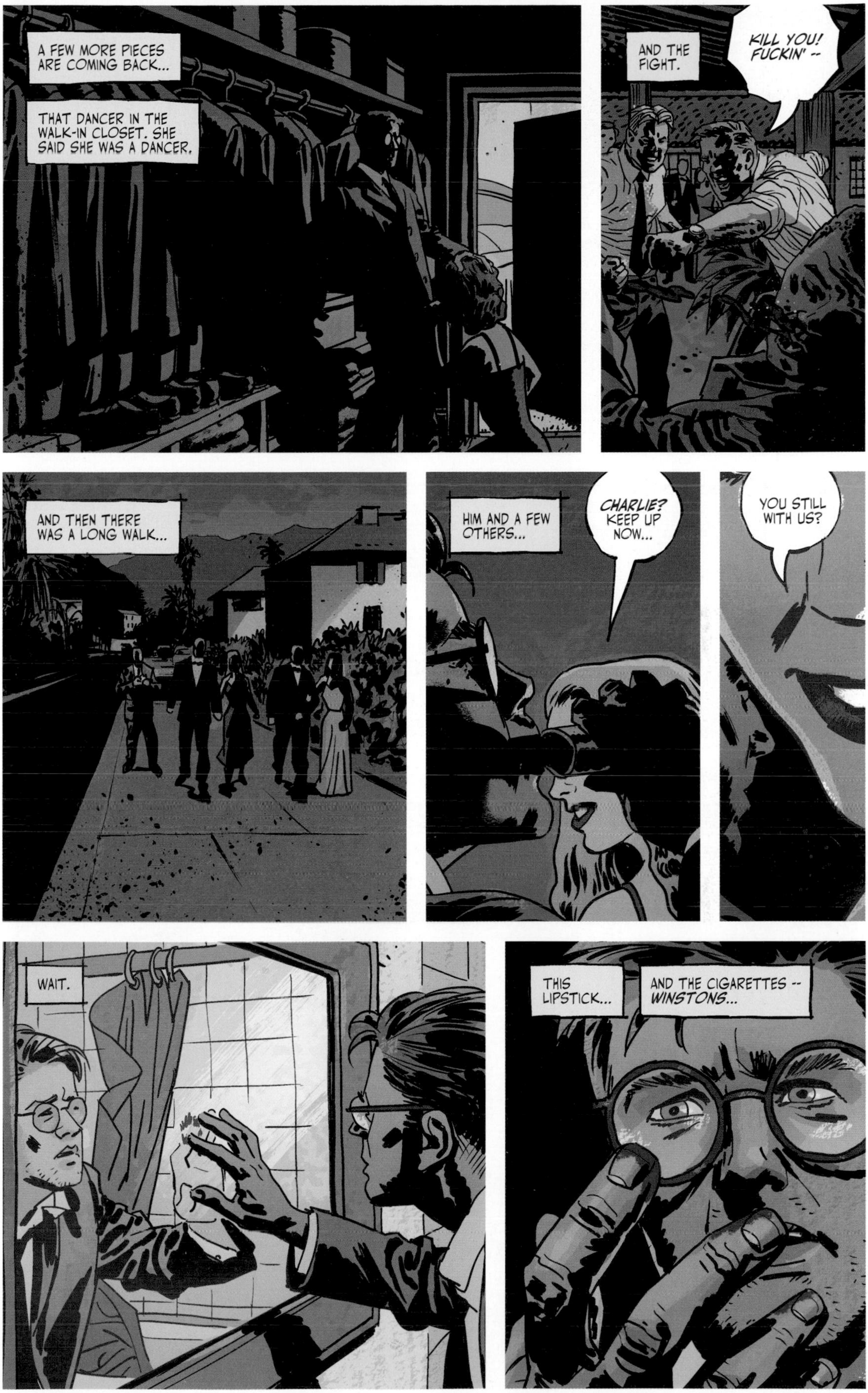
A FEW MORE PIECES ARE COMING BACK...
THAT DANCER IN THE WALK-IN CLOSET. SHE SAID SHE WAS A DANCER.
AND THE FIGHT.
KILL YOU! FUCKIN' --
AND THEN THERE WAS A LONG WALK...
HIM AND A FEW OTHERS...
CHARLIE? KEEP UP NOW...
YOU STILL WITH US?
WAIT.
THIS LIPSTICK...
AND THE CIGARETTES -- WINSTONS...

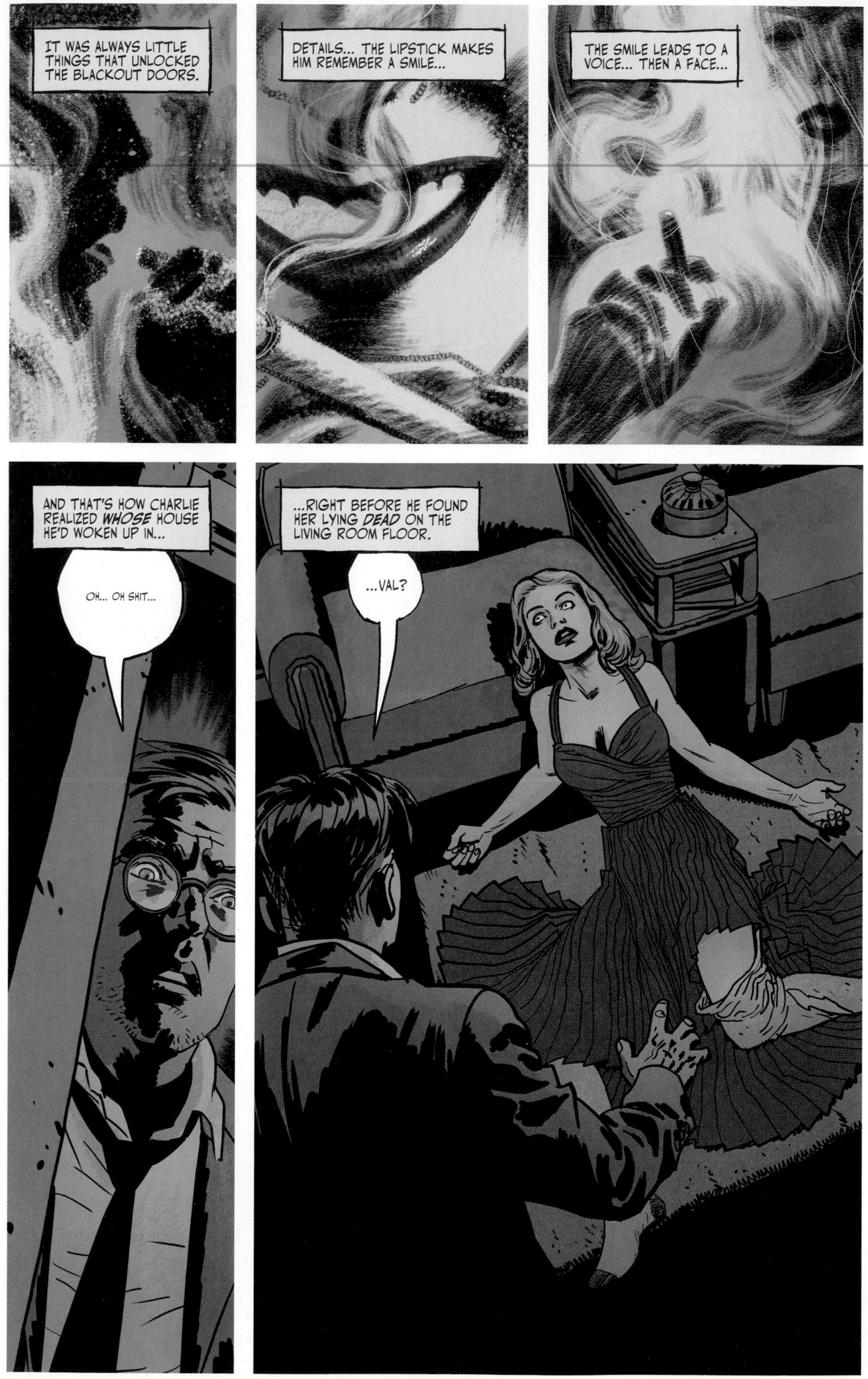
IT WAS ALWAYS LITTLE THINGS THAT UNLOCKED THE BLACKOUT DOORS.
DETAILS... THE LIPSTICK MAKES HIM REMEMBER A SMILE...
THE SMILE LEADS TO A VOICE... THEN A FACE...
AND THAT'S HOW CHARLIE REALIZED WHOSE HOUSE HE'D WOKEN UP IN...
OH... OH SHIT...
...RIGHT BEFORE HE FOUND HER LYING DEAD ON THE LIVING ROOM FLOOR.
...VAL?

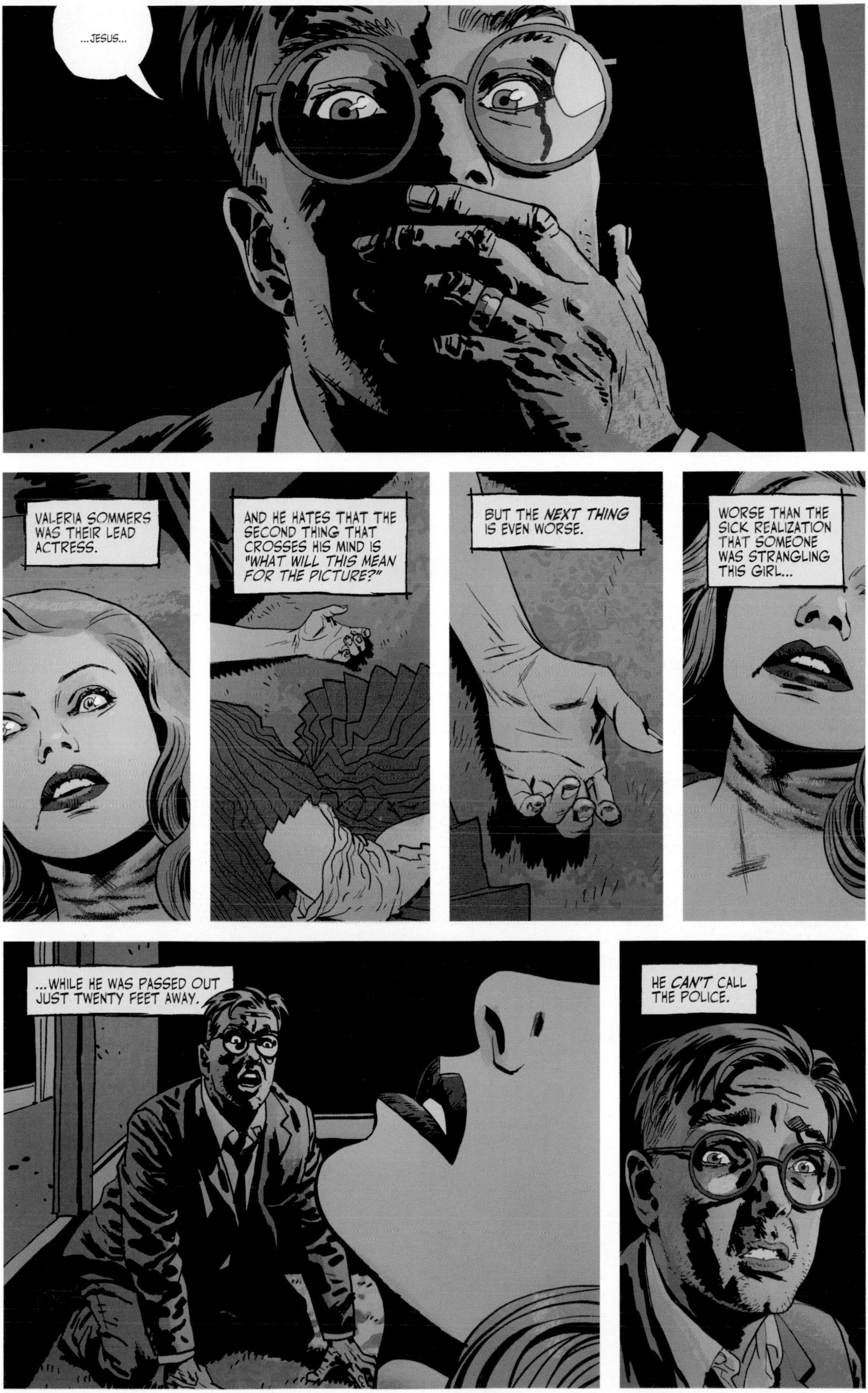
...JESUS...
VALERIA SOMMERS WAS THEIR LEAD ACTRESS.
AND HE HATES THAT THE SECOND THING THAT CROSSES HIS MIND IS "WHAT WILL THIS MEAN FOR THE PICTURE?"
BUT THE NEXT THING IS EVEN WORSE.
WORSE THAN THE SICK REALIZATION THAT SOMEONE WAS STRANGLING THIS GIRL...
...WHILE HE WAS PASSED OUT JUST TWENTY FEET AWAY.
HE CAN'T CALL THE POLICE.

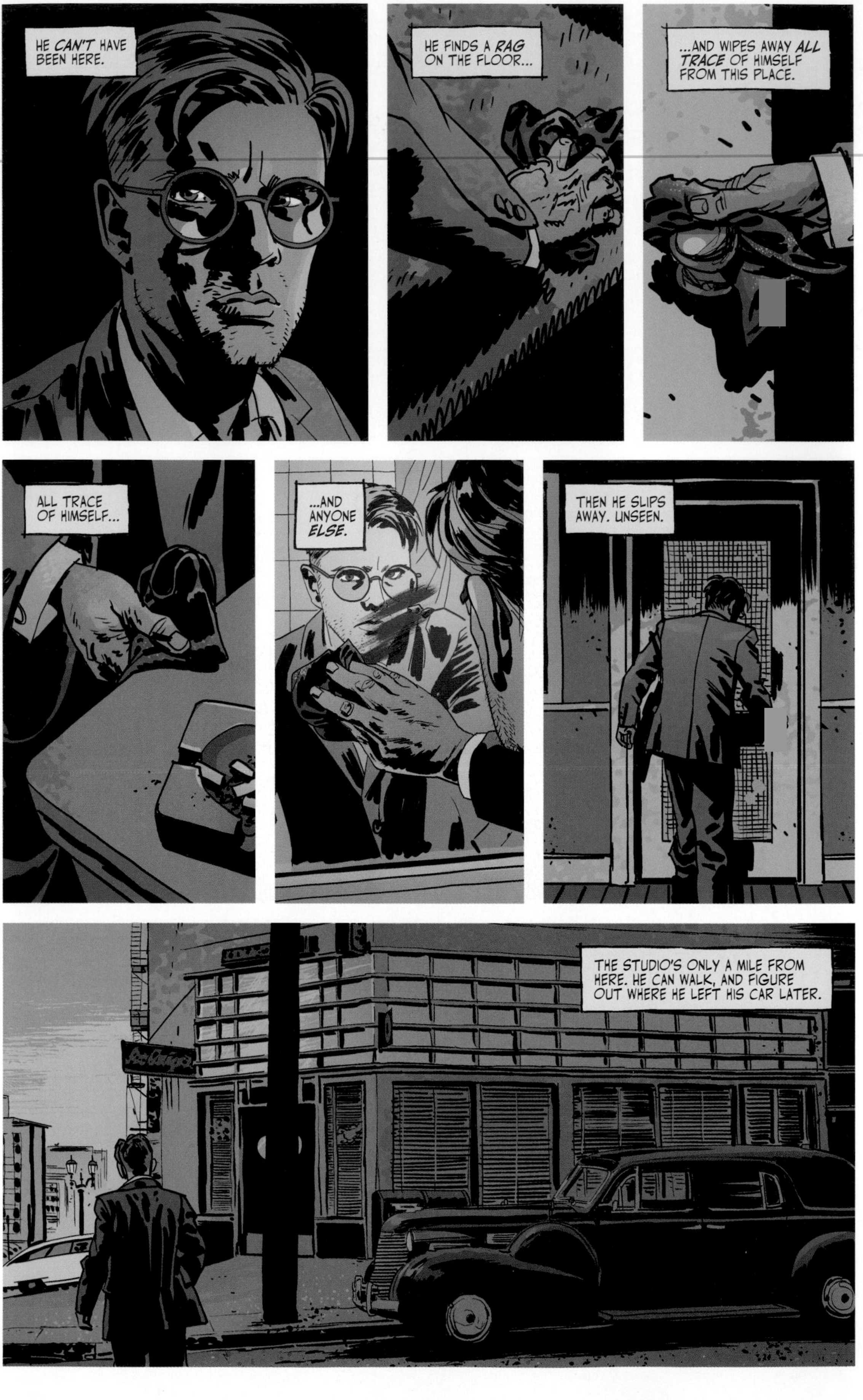
HE *CAN'T* HAVE BEEN HERE.
HE FINDS A *RAG* ON THE FLOOR...
...AND WIPES AWAY *ALL TRACE* OF HIMSELF FROM THIS PLACE.
ALL TRACE OF HIMSELF...
...AND ANYONE *ELSE*.
THEN HE SLIPS AWAY. UNSEEN.
THE STUDIO'S ONLY A MILE FROM HERE. HE CAN WALK, AND FIGURE OUT WHERE HE LEFT HIS CAR LATER.

VICTORY STREET PICTURES

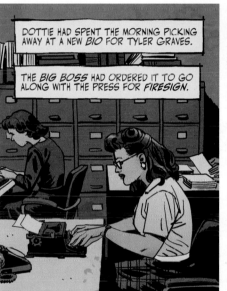

DOTTIE HAD SPENT THE MORNING PICKING AWAY AT A NEW *BIO* FOR TYLER GRAVES.

THE *BIG BOSS* HAD ORDERED IT TO GO ALONG WITH THE PRESS FOR *FIRESIGN*.

THIS TIME SHE WAS TOLD TO PLAY UP HIS YEARS AS A *RANCH HAND* IN TEXAS.

DOTTIE, YOU'RE A *RIOT*... I'VE NEVER RIDDEN A HORSE IN MY LIFE.

I KNOW, I STILL PREFER THE *FIRST* ONE WE CAME UP WITH...

OH RIGHT. I WAS A *MECHANIC* SELZNICK DISCOVERED WHEN HE *BROKE DOWN* IN PALM SPRINGS.

IT WAS YOUR OWN LITTLE *CINDERELLA* STORY.

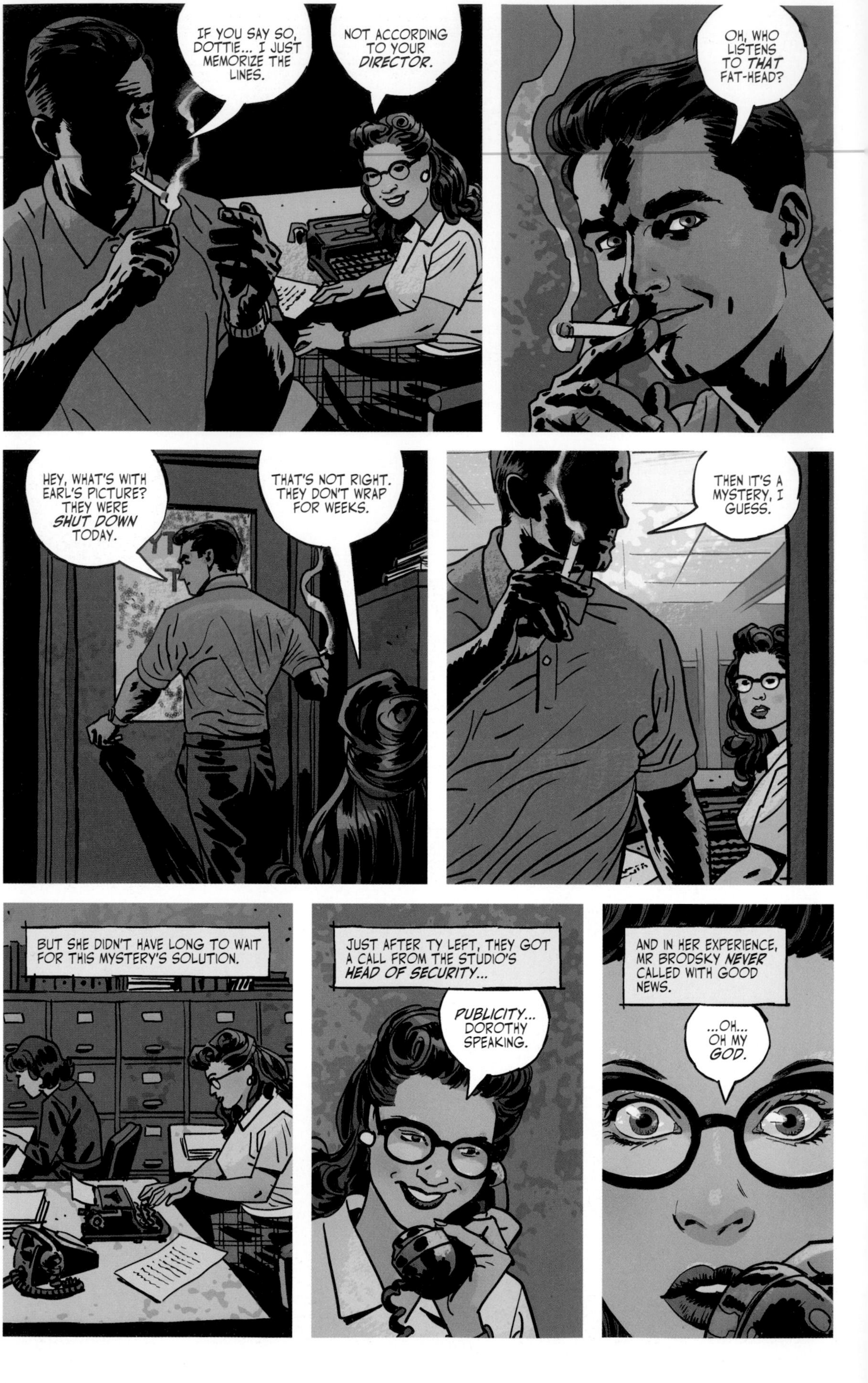
IF YOU SAY SO, DOTTIE... I JUST MEMORIZE THE LINES.
NOT ACCORDING TO YOUR *DIRECTOR*.
OH, WHO LISTENS TO *THAT* FAT-HEAD?
HEY, WHAT'S WITH EARL'S PICTURE? THEY WERE *SHUT DOWN* TODAY.
THAT'S NOT RIGHT. THEY DON'T WRAP FOR WEEKS.
THEN IT'S A MYSTERY, I GUESS.
BUT SHE DIDN'T HAVE LONG TO WAIT FOR THIS MYSTERY'S SOLUTION.
JUST AFTER TY LEFT, THEY GOT A CALL FROM THE STUDIO'S *HEAD OF SECURITY*...
PUBLICITY... DOROTHY SPEAKING.
AND IN HER EXPERIENCE, MR BRODSKY *NEVER* CALLED WITH GOOD NEWS.
...OH... OH MY *GOD*.

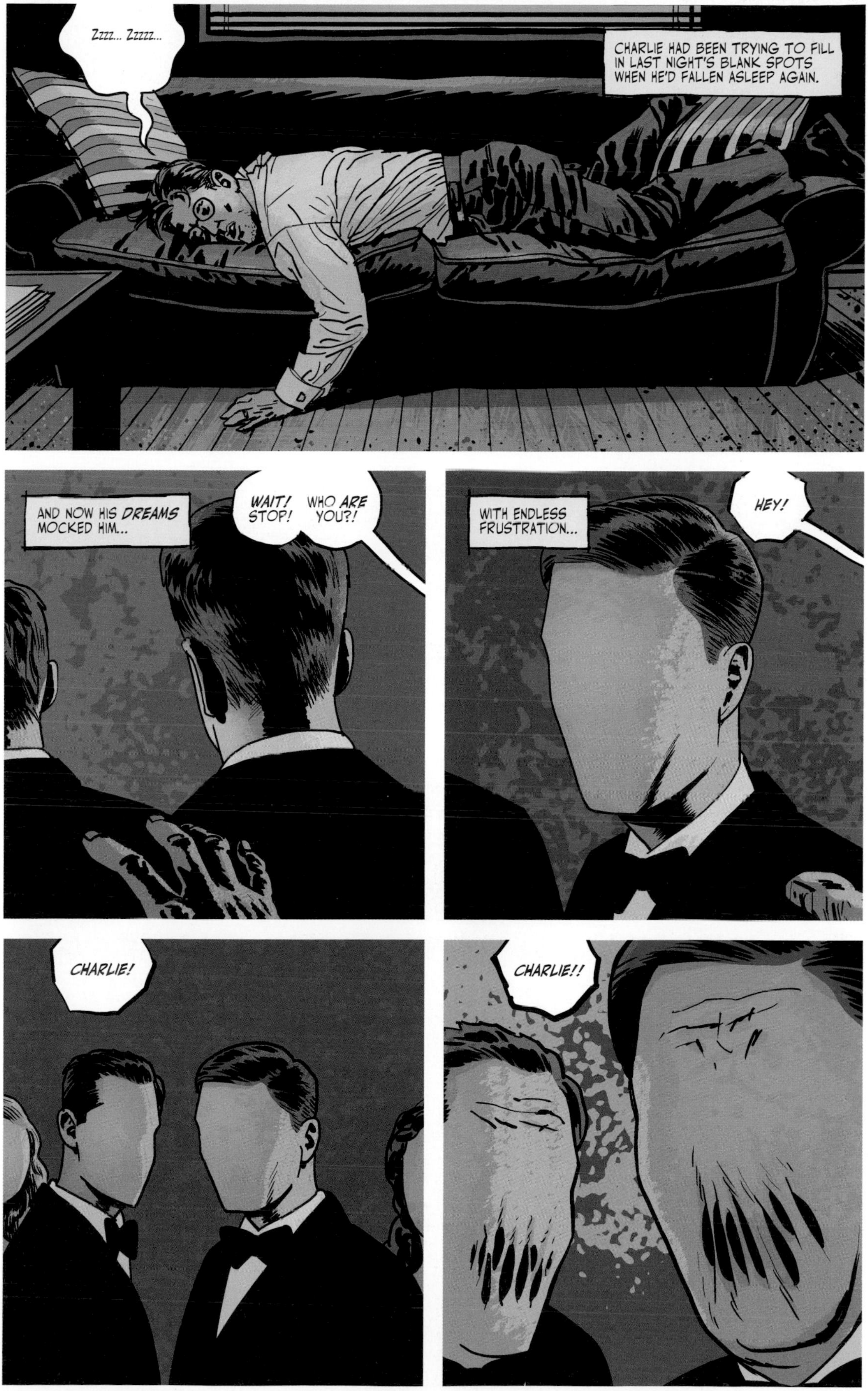
Zzzz... Zzzzz...
CHARLIE HAD BEEN TRYING TO FILL IN LAST NIGHT'S BLANK SPOTS WHEN HE'D FALLEN ASLEEP AGAIN.
AND NOW HIS *DREAMS* MOCKED HIM...
WAIT! STOP!
WHO *ARE* YOU?!
WITH ENDLESS FRUSTRATION...
HEY!
CHARLIE!
CHARLIE!!

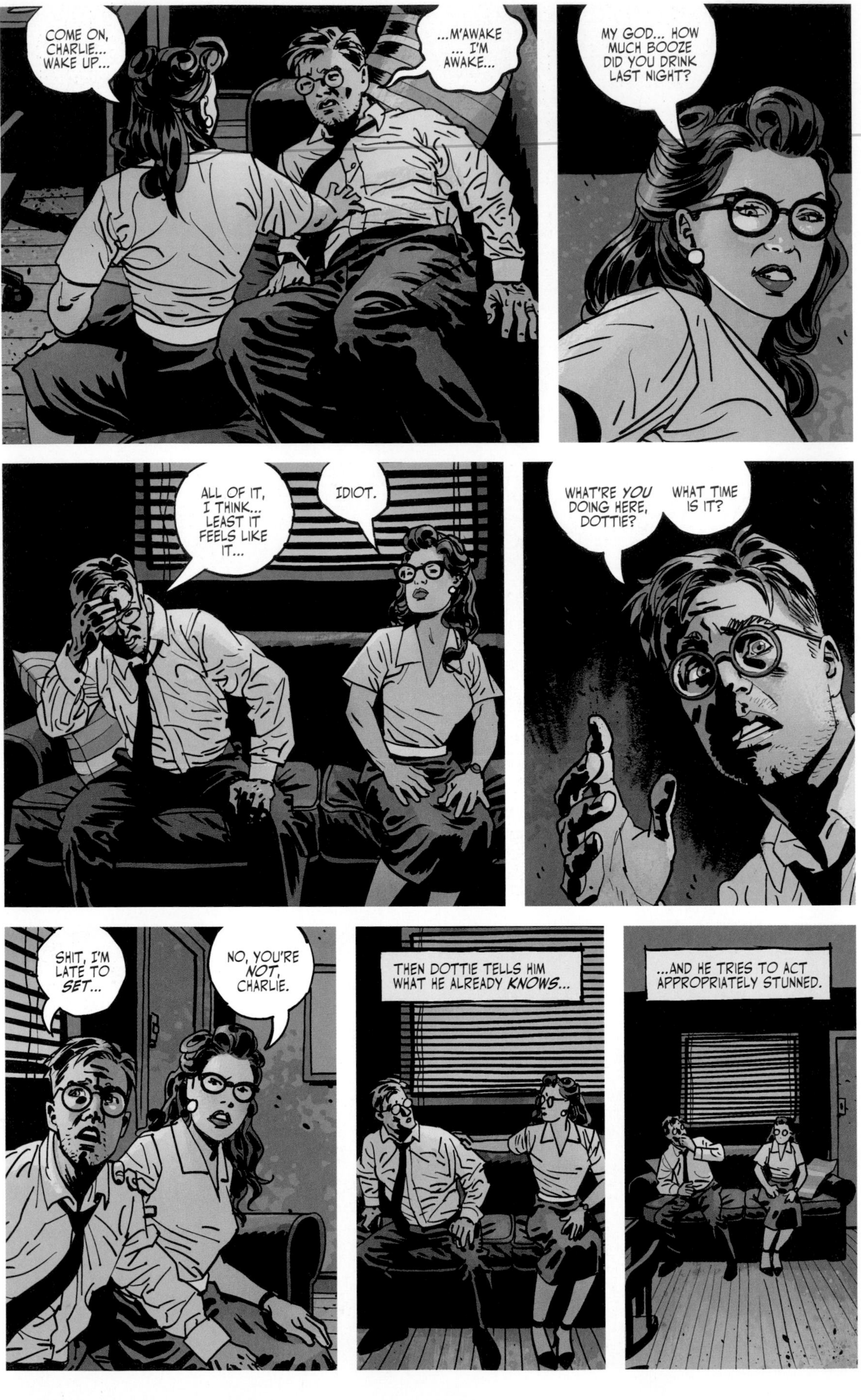
COME ON, CHARLIE... WAKE UP...
...M'AWAKE ... I'M AWAKE...
MY GOD... HOW MUCH BOOZE DID YOU DRINK LAST NIGHT?
ALL OF IT, I THINK... LEAST IT FEELS LIKE IT...
IDIOT.
WHAT'RE YOU DOING HERE, DOTTIE?
WHAT TIME IS IT?
SHIT, I'M LATE TO SET...
NO, YOU'RE NOT, CHARLIE.
THEN DOTTIE TELLS HIM WHAT HE ALREADY KNOWS...
...AND HE TRIES TO ACT APPROPRIATELY STUNNED.

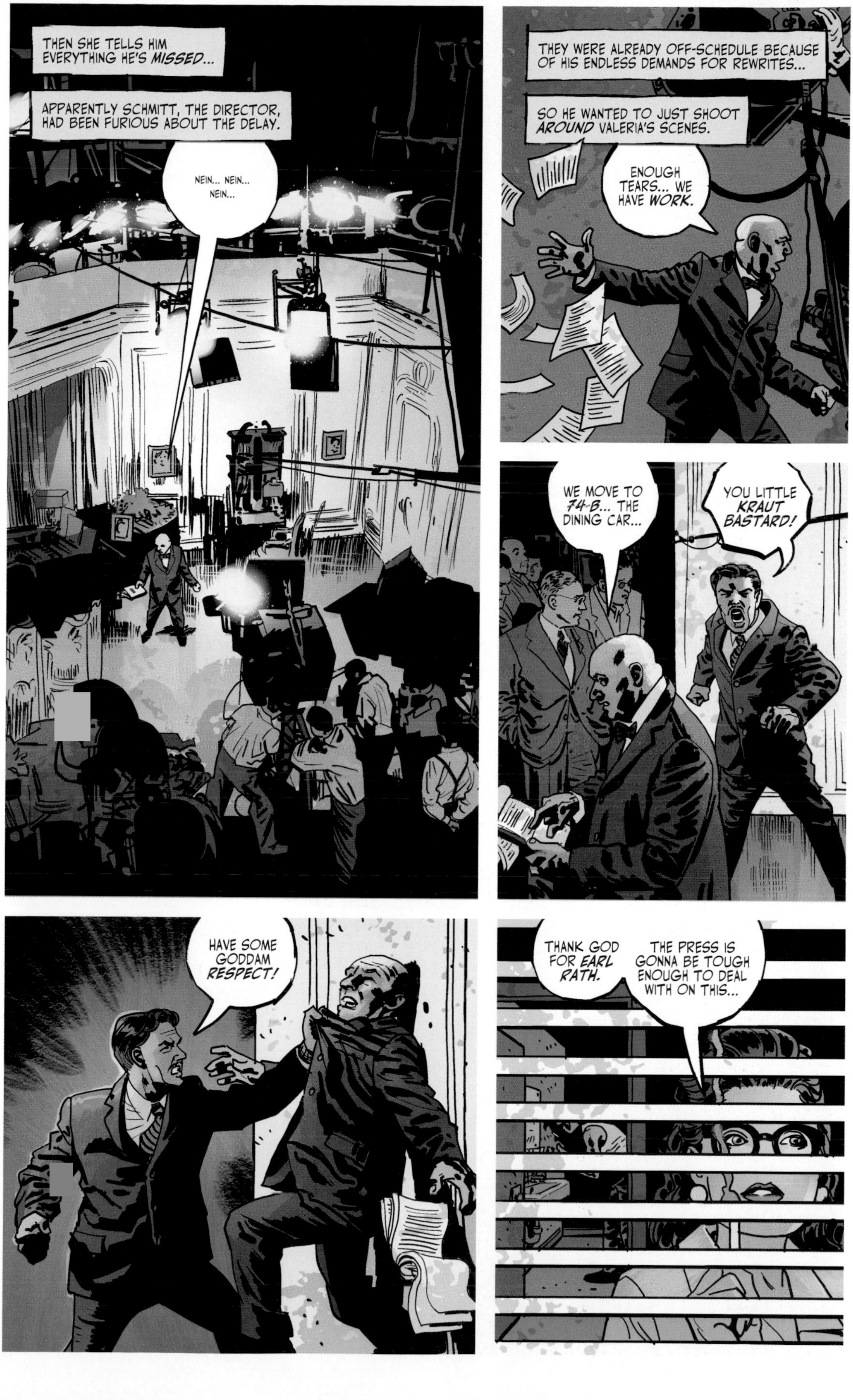
THEN SHE TELLS HIM EVERYTHING HE'S *MISSED*...
APPARENTLY SCHMITT, THE DIRECTOR, HAD BEEN FURIOUS ABOUT THE DELAY.
NEIN... NEIN... NEIN...
THEY WERE ALREADY OFF-SCHEDULE BECAUSE OF HIS ENDLESS DEMANDS FOR REWRITES...
SO HE WANTED TO JUST SHOOT *AROUND* VALERIA'S SCENES.
ENOUGH TEARS... WE HAVE *WORK*.
WE MOVE TO *74-B*... THE DINING CAR...
YOU LITTLE *KRAUT BASTARD!*
HAVE SOME GODDAM *RESPECT!*
THANK GOD FOR *EARL RATH.*
THE PRESS IS GONNA BE TOUGH ENOUGH TO DEAL WITH ON THIS...

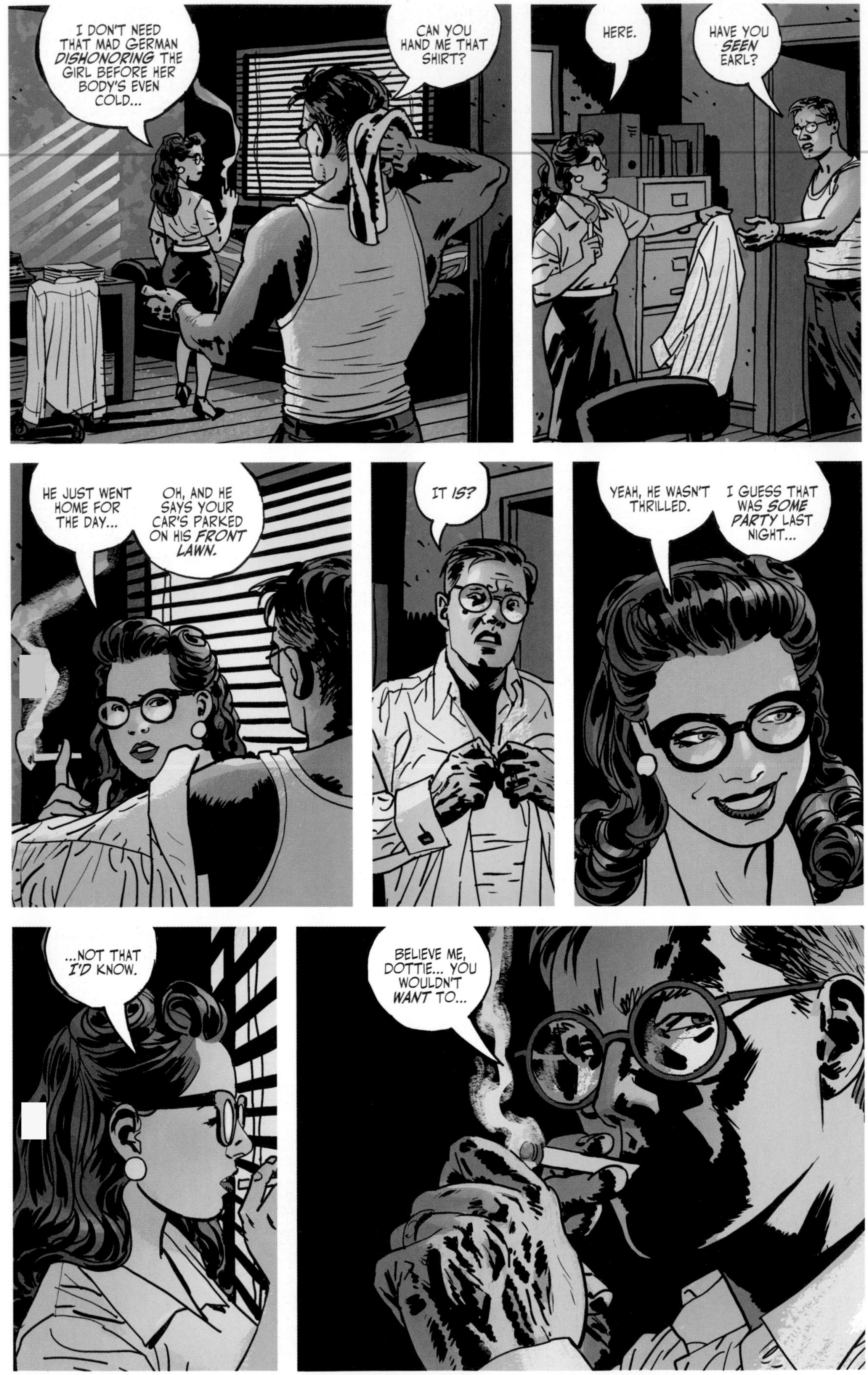
I DON'T NEED THAT MAD GERMAN *DISHONORING* THE GIRL BEFORE HER BODY'S EVEN COLD...
CAN YOU HAND ME THAT SHIRT?
HERE.
HAVE YOU *SEEN* EARL?
HE JUST WENT HOME FOR THE DAY...
OH, AND HE SAYS YOUR CAR'S PARKED ON HIS *FRONT LAWN.*
IT *IS?*
YEAH, HE WASN'T THRILLED.
I GUESS THAT WAS *SOME PARTY* LAST NIGHT...
...NOT THAT *I'D* KNOW.
BELIEVE ME, DOTTIE... YOU WOULDN'T *WANT* TO...

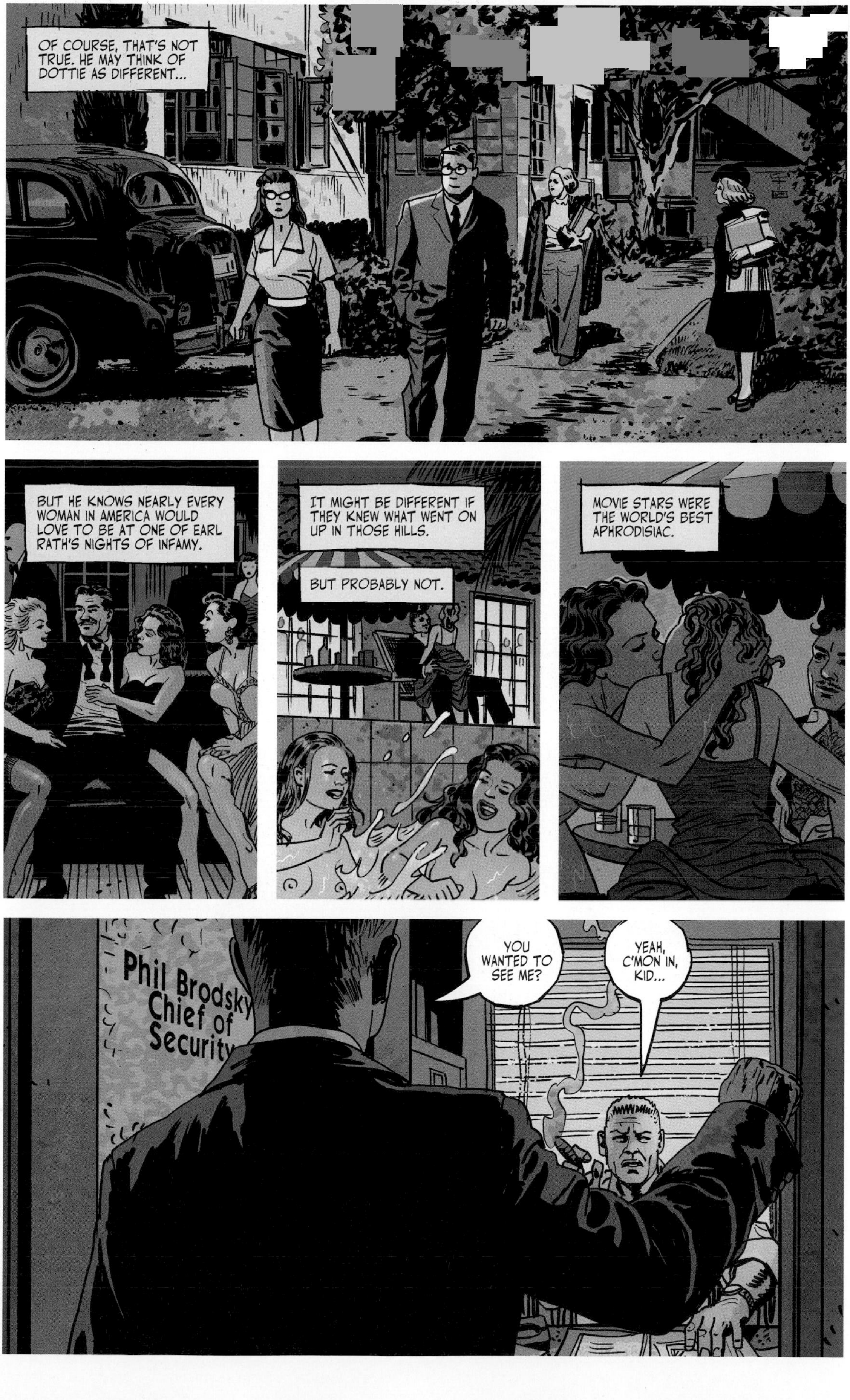
OF COURSE, THAT'S NOT TRUE. HE MAY THINK OF DOTTIE AS DIFFERENT...
BUT HE KNOWS NEARLY EVERY WOMAN IN AMERICA WOULD LOVE TO BE AT ONE OF EARL RATH'S NIGHTS OF INFAMY.
IT MIGHT BE DIFFERENT IF THEY KNEW WHAT WENT ON UP IN THOSE HILLS.
BUT PROBABLY NOT.
MOVIE STARS WERE THE WORLD'S BEST APHRODISIAC.
Phil Brodsky Chief of Security
YOU WANTED TO SEE ME?
YEAH, C'MON IN, KID...

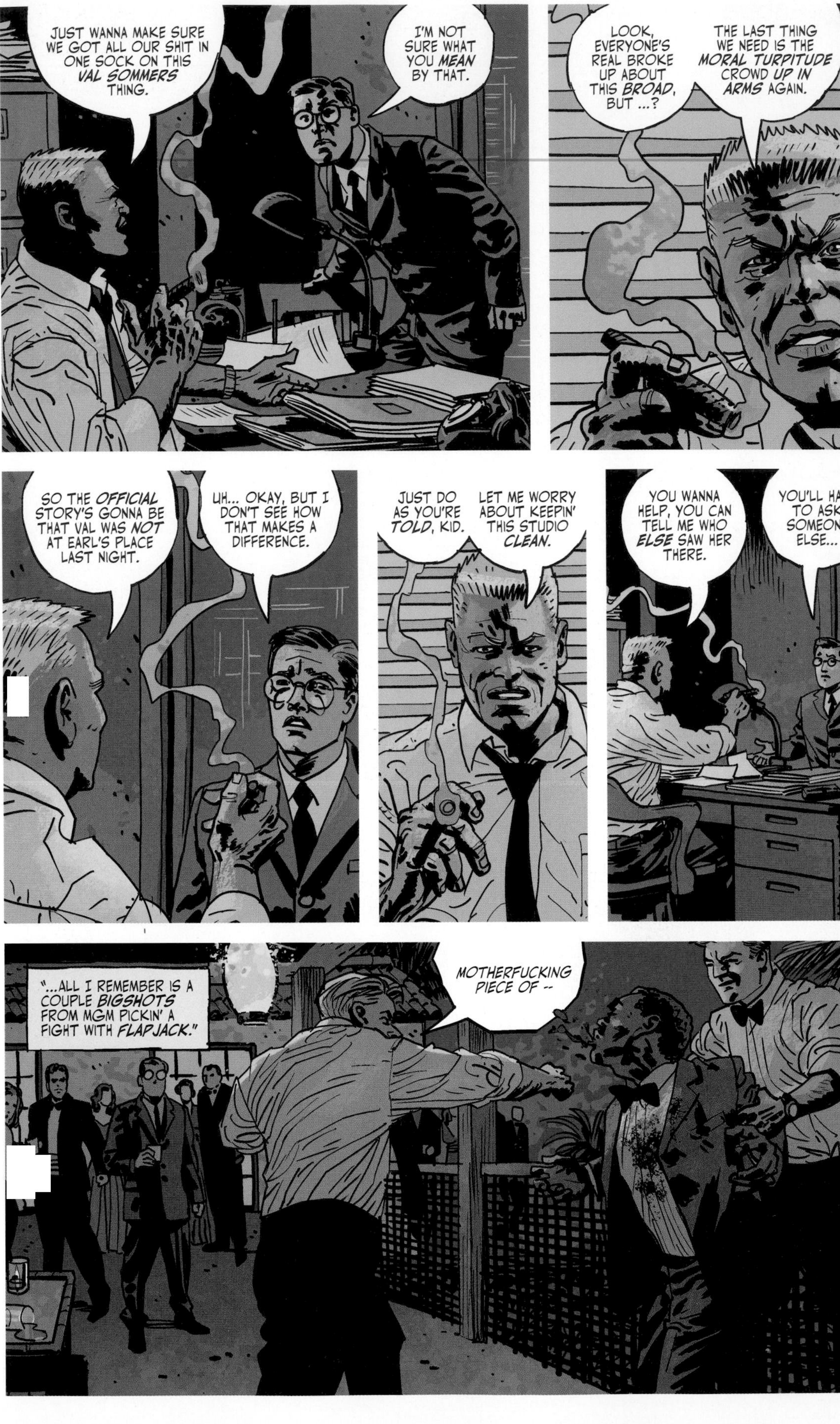
JUST WANNA MAKE SURE WE GOT ALL OUR SHIT IN ONE SOCK ON THIS VAL SOMMERS THING.
I'M NOT SURE WHAT YOU MEAN BY THAT.
LOOK, EVERYONE'S REAL BROKE UP ABOUT THIS BROAD, BUT ...?
THE LAST THING WE NEED IS THE MORAL TURPITUDE CROWD UP IN ARMS AGAIN.
SO THE OFFICIAL STORY'S GONNA BE THAT VAL WAS NOT AT EARL'S PLACE LAST NIGHT.
UH... OKAY, BUT I DON'T SEE HOW THAT MAKES A DIFFERENCE.
JUST DO AS YOU'RE TOLD, KID.
LET ME WORRY ABOUT KEEPIN' THIS STUDIO CLEAN.
YOU WANNA HELP, YOU CAN TELL ME WHO ELSE SAW HER THERE.
YOU'LL HAVE TO ASK SOMEONE ELSE...
"...ALL I REMEMBER IS A COUPLE BIGSHOTS FROM MGM PICKIN' A FIGHT WITH FLAPJACK."
MOTHERFUCKING PIECE OF --

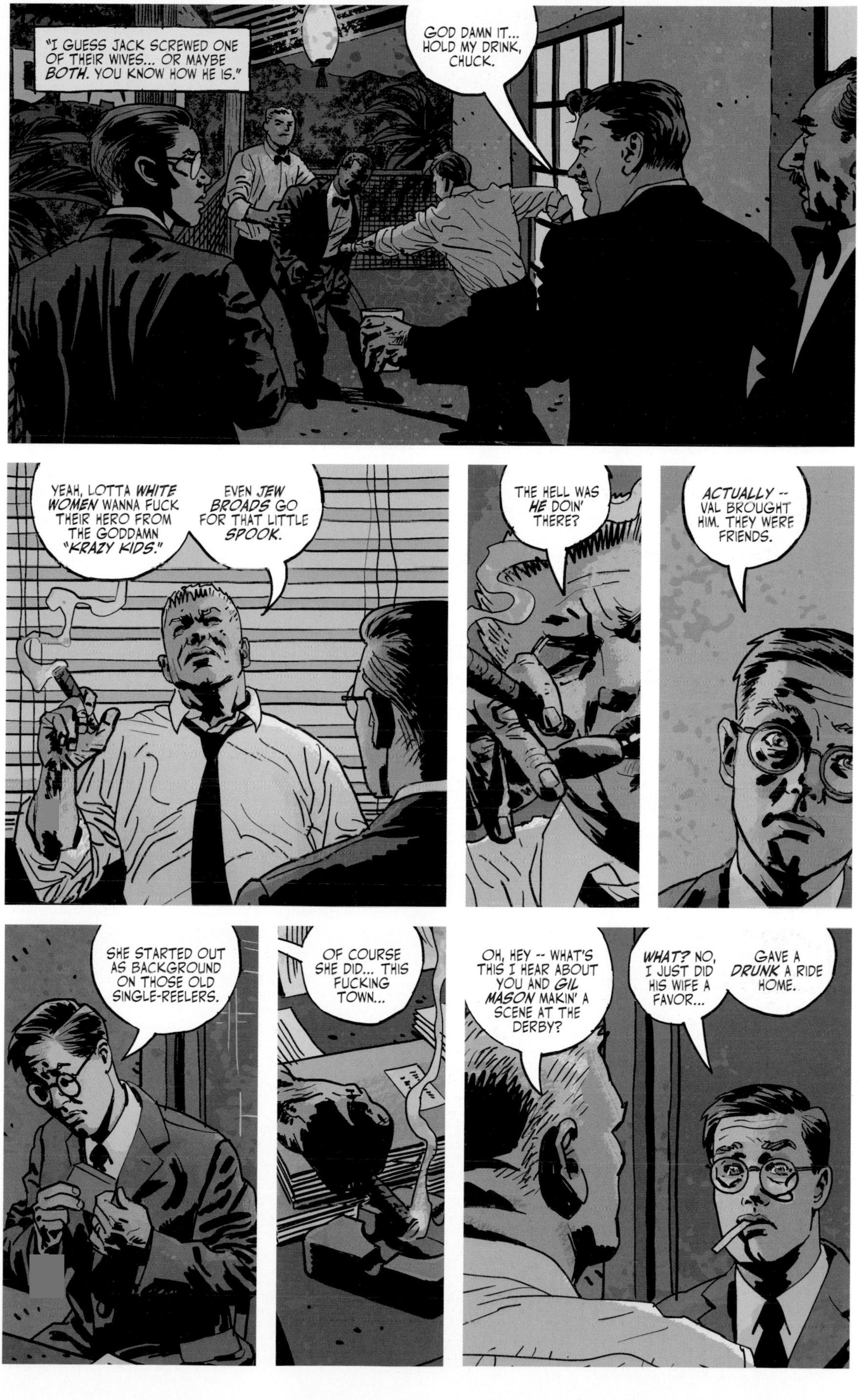
"I GUESS JACK SCREWED ONE OF THEIR WIVES... OR MAYBE BOTH. YOU KNOW HOW HE IS."
GOD DAMN IT... HOLD MY DRINK, CHUCK.
YEAH, LOTTA WHITE WOMEN WANNA FUCK THEIR HERO FROM THE GODDAMN "KRAZY KIDS."
EVEN JEW BROADS GO FOR THAT LITTLE SPOOK.
THE HELL WAS HE DOIN' THERE?
ACTUALLY -- VAL BROUGHT HIM. THEY WERE FRIENDS.
SHE STARTED OUT AS BACKGROUND ON THOSE OLD SINGLE-REELERS.
OF COURSE SHE DID... THIS FUCKING TOWN...
OH, HEY -- WHAT'S THIS I HEAR ABOUT YOU AND GIL MASON MAKIN' A SCENE AT THE DERBY?
WHAT? NO, I JUST DID HIS WIFE A FAVOR...
GAVE A DRUNK A RIDE HOME.

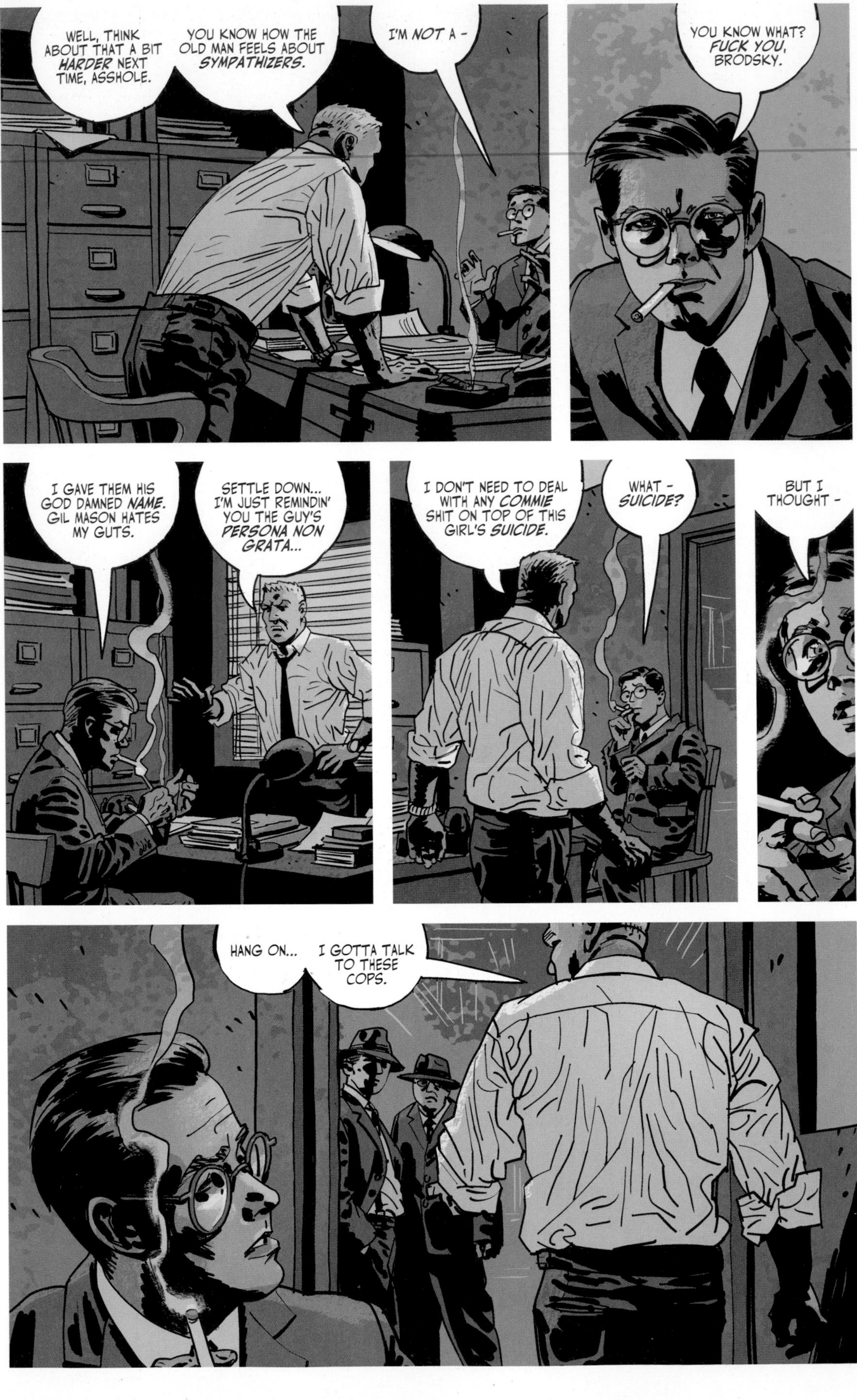
WELL, THINK ABOUT THAT A BIT HARDER NEXT TIME, ASSHOLE.
YOU KNOW HOW THE OLD MAN FEELS ABOUT SYMPATHIZERS.
I'M NOT A -
YOU KNOW WHAT? FUCK YOU, BRODSKY.
I GAVE THEM HIS GOD DAMNED NAME. GIL MASON HATES MY GUTS.
SETTLE DOWN... I'M JUST REMINDIN' YOU THE GUY'S PERSONA NON GRATA...
I DON'T NEED TO DEAL WITH ANY COMMIE SHIT ON TOP OF THIS GIRL'S SUICIDE.
WHAT - SUICIDE?
BUT I THOUGHT -
HANG ON...
I GOTTA TALK TO THESE COPS.

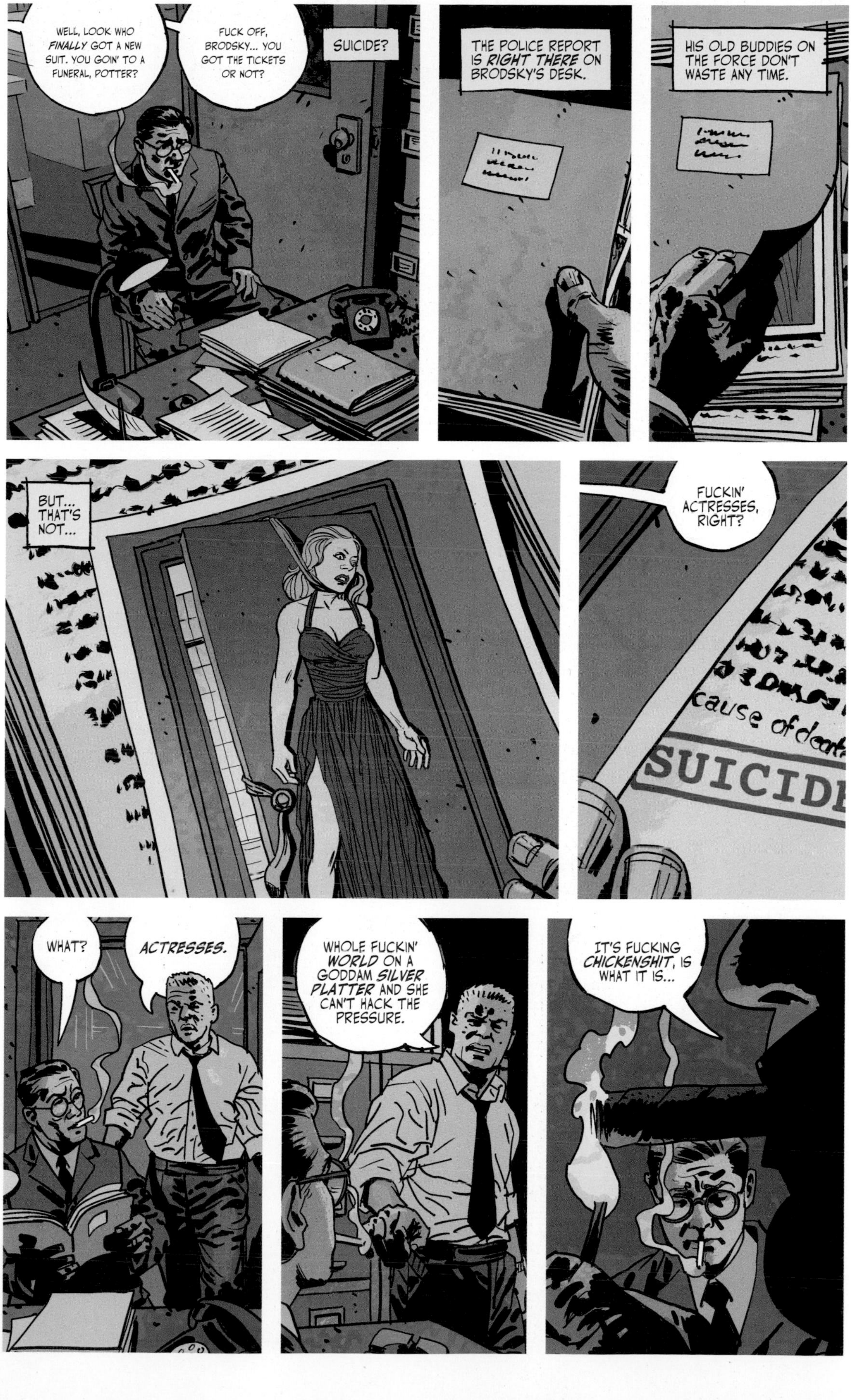
WELL, LOOK WHO FINALLY GOT A NEW SUIT. YOU GOIN' TO A FUNERAL, POTTER?
FUCK OFF, BRODSKY... YOU GOT THE TICKETS OR NOT?
SUICIDE?
THE POLICE REPORT IS RIGHT THERE ON BRODSKY'S DESK.
HIS OLD BUDDIES ON THE FORCE DON'T WASTE ANY TIME.
BUT... THAT'S NOT...
FUCKIN' ACTRESSES, RIGHT?
cause of death
SUICIDE
WHAT?
ACTRESSES.
WHOLE FUCKIN' WORLD ON A GODDAM SILVER PLATTER AND SHE CAN'T HACK THE PRESSURE.
IT'S FUCKING CHICKENSHIT, IS WHAT IT IS...

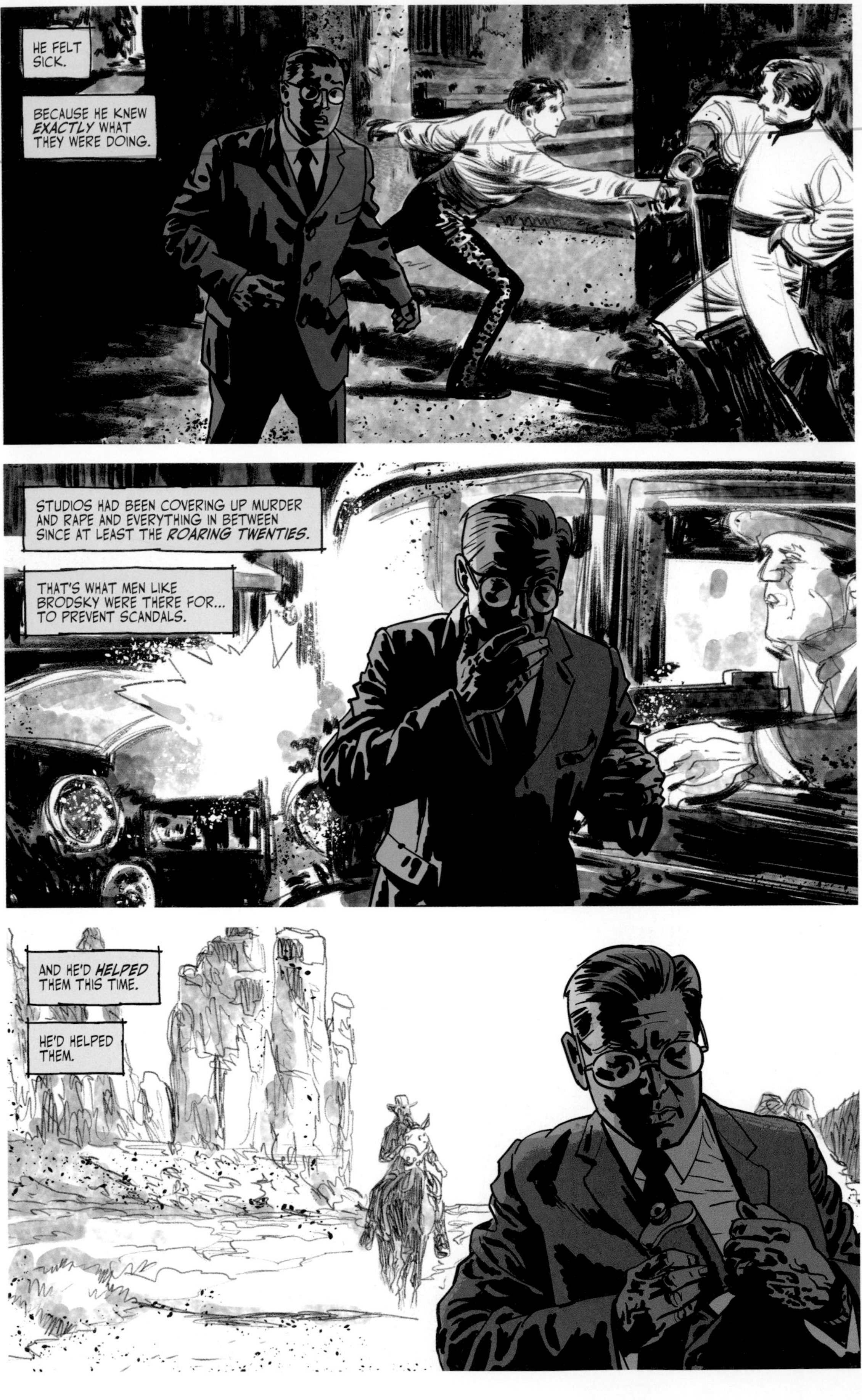
HE FELT SICK.
BECAUSE HE KNEW *EXACTLY* WHAT THEY WERE DOING.
STUDIOS HAD BEEN COVERING UP MURDER AND RAPE AND EVERYTHING IN BETWEEN SINCE AT LEAST THE *ROARING TWENTIES*.
THAT'S WHAT MEN LIKE BRODSKY WERE THERE FOR... TO PREVENT SCANDALS.
AND HE'D *HELPED* THEM THIS TIME.
HE'D HELPED THEM.

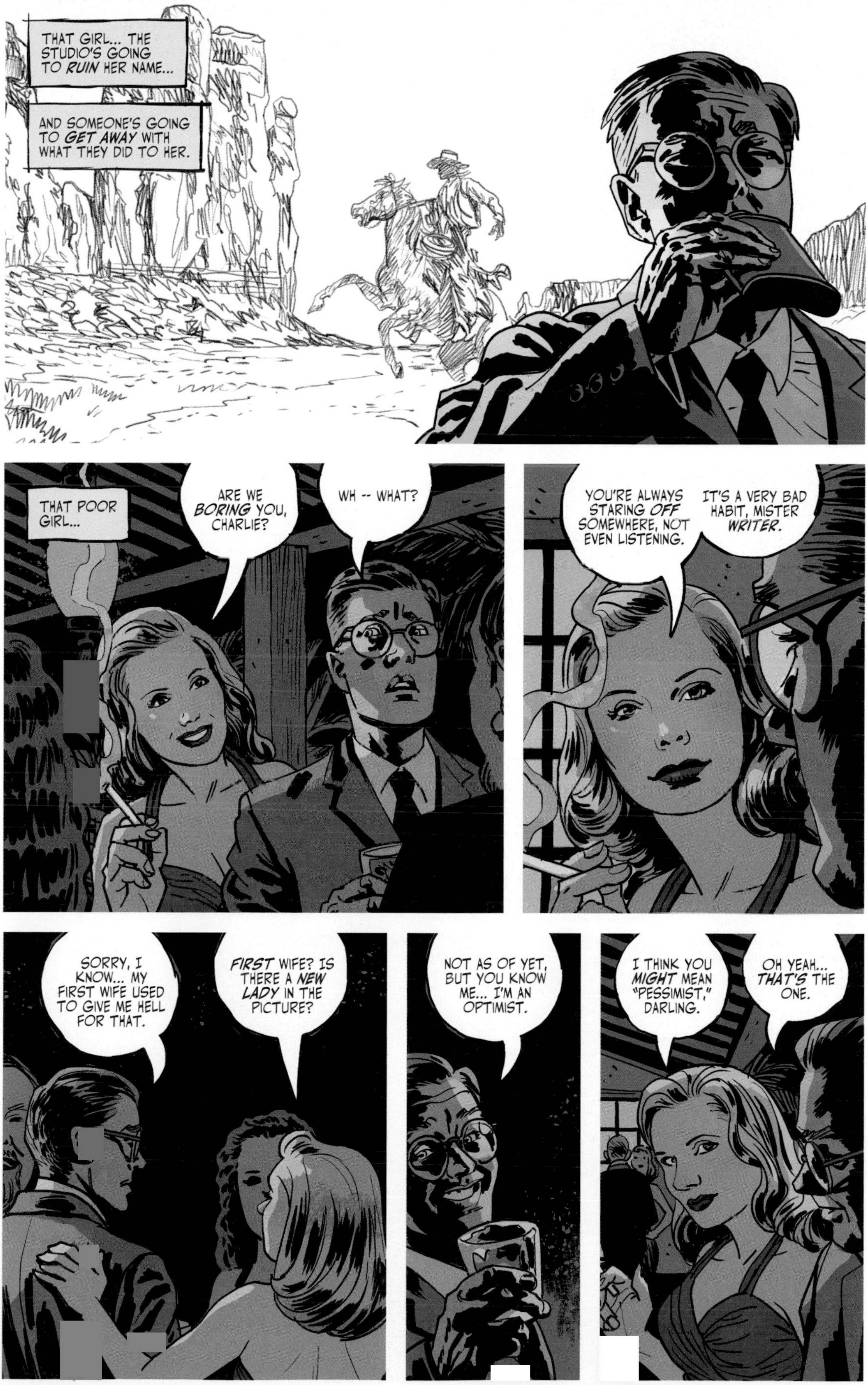

THAT GIRL... THE STUDIO'S GOING TO *RUIN* HER NAME...
AND SOMEONE'S GOING TO *GET AWAY* WITH WHAT THEY DID TO HER.
THAT POOR GIRL...
ARE WE *BORING* YOU, CHARLIE?
WH -- WHAT?
YOU'RE ALWAYS STARING *OFF* SOMEWHERE, NOT EVEN LISTENING.
IT'S A VERY BAD HABIT, MISTER *WRITER.*
SORRY, I KNOW... MY FIRST WIFE USED TO GIVE ME HELL FOR THAT.
FIRST WIFE? IS THERE A *NEW LADY* IN THE PICTURE?
NOT AS OF YET, BUT YOU KNOW ME... I'M AN OPTIMIST.
I THINK YOU *MIGHT* MEAN "PESSIMIST," DARLING.
OH YEAH... *THAT'S* THE ONE.

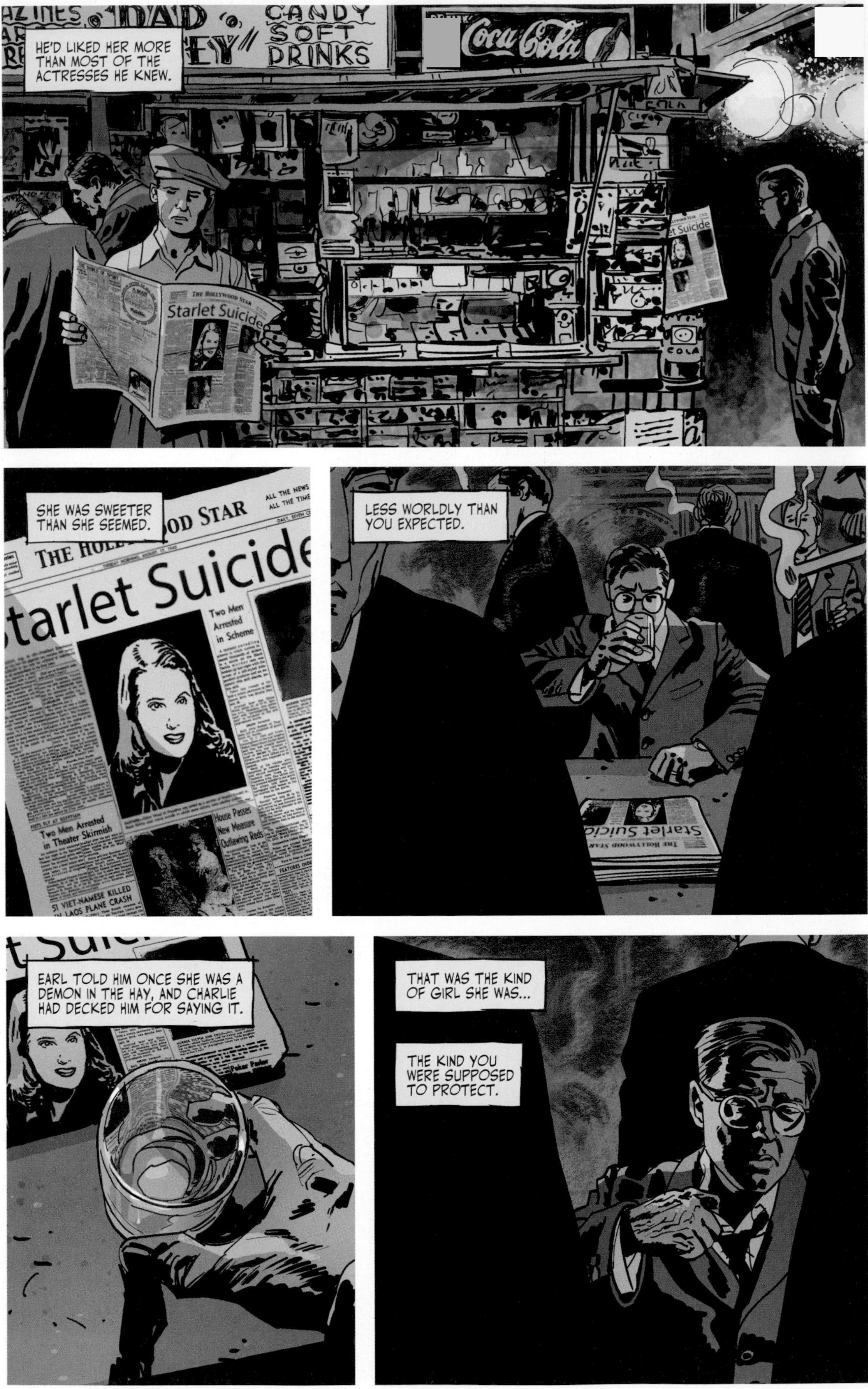
CANDY
SOFT
DRINKS
Coca-Cola
HE'D LIKED HER MORE THAN MOST OF THE ACTRESSES HE KNEW.
THE HOLLYWOOD STAR
Starlet Suicide
COLA
SHE WAS SWEETER THAN SHE SEEMED.
ALL THE NEWS ALL THE TIME
Starlet Suicide
Two Men Arrested in Scheme
Two Men Arrested in Theater Skirmish
House Passes New Measure Outlawing Reds
51 VIET-NAMESE KILLED IN LAOS PLANE CRASH
LESS WORLDLY THAN YOU EXPECTED.
EARL TOLD HIM ONCE SHE WAS A DEMON IN THE HAY, AND CHARLIE HAD DECKED HIM FOR SAYING IT.
THAT WAS THE KIND OF GIRL SHE WAS...
THE KIND YOU WERE SUPPOSED TO PROTECT.

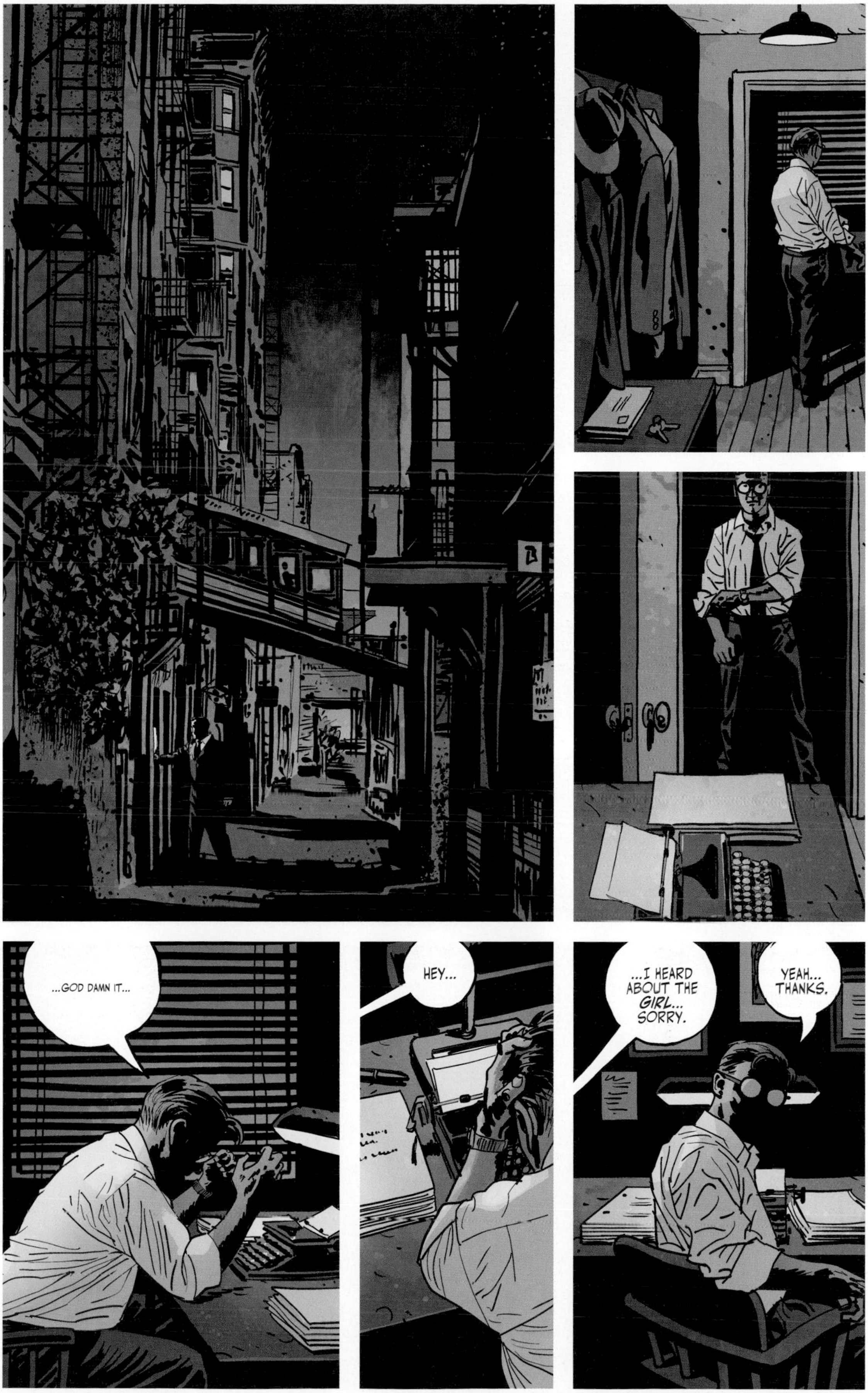
...GOD DAMN IT...
HEY...
...I HEARD ABOUT THE GIRL... SORRY.
YEAH... THANKS.

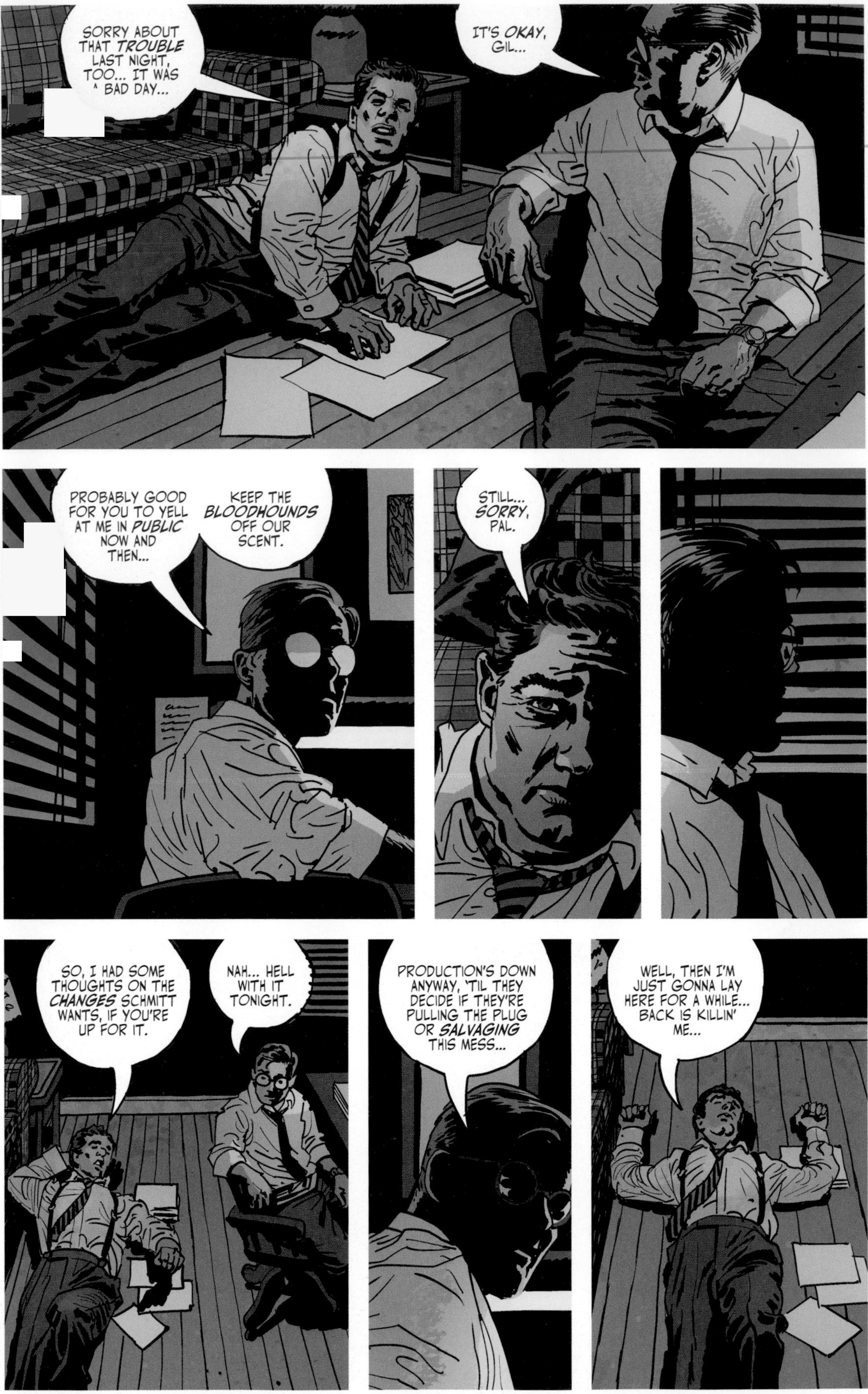
SORRY ABOUT THAT *TROUBLE* LAST NIGHT, TOO... IT WAS A BAD DAY...
IT'S *OKAY*, GIL...
PROBABLY GOOD FOR YOU TO YELL AT ME IN *PUBLIC* NOW AND THEN...
KEEP THE *BLOODHOUNDS* OFF OUR SCENT.
STILL... *SORRY*, PAL.
SO, I HAD SOME THOUGHTS ON THE *CHANGES* SCHMITT WANTS, IF YOU'RE UP FOR IT.
NAH... HELL WITH IT TONIGHT.
PRODUCTION'S DOWN ANYWAY, 'TIL THEY DECIDE IF THEY'RE PULLING THE PLUG OR *SALVAGING* THIS MESS...
WELL, THEN I'M JUST GONNA LAY HERE FOR A WHILE... BACK IS KILLIN' ME...

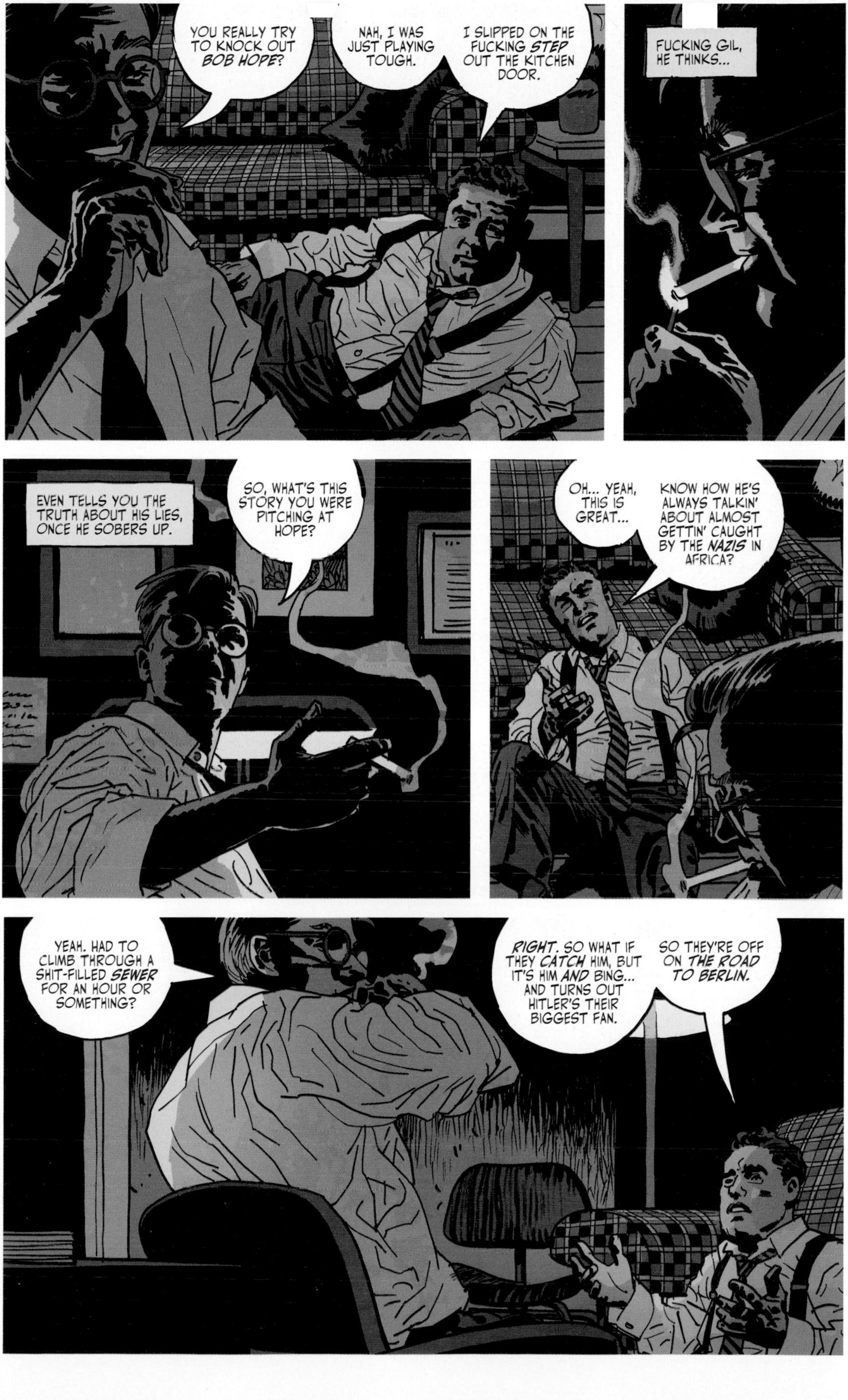
YOU REALLY TRY TO KNOCK OUT BOB HOPE?
NAH, I WAS JUST PLAYING TOUGH.
I SLIPPED ON THE FUCKING STEP OUT THE KITCHEN DOOR.
FUCKING GIL, HE THINKS...
EVEN TELLS YOU THE TRUTH ABOUT HIS LIES, ONCE HE SOBERS UP.
SO, WHAT'S THIS STORY YOU WERE PITCHING AT HOPE?
OH... YEAH, THIS IS GREAT...
KNOW HOW HE'S ALWAYS TALKIN' ABOUT ALMOST GETTIN' CAUGHT BY THE NAZIS IN AFRICA?
YEAH. HAD TO CLIMB THROUGH A SHIT-FILLED SEWER FOR AN HOUR OR SOMETHING?
RIGHT. SO WHAT IF THEY CATCH HIM, BUT IT'S HIM AND BING... AND TURNS OUT HITLER'S THEIR BIGGEST FAN.
SO THEY'RE OFF ON THE ROAD TO BERLIN.

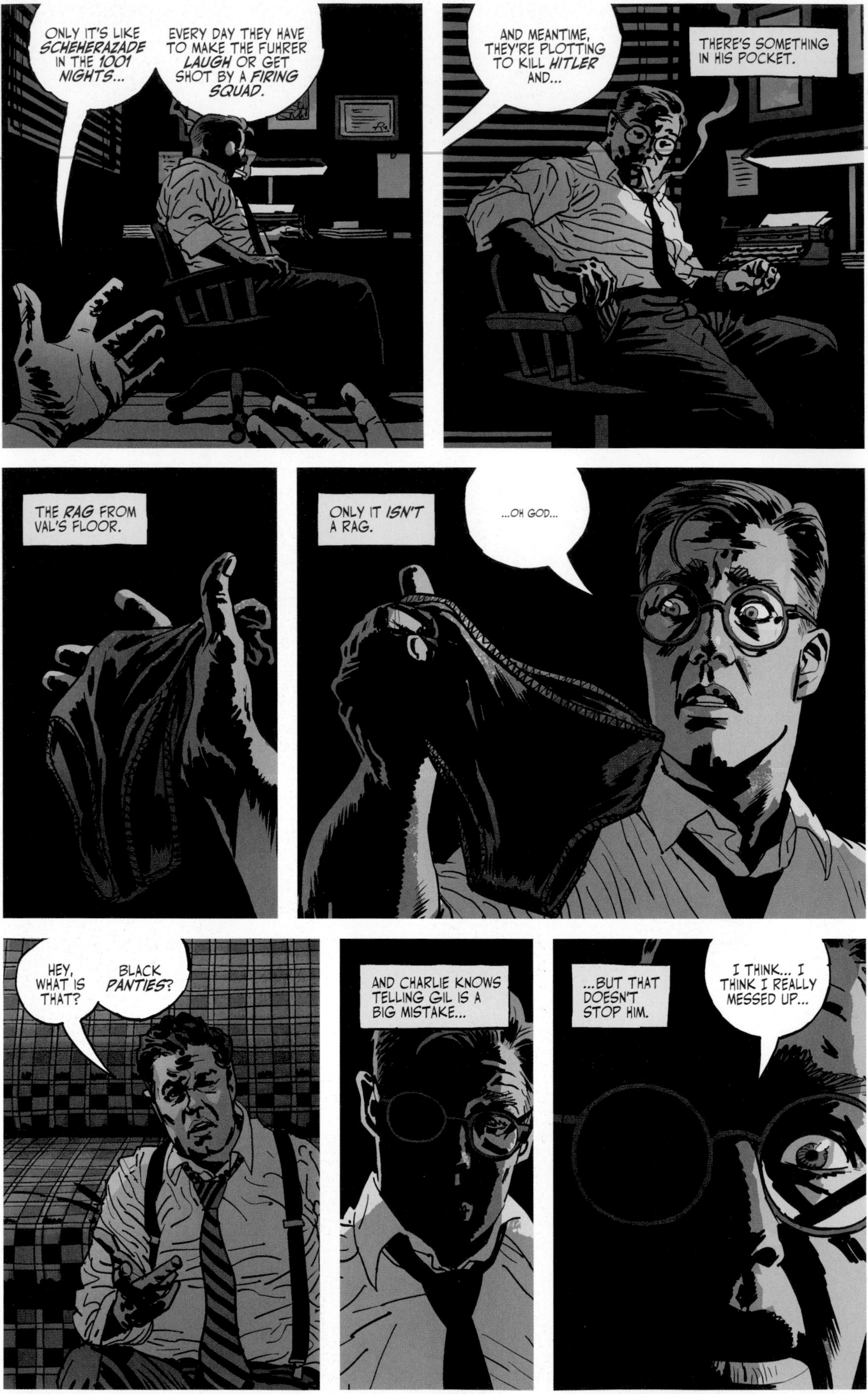
ONLY IT'S LIKE SCHEHERAZADE IN THE 1001 NIGHTS...
EVERY DAY THEY HAVE TO MAKE THE FUHRER LAUGH OR GET SHOT BY A FIRING SQUAD.
AND MEANTIME, THEY'RE PLOTTING TO KILL HITLER AND...
THERE'S SOMETHING IN HIS POCKET.
THE RAG FROM VAL'S FLOOR.
ONLY IT ISN'T A RAG.
...OH GOD...
HEY, WHAT IS THAT?
BLACK PANTIES?
AND CHARLIE KNOWS TELLING GIL IS A BIG MISTAKE...
...BUT THAT DOESN'T STOP HIM.
I THINK... I THINK I REALLY MESSED UP...

The Death of Me

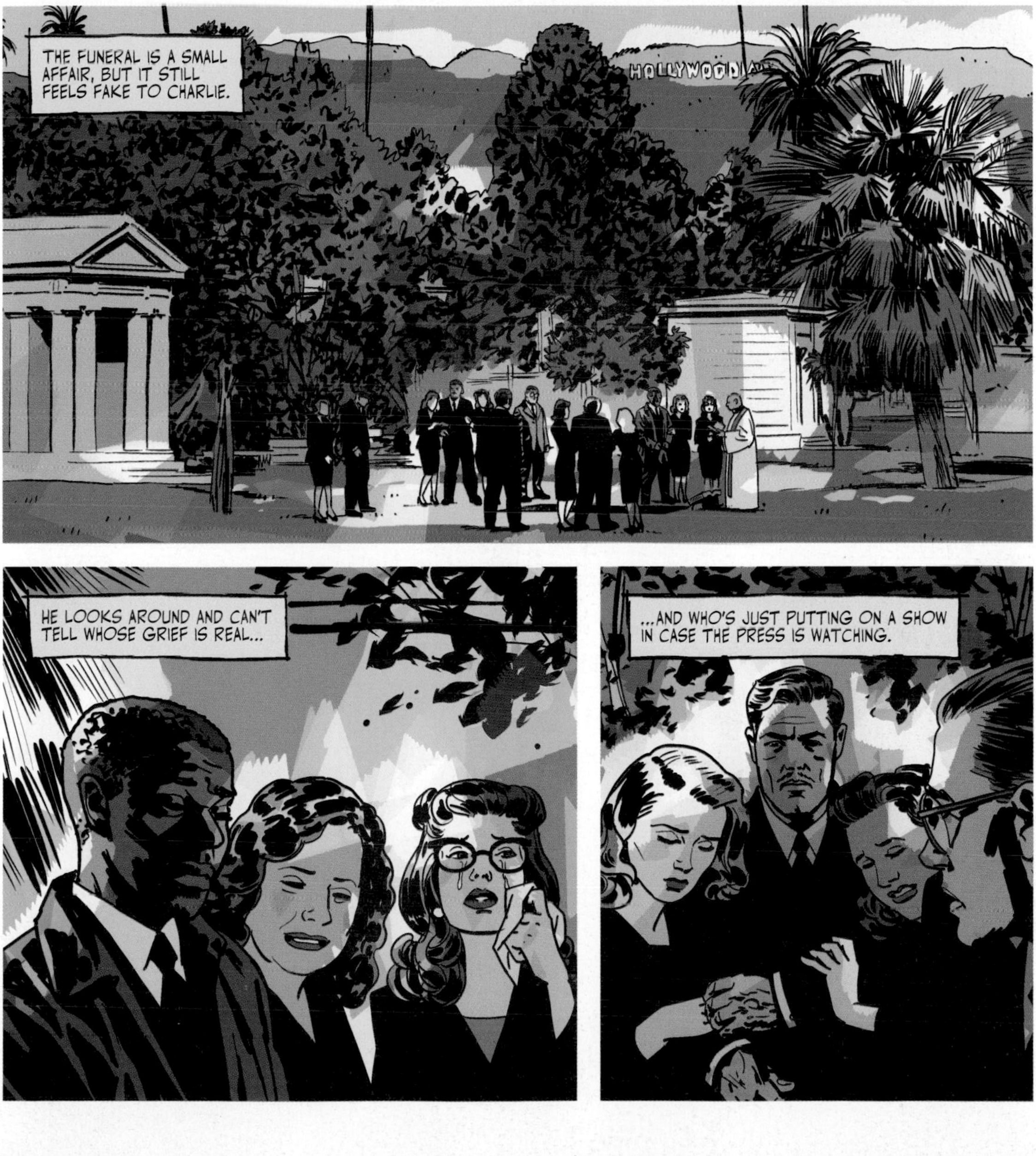
THE FUNERAL IS A SMALL AFFAIR, BUT IT STILL FEELS FAKE TO CHARLIE.
HOLLYWOOD
HE LOOKS AROUND AND CAN'T TELL WHOSE GRIEF IS REAL...
...AND WHO'S JUST PUTTING ON A SHOW IN CASE THE PRESS IS WATCHING.

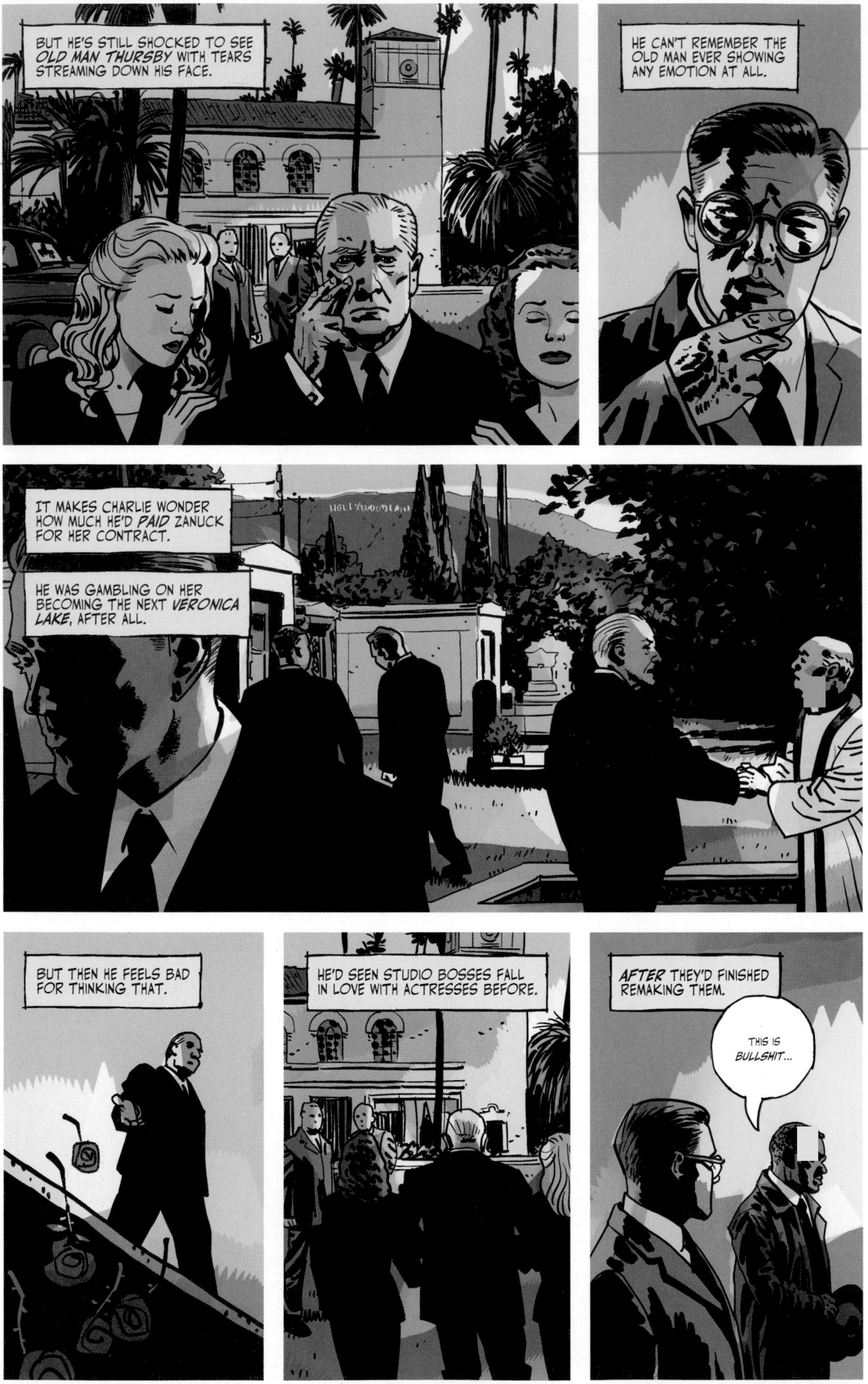
BUT HE'S STILL SHOCKED TO SEE *OLD MAN THURSBY* WITH TEARS STREAMING DOWN HIS FACE.
HE CAN'T REMEMBER THE OLD MAN EVER SHOWING ANY EMOTION AT ALL.
IT MAKES CHARLIE WONDER HOW MUCH HE'D *PAID* ZANUCK FOR HER CONTRACT.
HE WAS GAMBLING ON HER BECOMING THE NEXT *VERONICA LAKE*, AFTER ALL.
BUT THEN HE FEELS BAD FOR THINKING THAT.
HE'D SEEN STUDIO BOSSES FALL IN LOVE WITH ACTRESSES BEFORE.
AFTER THEY'D FINISHED REMAKING THEM.
THIS IS *BULLSHIT*...

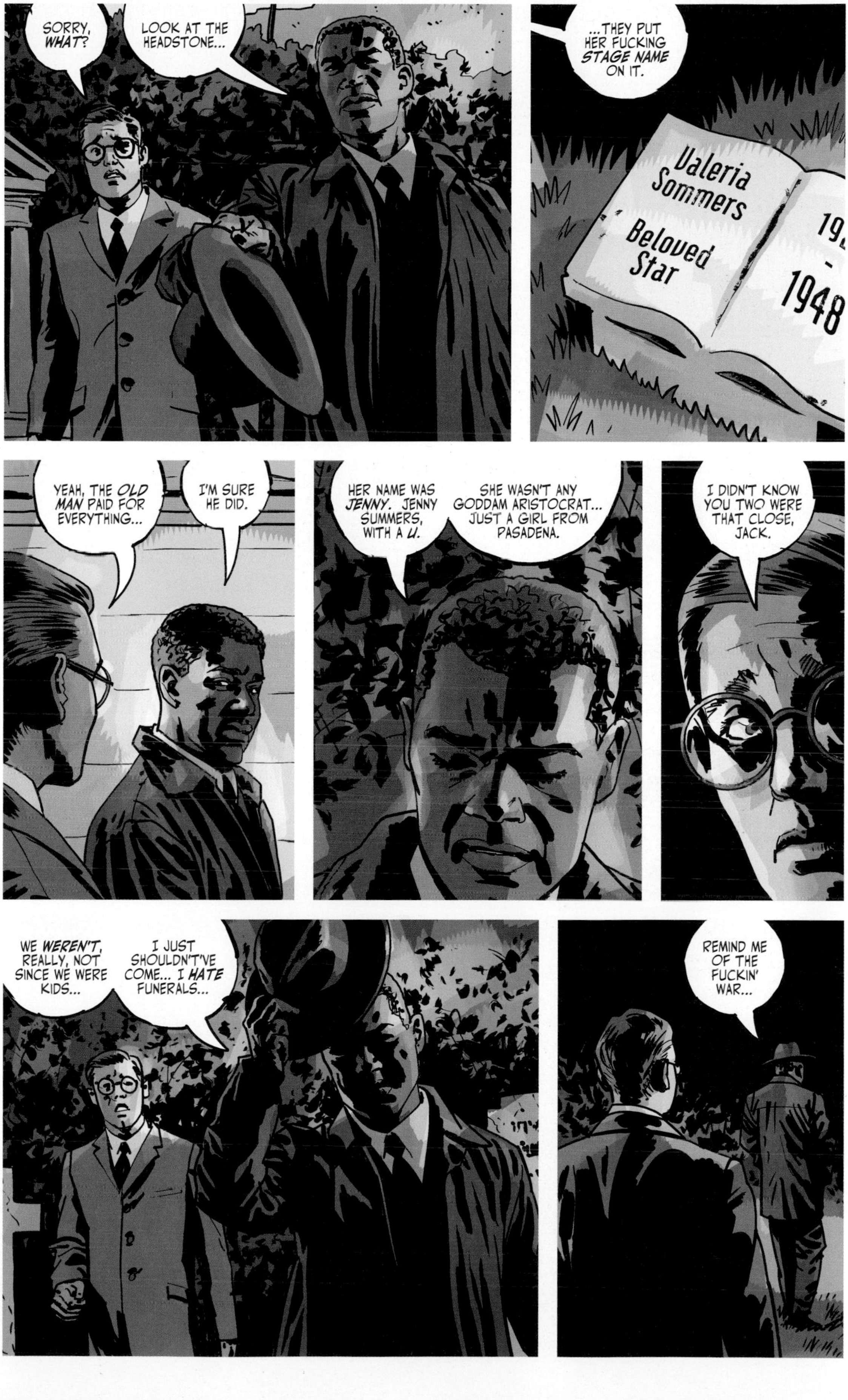
SORRY, WHAT?
LOOK AT THE HEADSTONE...
...THEY PUT HER FUCKING STAGE NAME ON IT.
Valeria Sommers
Beloved Star
1948
YEAH, THE OLD MAN PAID FOR EVERYTHING...
I'M SURE HE DID.
HER NAME WAS JENNY. JENNY SUMMERS, WITH A U.
SHE WASN'T ANY GODDAM ARISTOCRAT... JUST A GIRL FROM PASADENA.
I DIDN'T KNOW YOU TWO WERE THAT CLOSE, JACK.
WE WEREN'T, REALLY, NOT SINCE WE WERE KIDS...
I JUST SHOULDN'T'VE COME... I HATE FUNERALS...
REMIND ME OF THE FUCKIN' WAR...

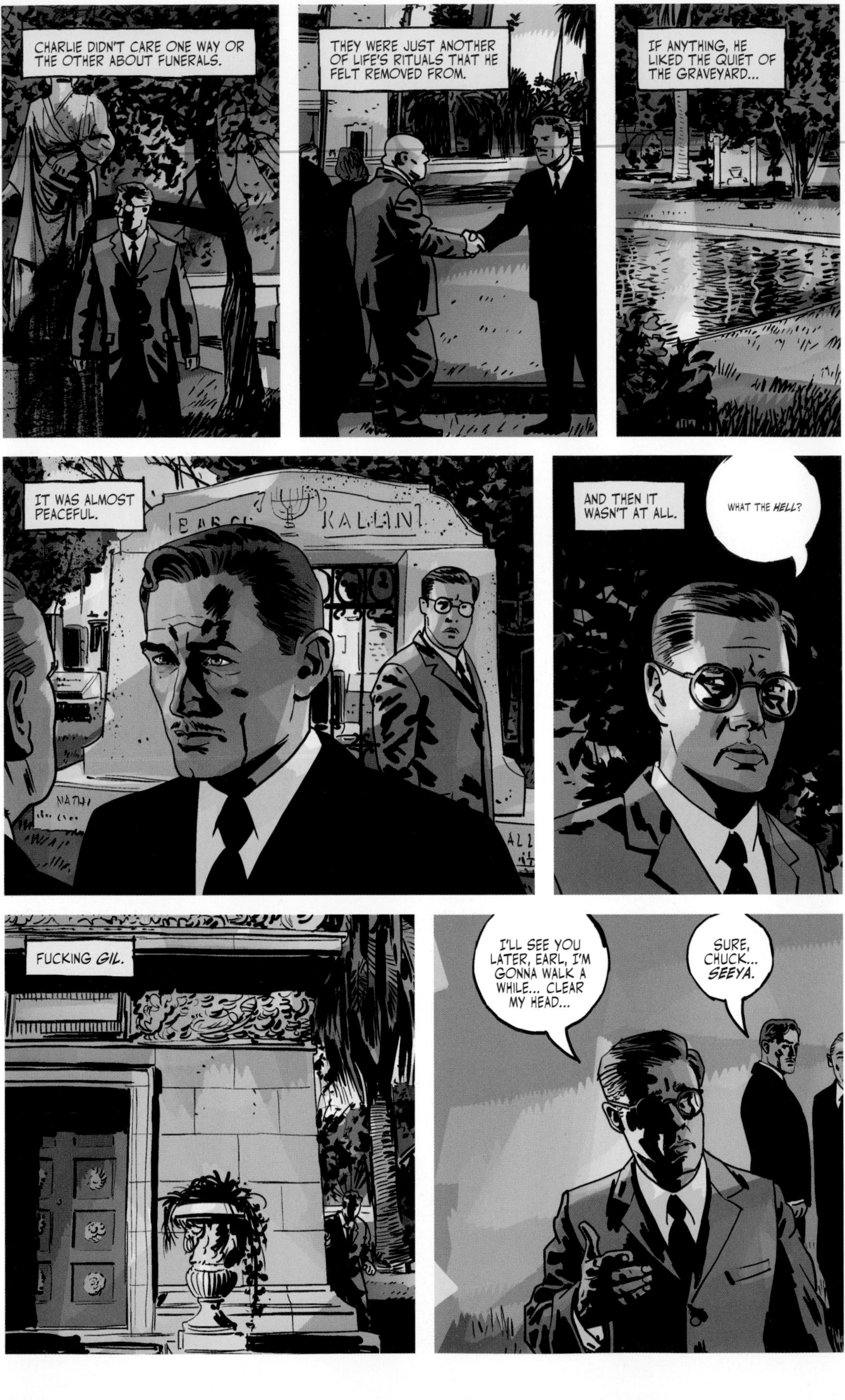
CHARLIE DIDN'T CARE ONE WAY OR THE OTHER ABOUT FUNERALS.
THEY WERE JUST ANOTHER OF LIFE'S RITUALS THAT HE FELT REMOVED FROM.
IF ANYTHING, HE LIKED THE QUIET OF THE GRAVEYARD...
IT WAS ALMOST PEACEFUL.
KALLIN
AND THEN IT WASN'T AT ALL.
WHAT THE HELL?
FUCKING GIL.
I'LL SEE YOU LATER, EARL, I'M GONNA WALK A WHILE... CLEAR MY HEAD...
SURE, CHUCK... SEEYA.

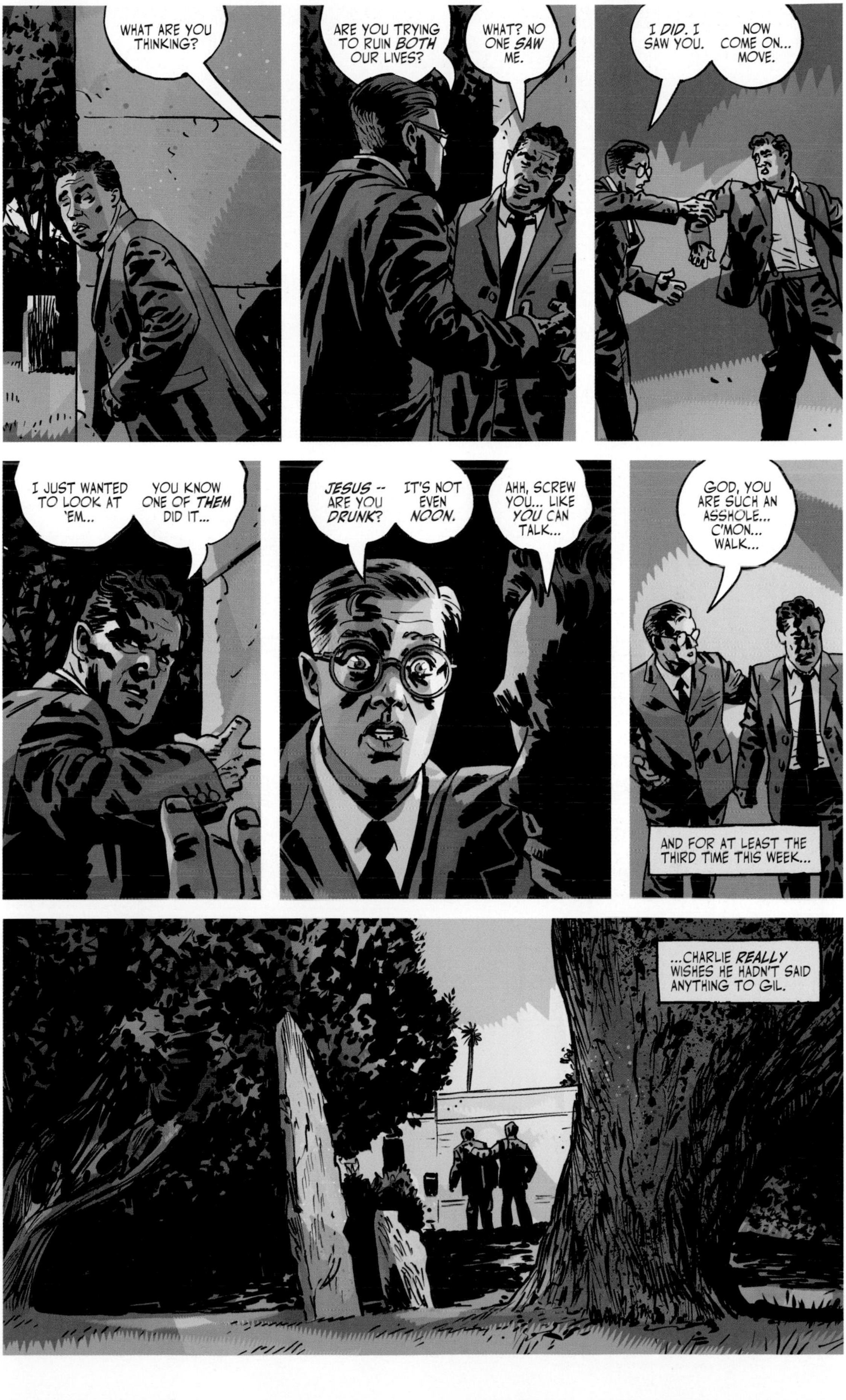
WHAT ARE YOU THINKING?
ARE YOU TRYING TO RUIN BOTH OUR LIVES?
WHAT? NO ONE SAW ME.
I DID. I SAW YOU.
NOW COME ON... MOVE.
I JUST WANTED TO LOOK AT 'EM...
YOU KNOW ONE OF THEM DID IT...
JESUS -- ARE YOU DRUNK?
IT'S NOT EVEN NOON.
AHH, SCREW YOU... LIKE YOU CAN TALK...
GOD, YOU ARE SUCH AN ASSHOLE... C'MON... WALK...
AND FOR AT LEAST THE THIRD TIME THIS WEEK...
...CHARLIE REALLY WISHES HE HADN'T SAID ANYTHING TO GIL.

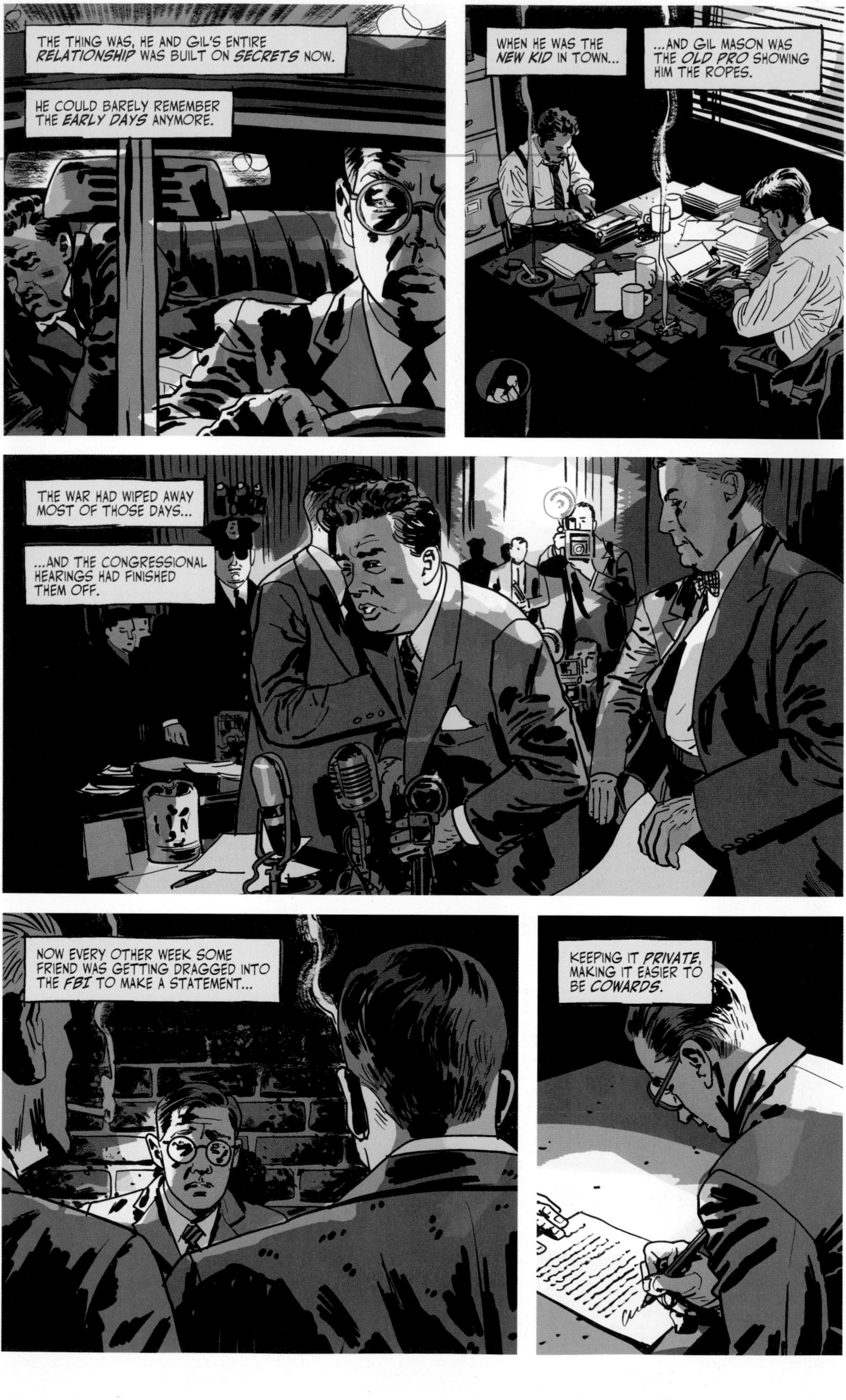
THE THING WAS, HE AND GIL'S ENTIRE RELATIONSHIP WAS BUILT ON SECRETS NOW.
HE COULD BARELY REMEMBER THE EARLY DAYS ANYMORE.
WHEN HE WAS THE NEW KID IN TOWN...
...AND GIL MASON WAS THE OLD PRO SHOWING HIM THE ROPES.
THE WAR HAD WIPED AWAY MOST OF THOSE DAYS...
...AND THE CONGRESSIONAL HEARINGS HAD FINISHED THEM OFF.
NOW EVERY OTHER WEEK SOME FRIEND WAS GETTING DRAGGED INTO THE FBI TO MAKE A STATEMENT...
KEEPING IT PRIVATE, MAKING IT EASIER TO BE COWARDS.

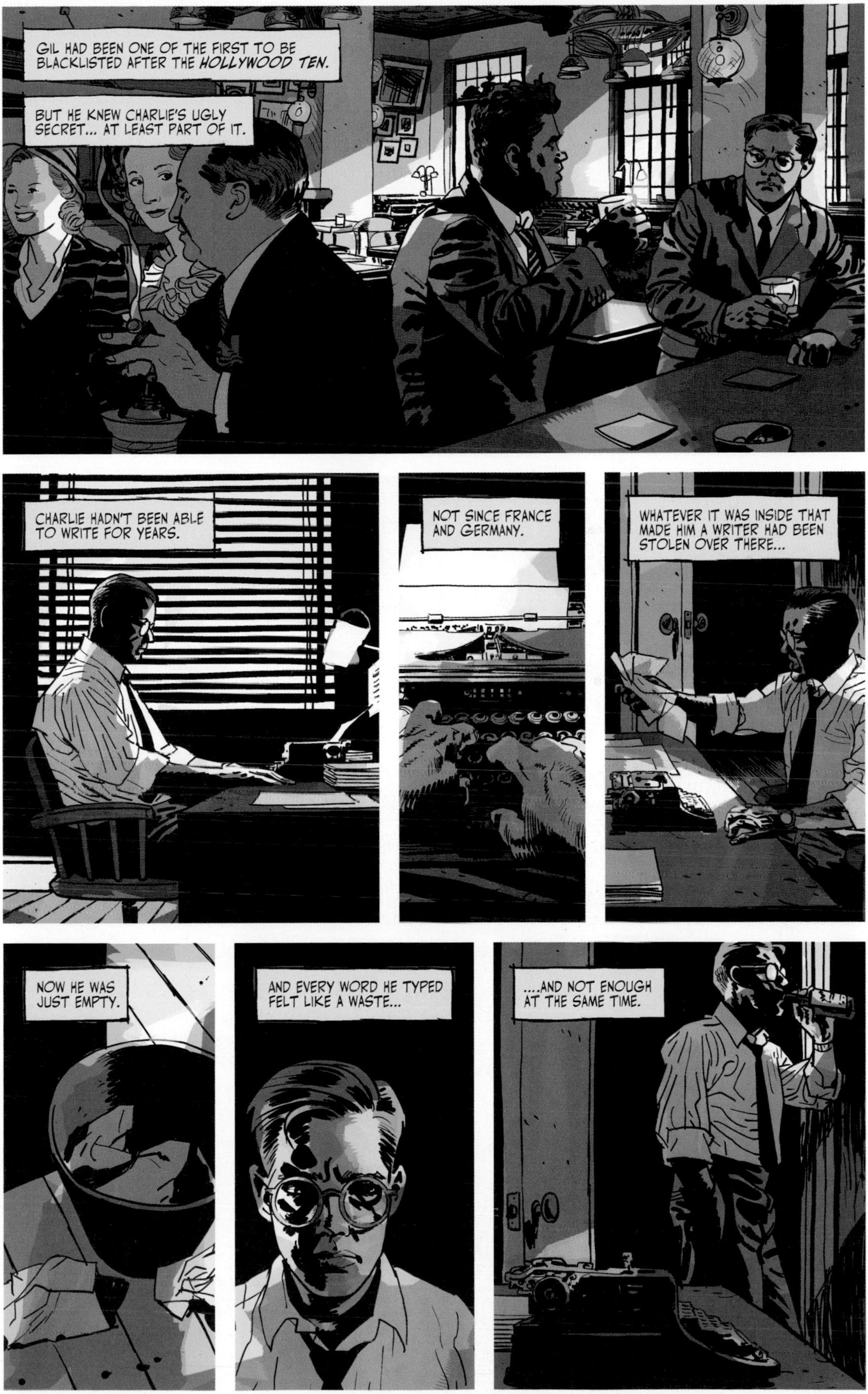
GIL HAD BEEN ONE OF THE FIRST TO BE BLACKLISTED AFTER THE *HOLLYWOOD TEN*.
BUT HE KNEW CHARLIE'S UGLY SECRET... AT LEAST PART OF IT.
CHARLIE HADN'T BEEN ABLE TO WRITE FOR YEARS.
NOT SINCE FRANCE AND GERMANY.
WHATEVER IT WAS INSIDE THAT MADE HIM A WRITER HAD BEEN STOLEN OVER THERE...
NOW HE WAS JUST EMPTY.
AND EVERY WORD HE TYPED FELT LIKE A WASTE...
....AND NOT ENOUGH AT THE SAME TIME.

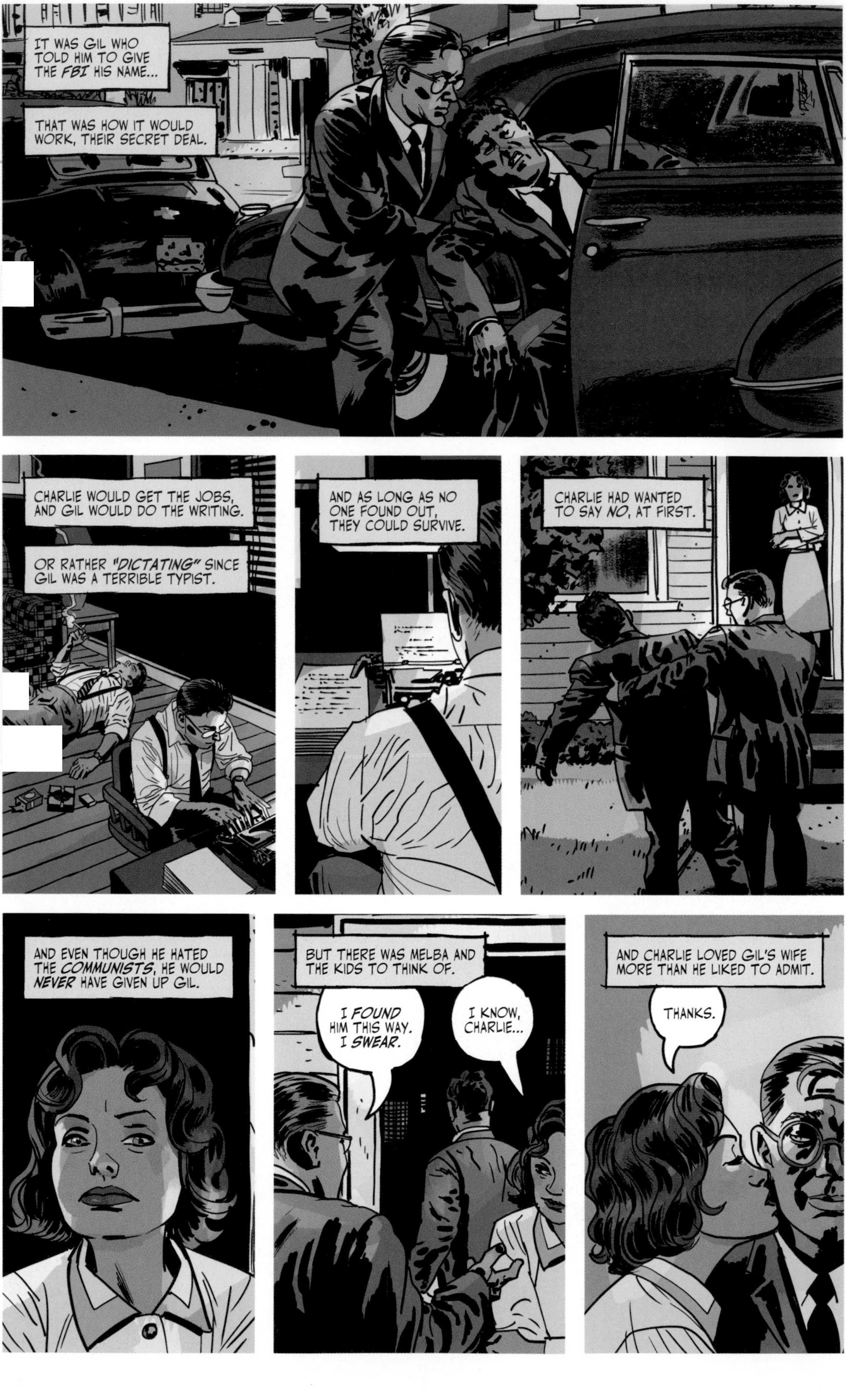
IT WAS GIL WHO TOLD HIM TO GIVE THE FBI HIS NAME...
THAT WAS HOW IT WOULD WORK, THEIR SECRET DEAL.
CHARLIE WOULD GET THE JOBS, AND GIL WOULD DO THE WRITING.
OR RATHER "DICTATING" SINCE GIL WAS A TERRIBLE TYPIST.
AND AS LONG AS NO ONE FOUND OUT, THEY COULD SURVIVE.
CHARLIE HAD WANTED TO SAY NO, AT FIRST.
AND EVEN THOUGH HE HATED THE COMMUNISTS, HE WOULD NEVER HAVE GIVEN UP GIL.
BUT THERE WAS MELBA AND THE KIDS TO THINK OF.
I FOUND HIM THIS WAY. I SWEAR.
I KNOW, CHARLIE...
AND CHARLIE LOVED GIL'S WIFE MORE THAN HE LIKED TO ADMIT.
THANKS.

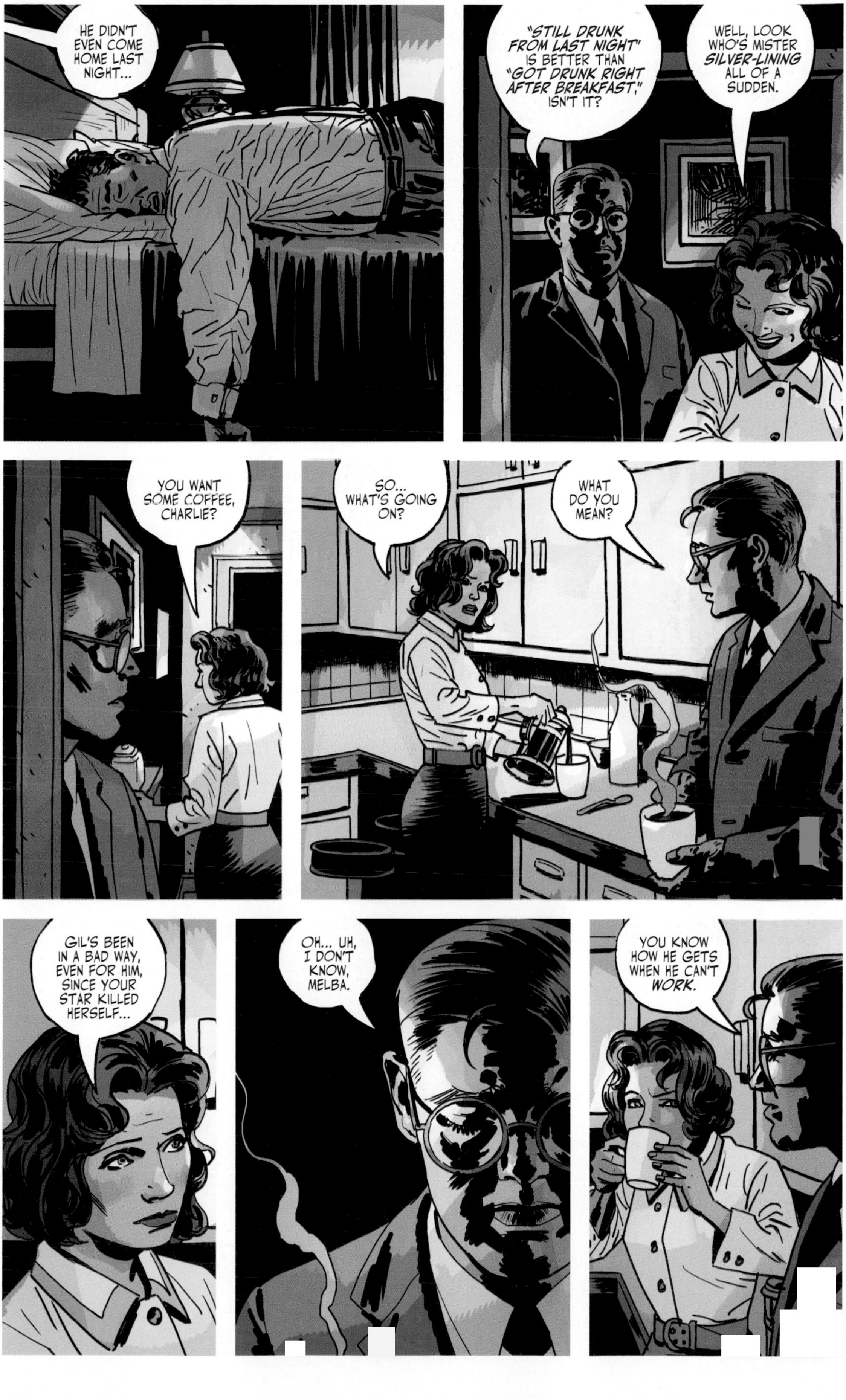
HE DIDN'T EVEN COME HOME LAST NIGHT...
"STILL DRUNK FROM LAST NIGHT" IS BETTER THAN "GOT DRUNK RIGHT AFTER BREAKFAST," ISN'T IT?
WELL, LOOK WHO'S MISTER SILVER-LINING ALL OF A SUDDEN.
YOU WANT SOME COFFEE, CHARLIE?
SO... WHAT'S GOING ON?
WHAT DO YOU MEAN?
GIL'S BEEN IN A BAD WAY, EVEN FOR HIM, SINCE YOUR STAR KILLED HERSELF...
OH... UH, I DON'T KNOW, MELBA.
YOU KNOW HOW HE GETS WHEN HE CAN'T WORK.

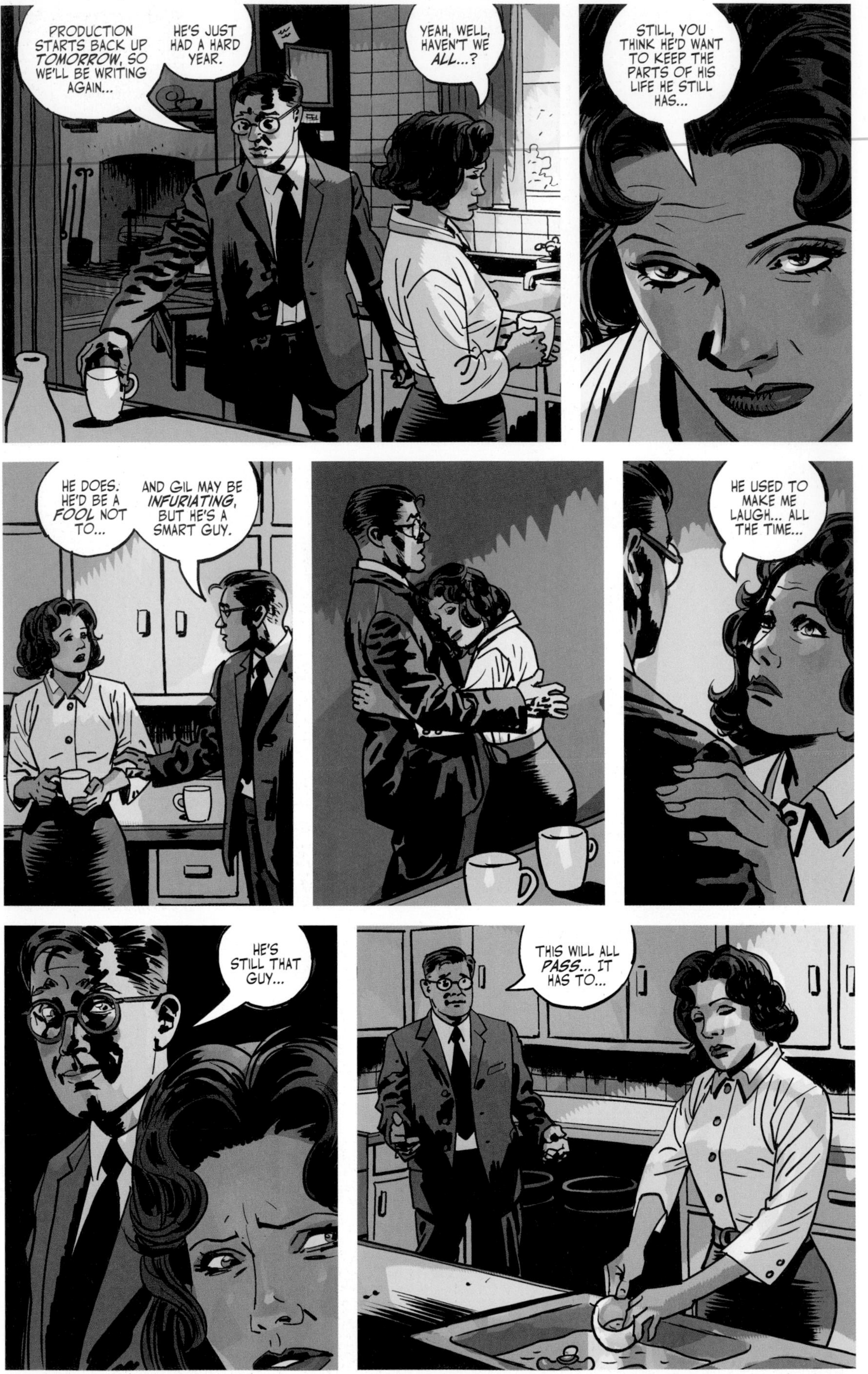
PRODUCTION STARTS BACK UP *TOMORROW*, SO WE'LL BE WRITING AGAIN...
HE'S JUST HAD A HARD YEAR.
YEAH, WELL, HAVEN'T WE *ALL*...?
STILL, YOU THINK HE'D WANT TO KEEP THE PARTS OF HIS LIFE HE STILL HAS...
HE DOES. HE'D BE A *FOOL* NOT TO...
AND GIL MAY BE *INFURIATING*, BUT HE'S A SMART GUY.
HE USED TO MAKE ME LAUGH... ALL THE TIME...
HE'S STILL THAT GUY...
THIS WILL ALL *PASS*... IT HAS TO...

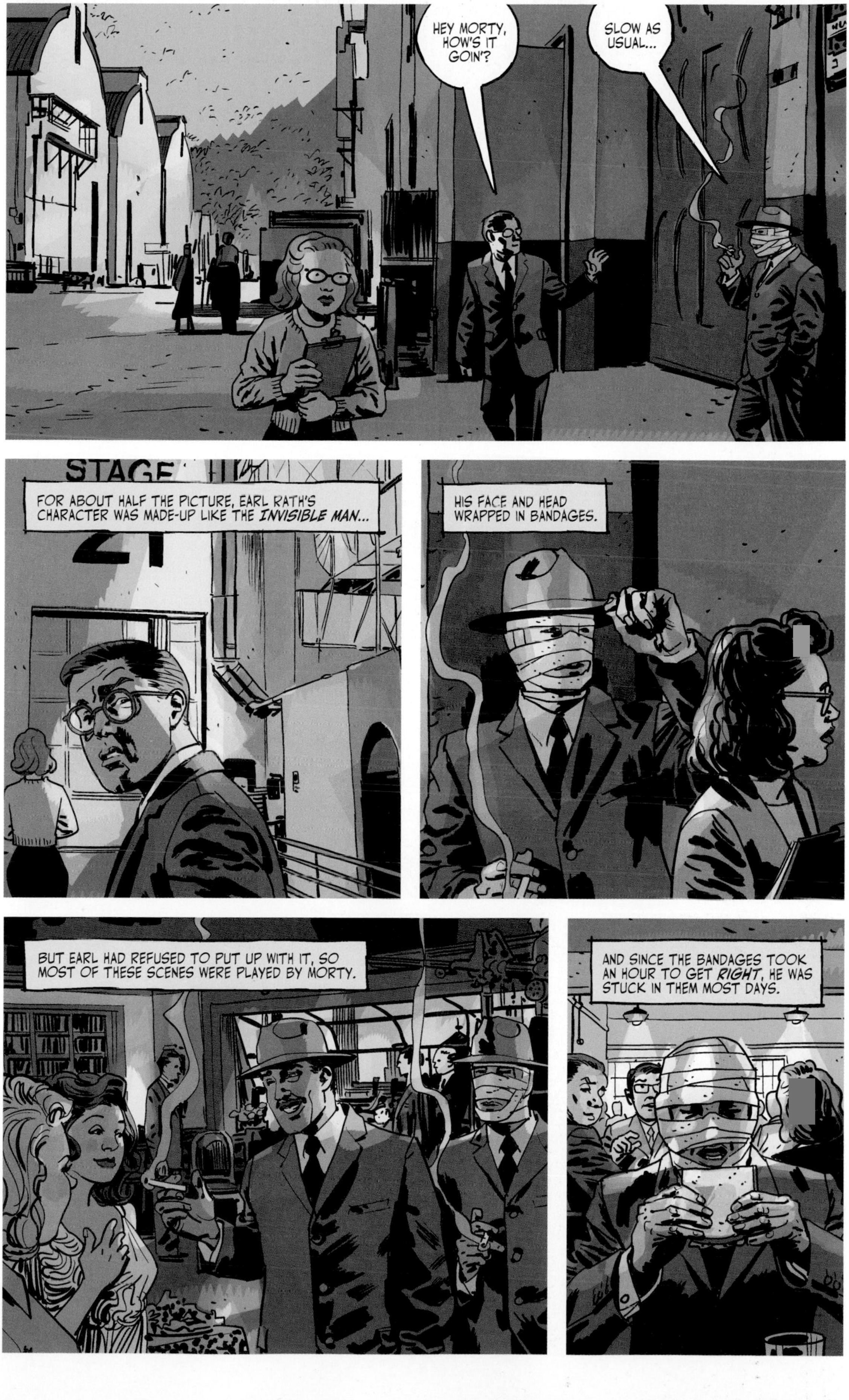
HEY MORTY, HOW'S IT GOIN'?
SLOW AS USUAL...
STAGE 21
FOR ABOUT HALF THE PICTURE, EARL RATH'S CHARACTER WAS MADE-UP LIKE THE *INVISIBLE MAN*...
HIS FACE AND HEAD WRAPPED IN BANDAGES.
BUT EARL HAD REFUSED TO PUT UP WITH IT, SO MOST OF THESE SCENES WERE PLAYED BY MORTY.
AND SINCE THE BANDAGES TOOK AN HOUR TO GET *RIGHT*, HE WAS STUCK IN THEM MOST DAYS.

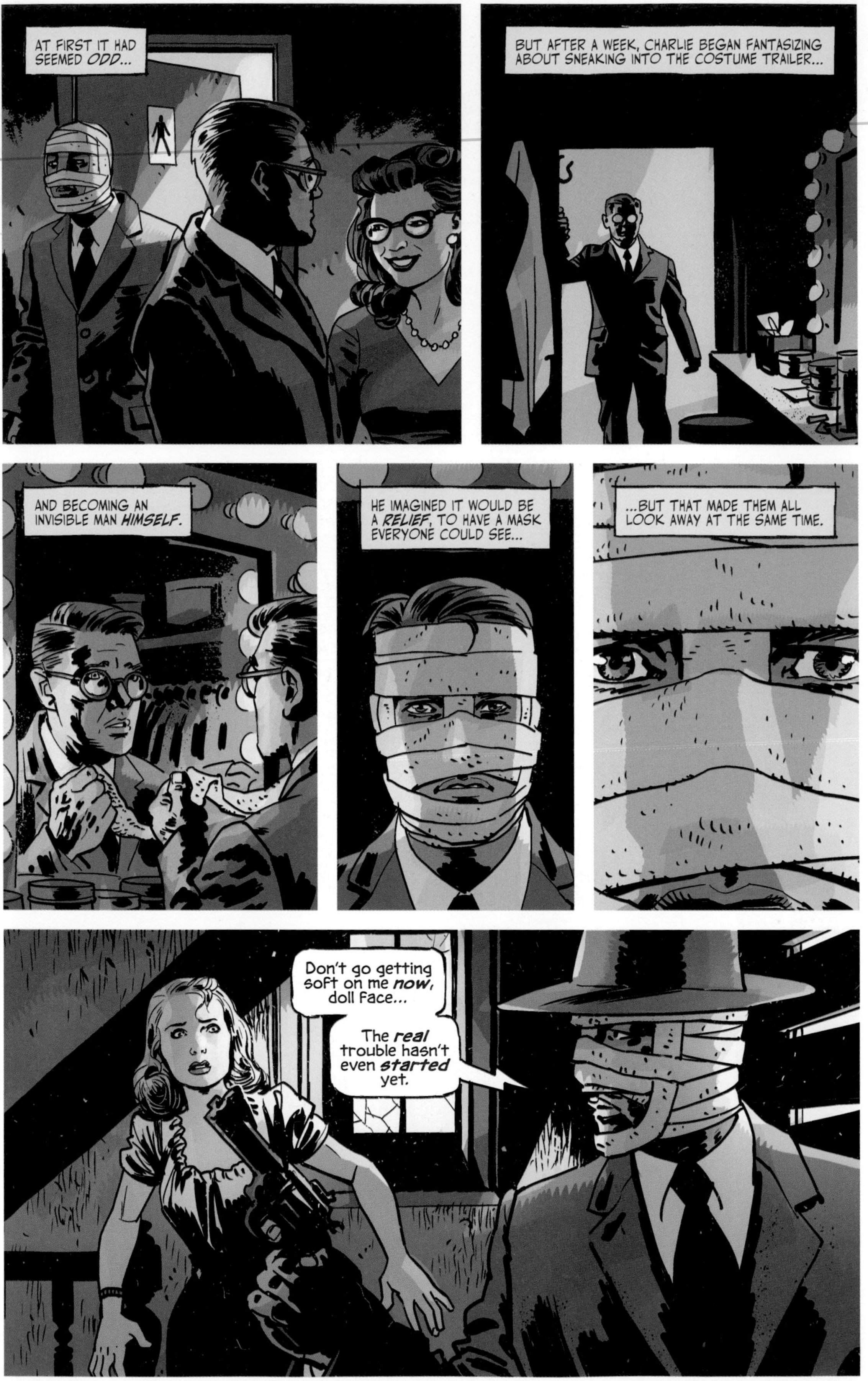
AT FIRST IT HAD SEEMED *ODD*...
BUT AFTER A WEEK, CHARLIE BEGAN FANTASIZING ABOUT SNEAKING INTO THE COSTUME TRAILER...
AND BECOMING AN INVISIBLE MAN *HIMSELF*.
HE IMAGINED IT WOULD BE A *RELIEF*, TO HAVE A MASK EVERYONE COULD SEE...
...BUT THAT MADE THEM ALL LOOK AWAY AT THE SAME TIME.
Don't go getting soft on me *now*, doll face...
The *real* trouble hasn't even *started* yet.

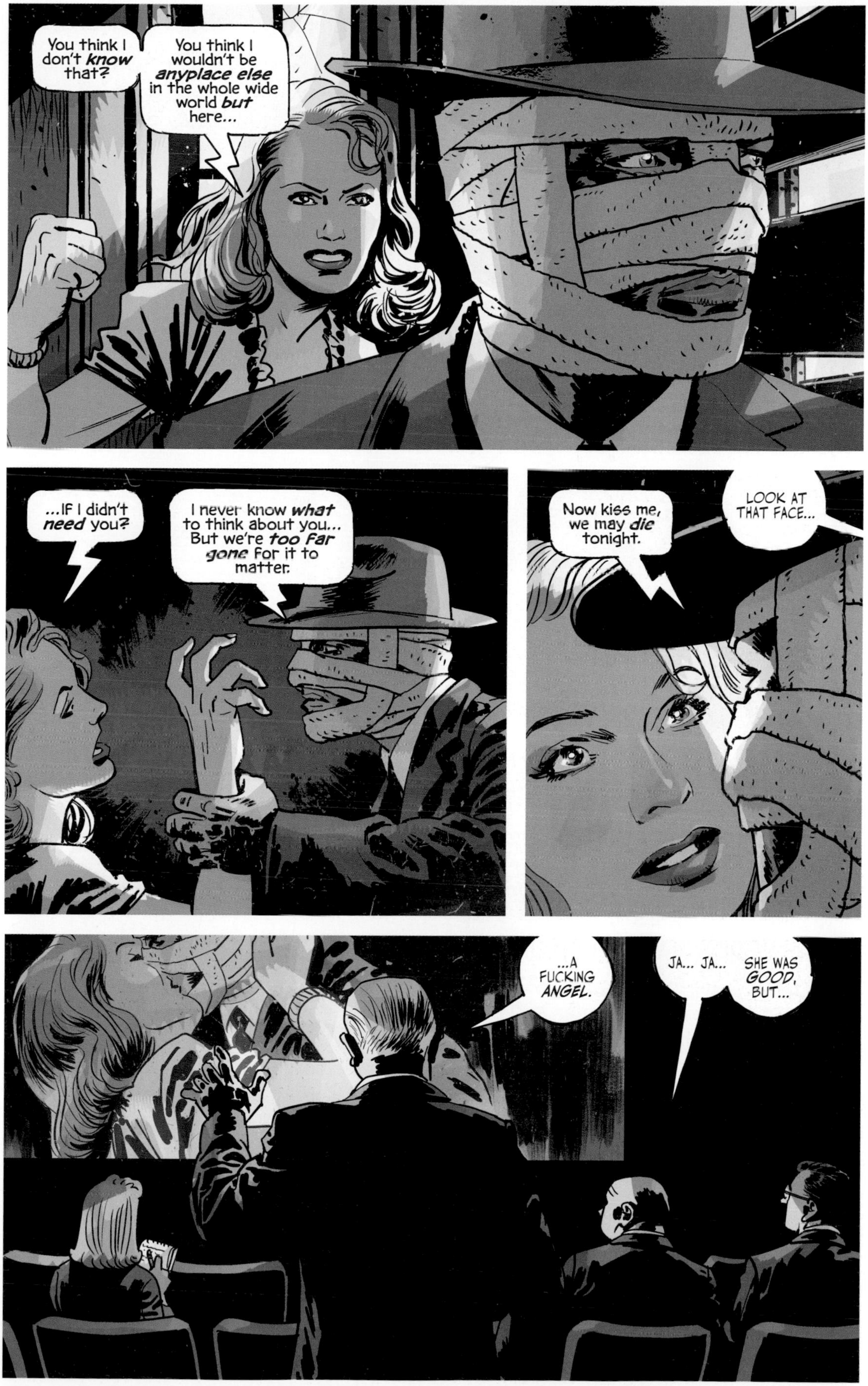
You think I don't *know* that?
You think I wouldn't be *anyplace else* in the whole wide world *but* here...
...If I didn't *need* you?
I never know *what* to think about you... But we're *too far gone* for it to matter.
Now kiss me, we may *die* tonight.
LOOK AT THAT FACE...
...A FUCKING *ANGEL.*
JA... JA...
SHE WAS *GOOD,* BUT...

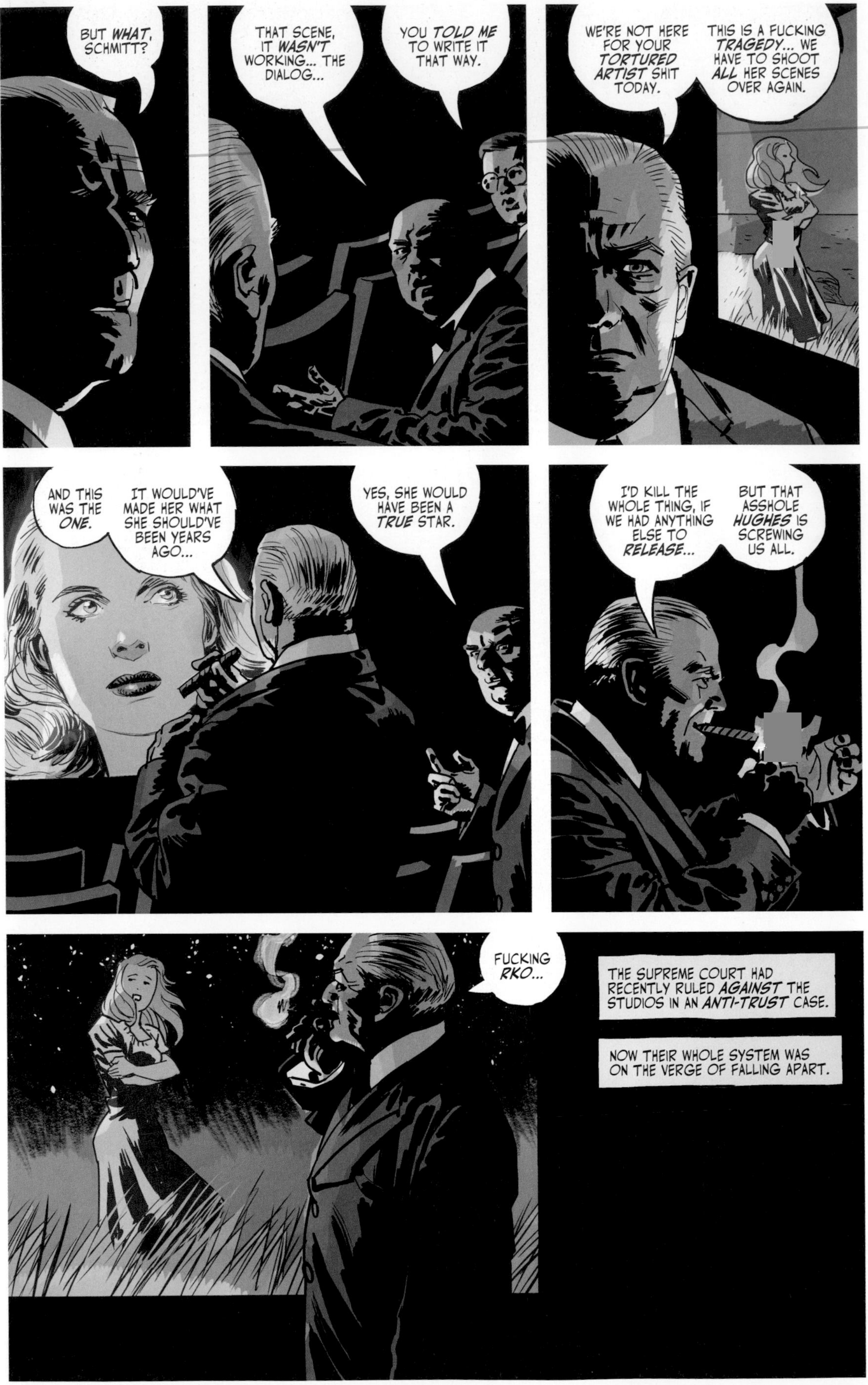

BUT *WHAT*, SCHMITT?
THAT SCENE, IT *WASN'T* WORKING... THE DIALOG...
YOU *TOLD ME* TO WRITE IT THAT WAY.
WE'RE NOT HERE FOR YOUR *TORTURED ARTIST* SHIT TODAY.
THIS IS A FUCKING *TRAGEDY*... WE HAVE TO SHOOT *ALL* HER SCENES OVER AGAIN.
AND THIS WAS THE *ONE*.
IT WOULD'VE MADE HER WHAT SHE SHOULD'VE BEEN YEARS AGO...
YES, SHE WOULD HAVE BEEN A *TRUE* STAR.
I'D KILL THE WHOLE THING, IF WE HAD ANYTHING ELSE TO *RELEASE*...
BUT THAT ASSHOLE *HUGHES* IS SCREWING US ALL.
FUCKING *RKO*...
THE SUPREME COURT HAD RECENTLY RULED *AGAINST* THE STUDIOS IN AN *ANTI-TRUST* CASE.
NOW THEIR WHOLE SYSTEM WAS ON THE VERGE OF FALLING APART.

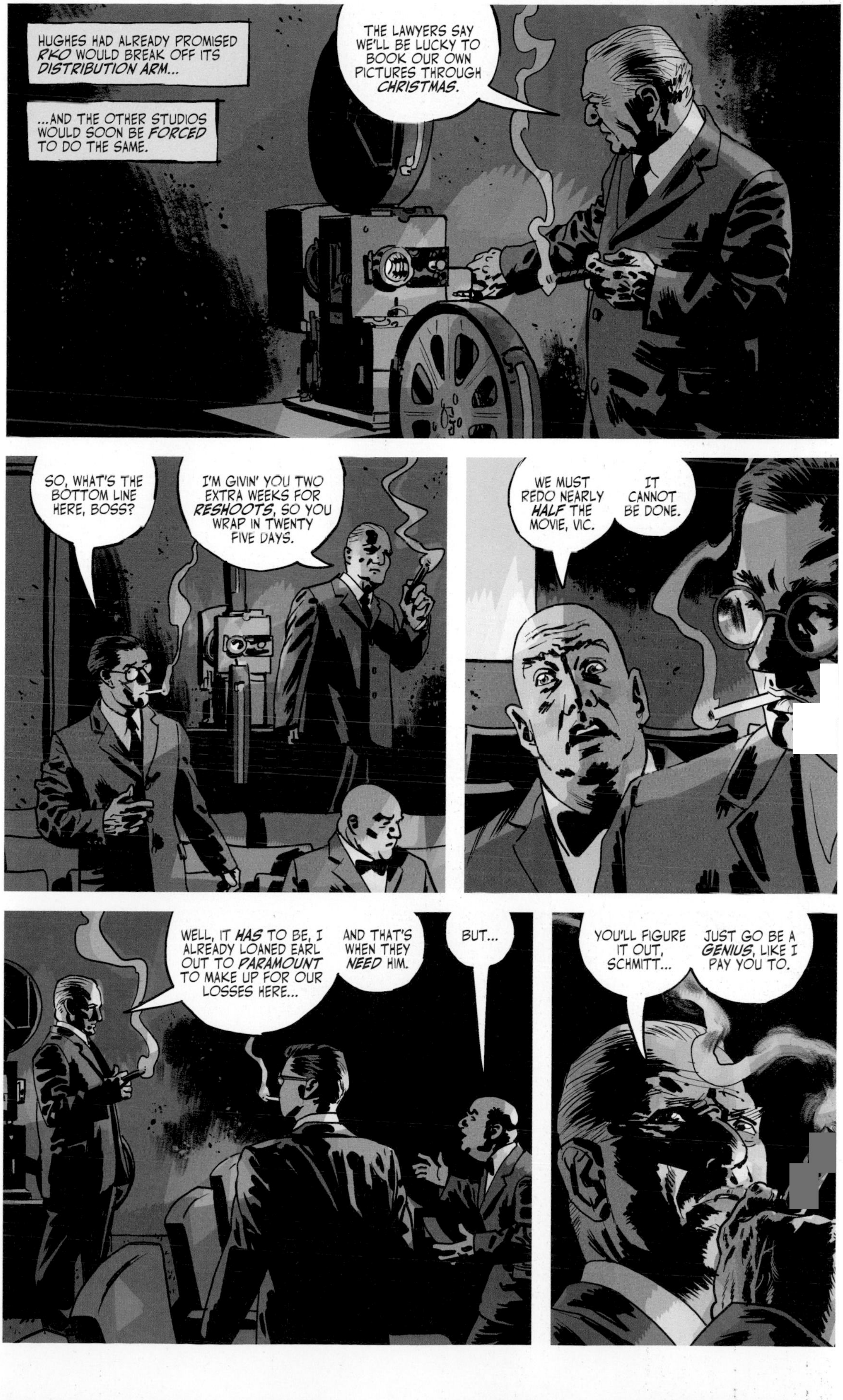
HUGHES HAD ALREADY PROMISED RKO WOULD BREAK OFF ITS DISTRIBUTION ARM...
...AND THE OTHER STUDIOS WOULD SOON BE FORCED TO DO THE SAME.
THE LAWYERS SAY WE'LL BE LUCKY TO BOOK OUR OWN PICTURES THROUGH CHRISTMAS.
SO, WHAT'S THE BOTTOM LINE HERE, BOSS?
I'M GIVIN' YOU TWO EXTRA WEEKS FOR RESHOOTS, SO YOU WRAP IN TWENTY FIVE DAYS.
WE MUST REDO NEARLY HALF THE MOVIE, VIC.
IT CANNOT BE DONE.
WELL, IT HAS TO BE, I ALREADY LOANED EARL OUT TO PARAMOUNT TO MAKE UP FOR OUR LOSSES HERE...
AND THAT'S WHEN THEY NEED HIM.
BUT...
YOU'LL FIGURE IT OUT, SCHMITT...
JUST GO BE A GENIUS, LIKE I PAY YOU TO.

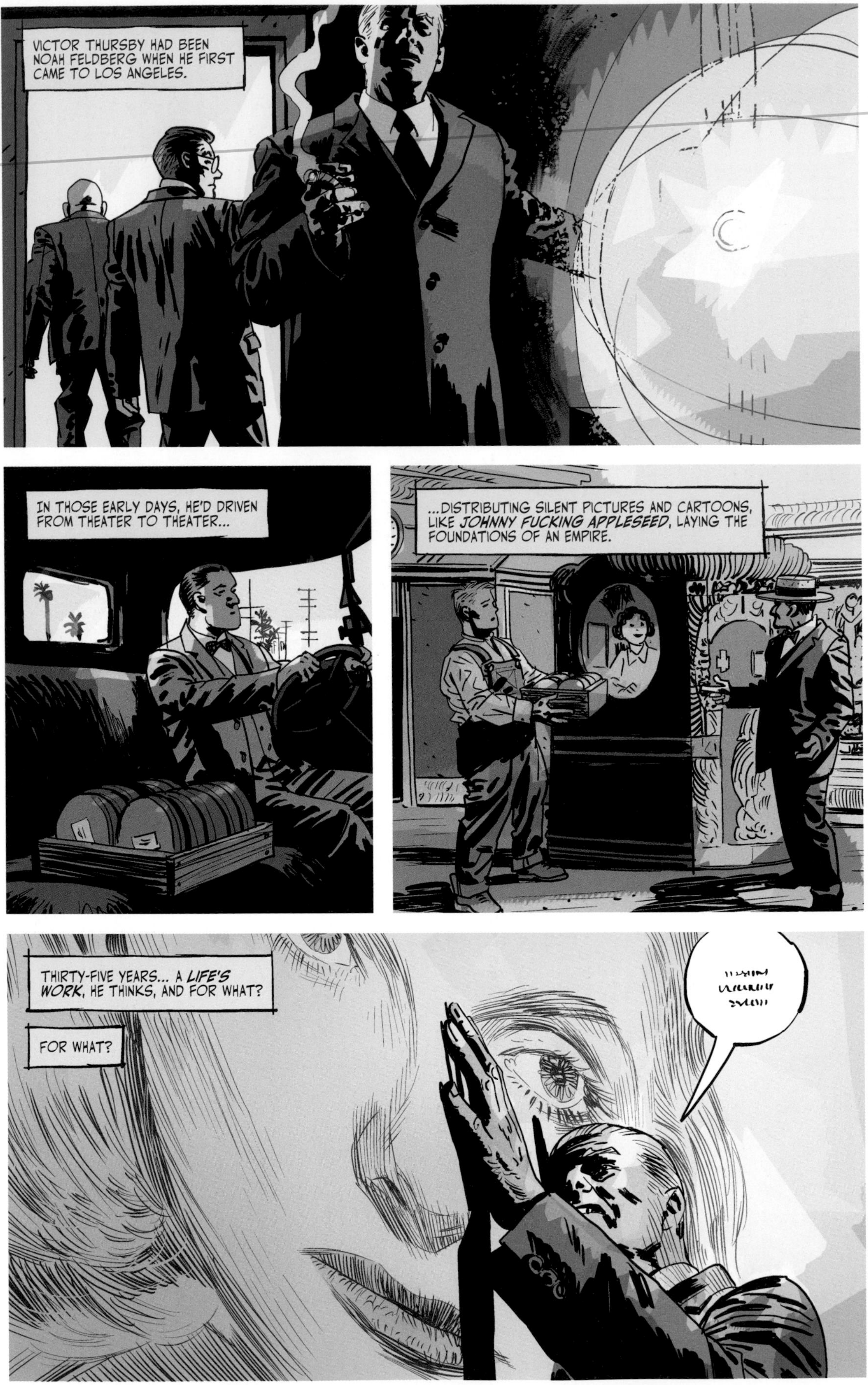
VICTOR THURSBY HAD BEEN NOAH FELDBERG WHEN HE FIRST CAME TO LOS ANGELES.
IN THOSE EARLY DAYS, HE'D DRIVEN FROM THEATER TO THEATER...
...DISTRIBUTING SILENT PICTURES AND CARTOONS, LIKE *JOHNNY FUCKING APPLESEED*, LAYING THE FOUNDATIONS OF AN EMPIRE.
THIRTY-FIVE YEARS... A *LIFE'S WORK*, HE THINKS, AND FOR WHAT?
FOR WHAT?

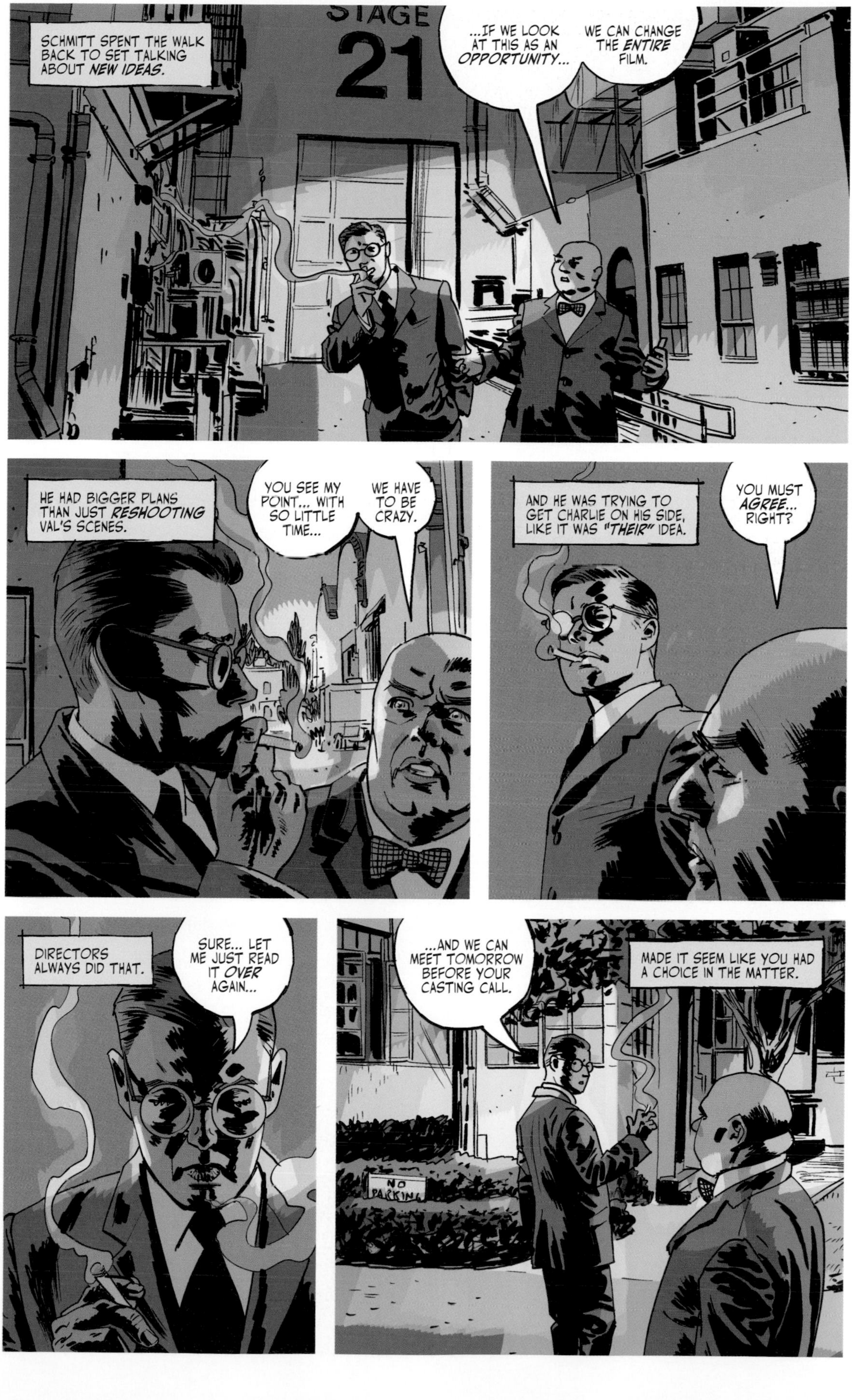

SCHMITT SPENT THE WALK BACK TO SET TALKING ABOUT NEW IDEAS.
STAGE 21
...IF WE LOOK AT THIS AS AN OPPORTUNITY...
WE CAN CHANGE THE ENTIRE FILM.
HE HAD BIGGER PLANS THAN JUST RESHOOTING VAL'S SCENES.
YOU SEE MY POINT... WITH SO LITTLE TIME...
WE HAVE TO BE CRAZY.
AND HE WAS TRYING TO GET CHARLIE ON HIS SIDE, LIKE IT WAS "THEIR" IDEA.
YOU MUST AGREE... RIGHT?
DIRECTORS ALWAYS DID THAT.
SURE... LET ME JUST READ IT OVER AGAIN...
...AND WE CAN MEET TOMORROW BEFORE YOUR CASTING CALL.
MADE IT SEEM LIKE YOU HAD A CHOICE IN THE MATTER.
NO PARKING

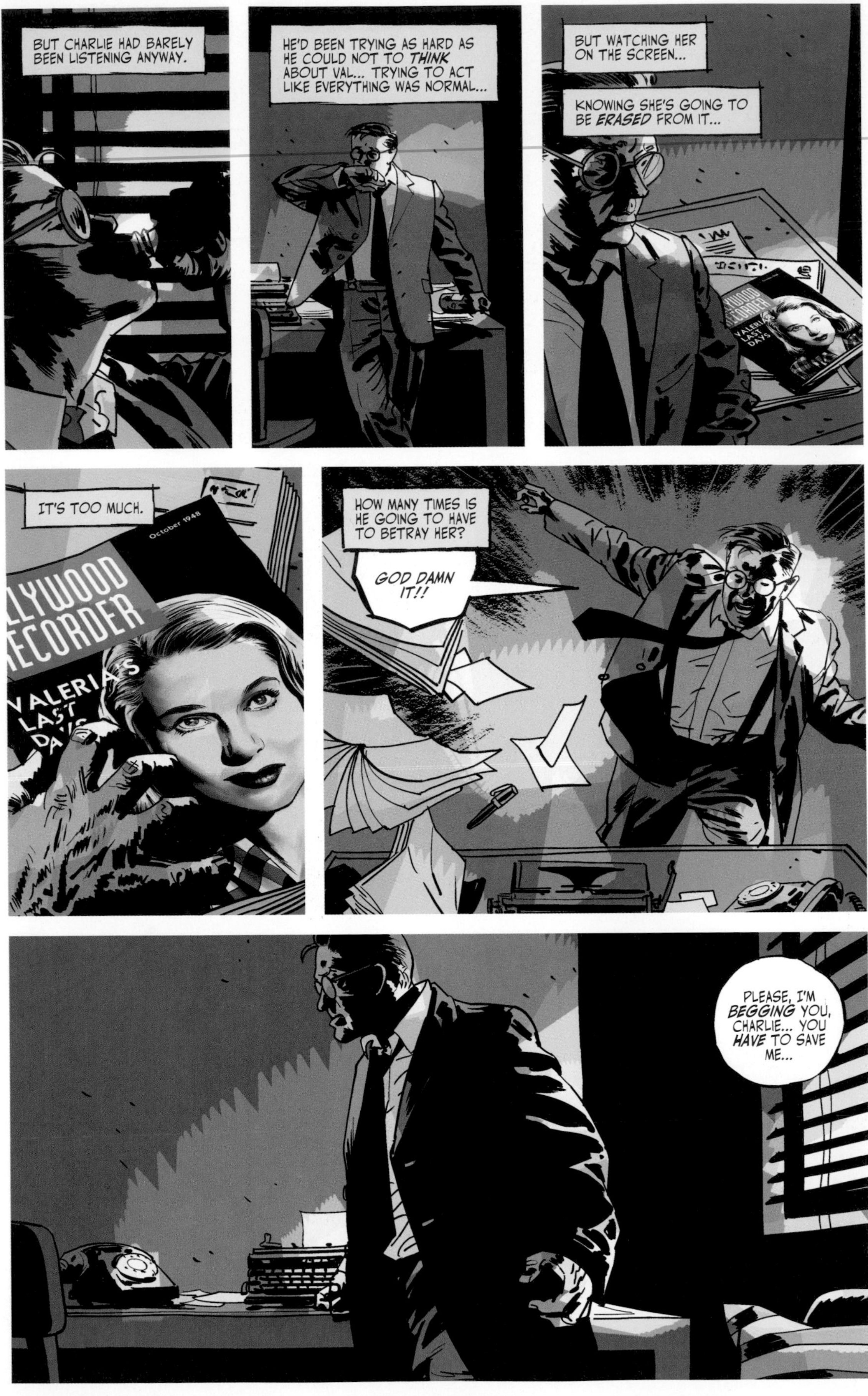
BUT CHARLIE HAD BARELY BEEN LISTENING ANYWAY.
HE'D BEEN TRYING AS HARD AS HE COULD NOT TO *THINK* ABOUT VAL... TRYING TO ACT LIKE EVERYTHING WAS NORMAL...
BUT WATCHING HER ON THE SCREEN...
KNOWING SHE'S GOING TO BE *ERASED* FROM IT...
IT'S TOO MUCH.
October 1948
LLYWOOD
ECORDER
VALERIA'S LAST DAYS
HOW MANY TIMES IS HE GOING TO HAVE TO BETRAY HER?
GOD DAMN IT!!
PLEASE, I'M *BEGGING* YOU, CHARLIE... YOU *HAVE* TO SAVE ME...

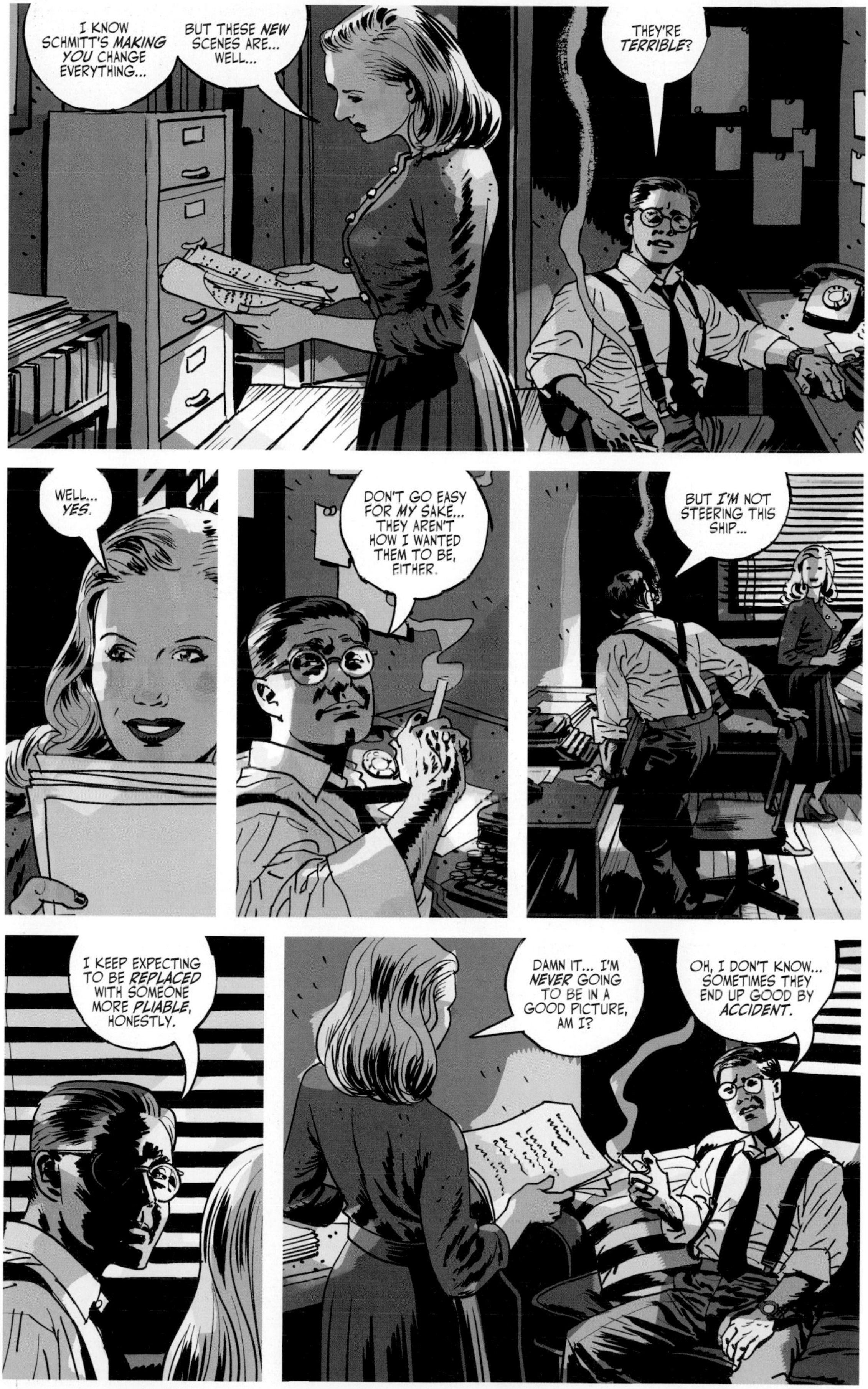
I KNOW SCHMITT'S *MAKING YOU* CHANGE EVERYTHING...
BUT THESE *NEW* SCENES ARE... WELL...
THEY'RE *TERRIBLE*?
WELL... *YES*.
DON'T GO EASY FOR *MY* SAKE... THEY AREN'T HOW I WANTED THEM TO BE, EITHER.
BUT *I'M* NOT STEERING THIS SHIP...
I KEEP EXPECTING TO BE *REPLACED* WITH SOMEONE MORE *PLIABLE*, HONESTLY.
DAMN IT... I'M *NEVER* GOING TO BE IN A GOOD PICTURE, AM I?
OH, I DON'T KNOW... SOMETIMES THEY END UP GOOD BY *ACCIDENT*.

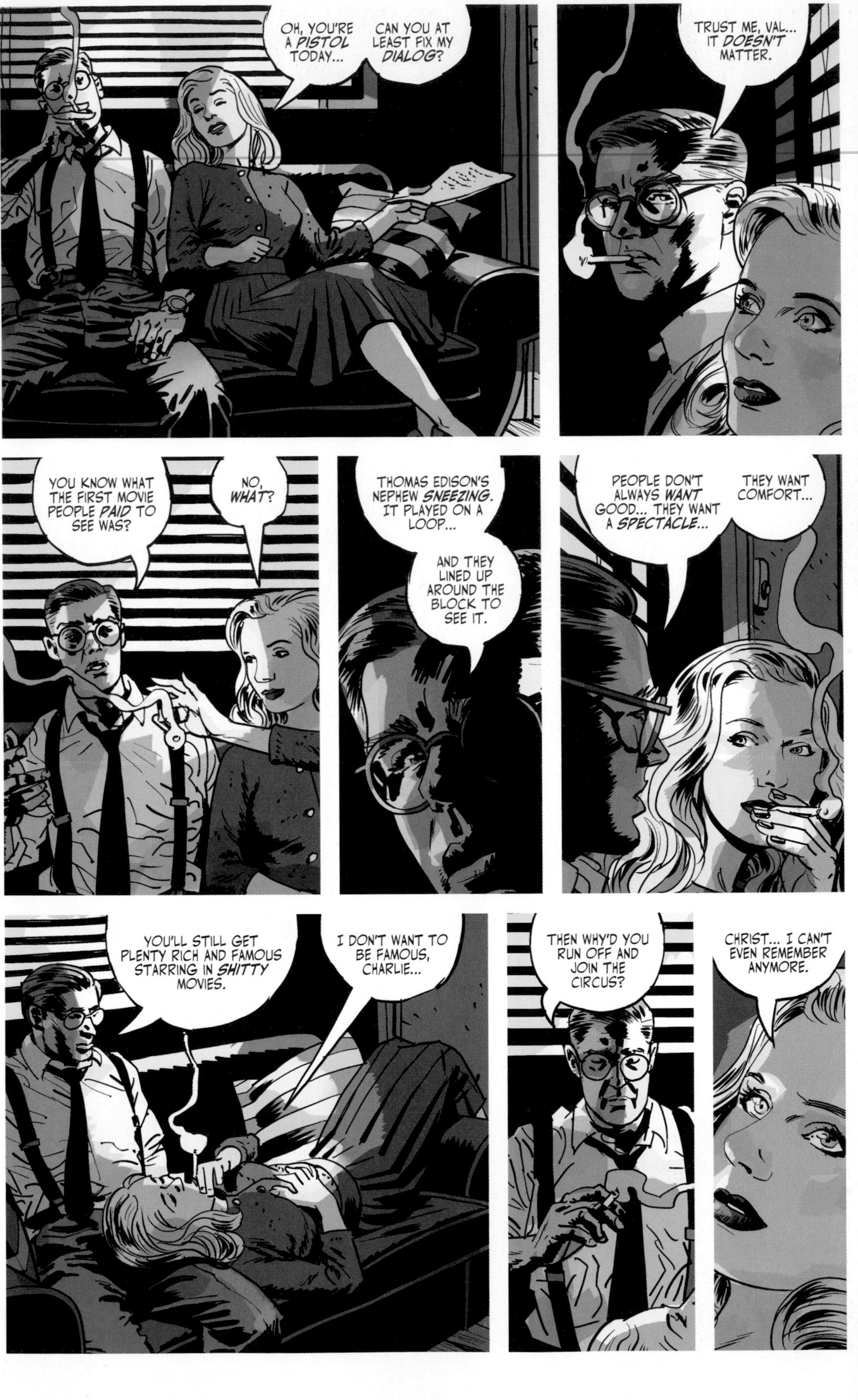
OH, YOU'RE A *PISTOL* TODAY...
CAN YOU AT LEAST FIX MY *DIALOG*?
TRUST ME, VAL... IT *DOESN'T* MATTER.
YOU KNOW WHAT THE FIRST MOVIE PEOPLE *PAID* TO SEE WAS?
NO, *WHAT*?
THOMAS EDISON'S NEPHEW *SNEEZING*. IT PLAYED ON A LOOP...
AND THEY LINED UP AROUND THE BLOCK TO SEE IT.
PEOPLE DON'T ALWAYS *WANT* GOOD... THEY WANT A *SPECTACLE*...
THEY WANT COMFORT...
YOU'LL STILL GET PLENTY RICH AND FAMOUS STARRING IN *SHITTY* MOVIES.
I DON'T WANT TO BE FAMOUS, CHARLIE...
THEN WHY'D YOU RUN OFF AND JOIN THE CIRCUS?
CHRIST... I CAN'T EVEN REMEMBER ANYMORE.

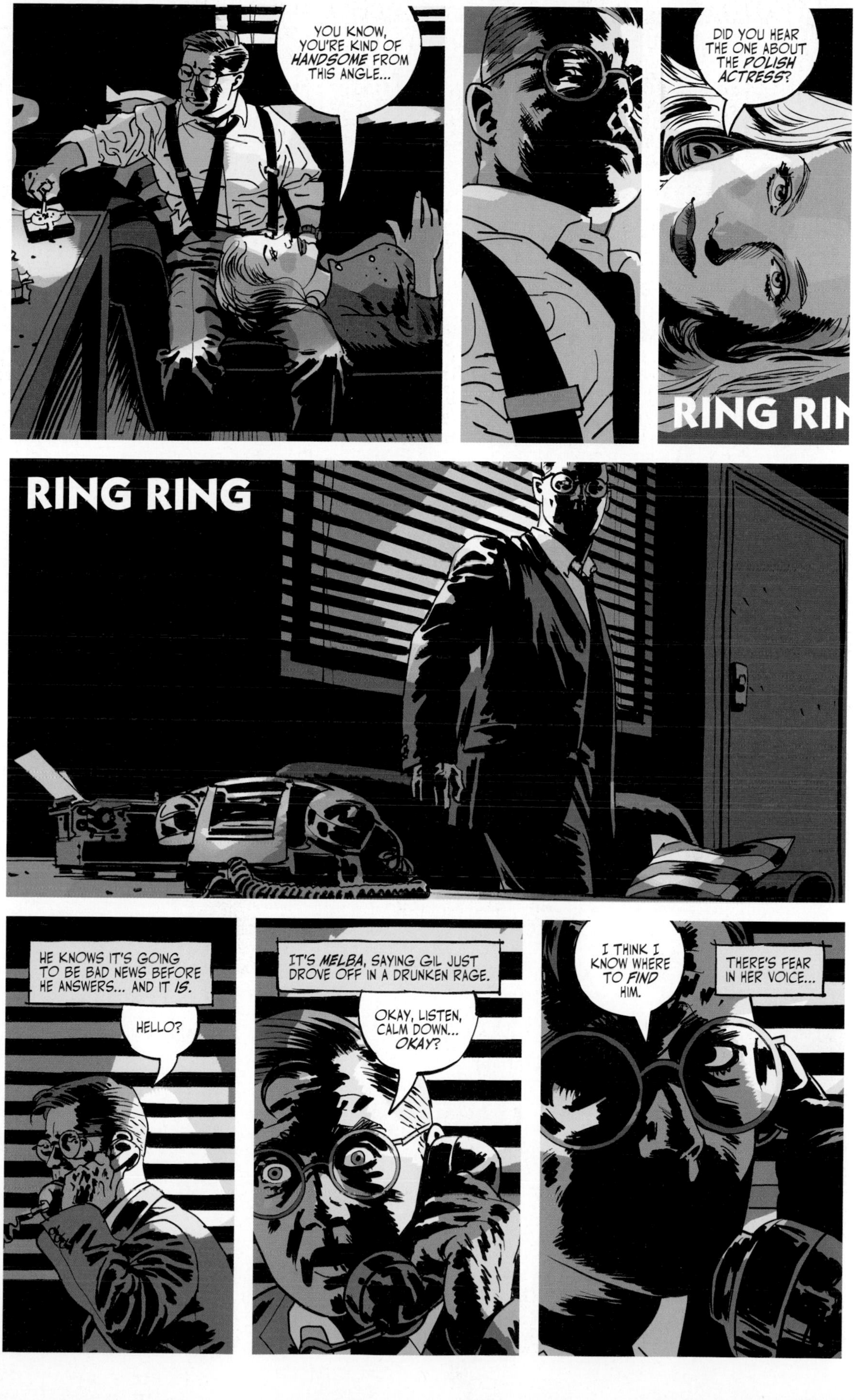
YOU KNOW, YOU'RE KIND OF HANDSOME FROM THIS ANGLE...
DID YOU HEAR THE ONE ABOUT THE POLISH ACTRESS?
RING RIN
RING RING
HE KNOWS IT'S GOING TO BE BAD NEWS BEFORE HE ANSWERS... AND IT IS.
HELLO?
IT'S MELBA, SAYING GIL JUST DROVE OFF IN A DRUNKEN RAGE.
OKAY, LISTEN, CALM DOWN... OKAY?
I THINK I KNOW WHERE TO FIND HIM.
THERE'S FEAR IN HER VOICE...

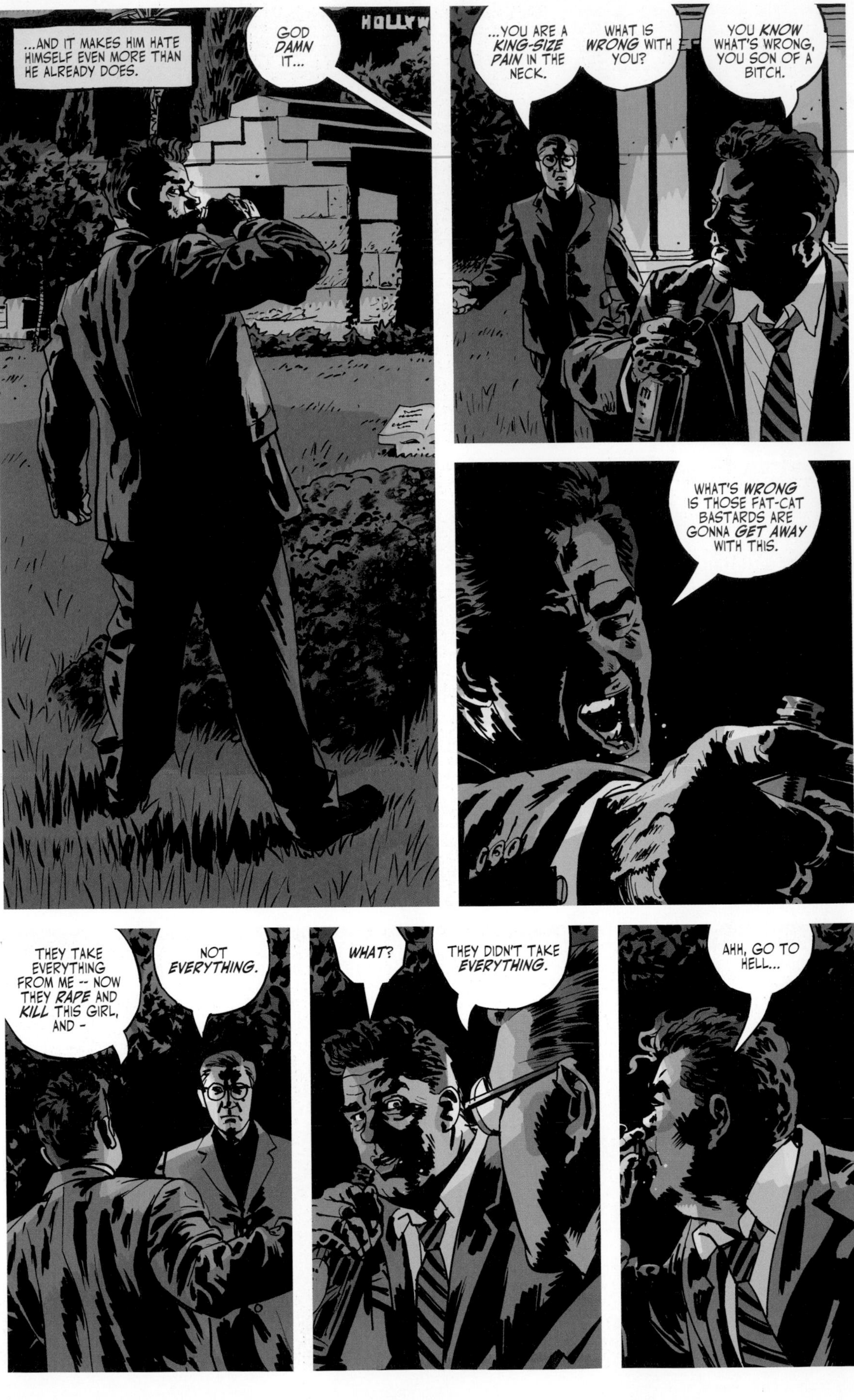
...AND IT MAKES HIM HATE HIMSELF EVEN MORE THAN HE ALREADY DOES.
GOD DAMN IT...
HOLLYW
...YOU ARE A KING-SIZE PAIN IN THE NECK.
WHAT IS WRONG WITH YOU?
YOU KNOW WHAT'S WRONG, YOU SON OF A BITCH.
WHAT'S WRONG IS THOSE FAT-CAT BASTARDS ARE GONNA GET AWAY WITH THIS.
THEY TAKE EVERYTHING FROM ME -- NOW THEY RAPE AND KILL THIS GIRL, AND -
NOT EVERYTHING.
WHAT?
THEY DIDN'T TAKE EVERYTHING.
AHH, GO TO HELL...

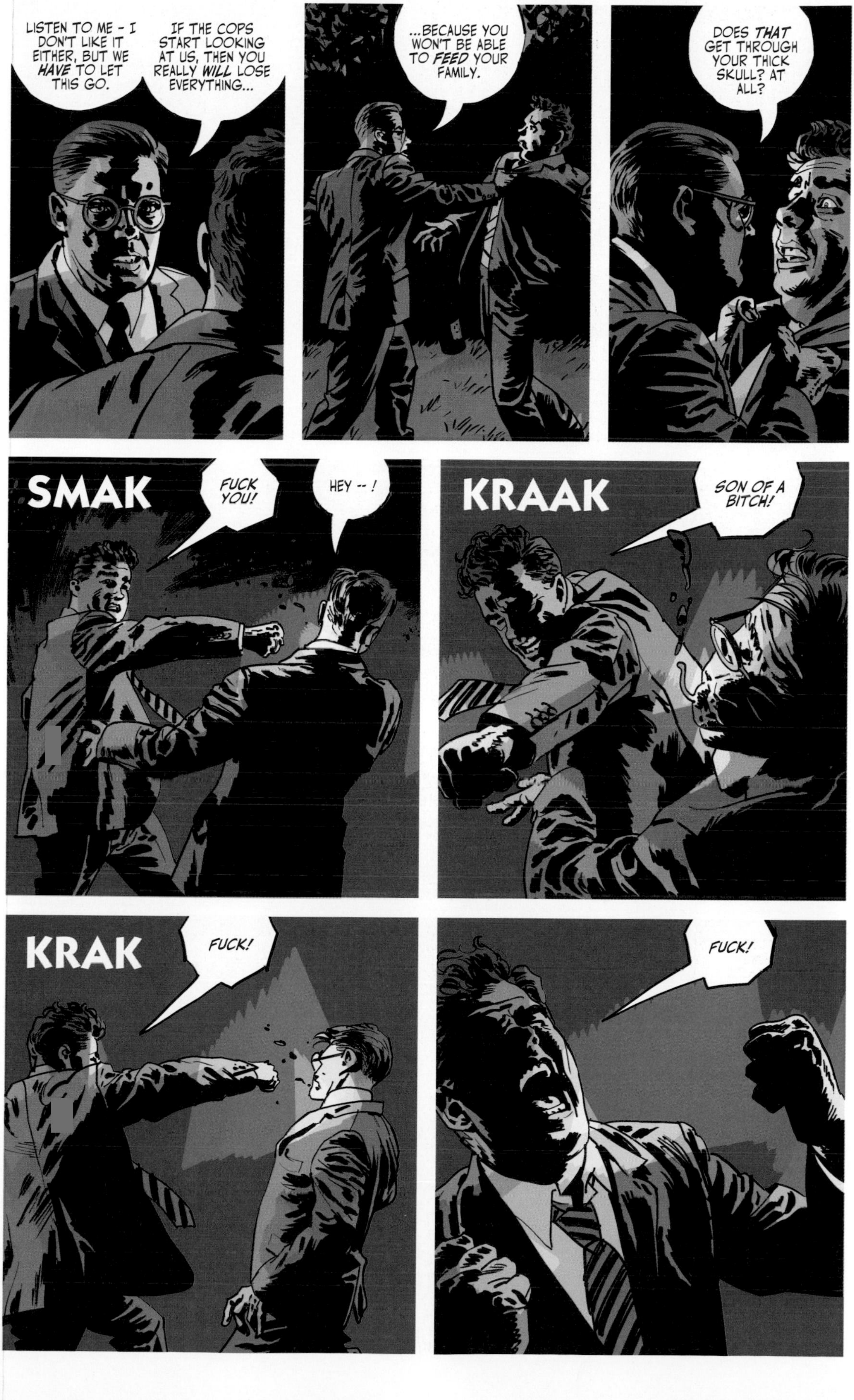

LISTEN TO ME - I DON'T LIKE IT EITHER, BUT WE HAVE TO LET THIS GO.
IF THE COPS START LOOKING AT US, THEN YOU REALLY WILL LOSE EVERYTHING...
...BECAUSE YOU WON'T BE ABLE TO FEED YOUR FAMILY.
DOES THAT GET THROUGH YOUR THICK SKULL? AT ALL?
SMAK
FUCK YOU!
HEY -- !
KRAAK
SON OF A BITCH!
KRAK
FUCK!
FUCK!

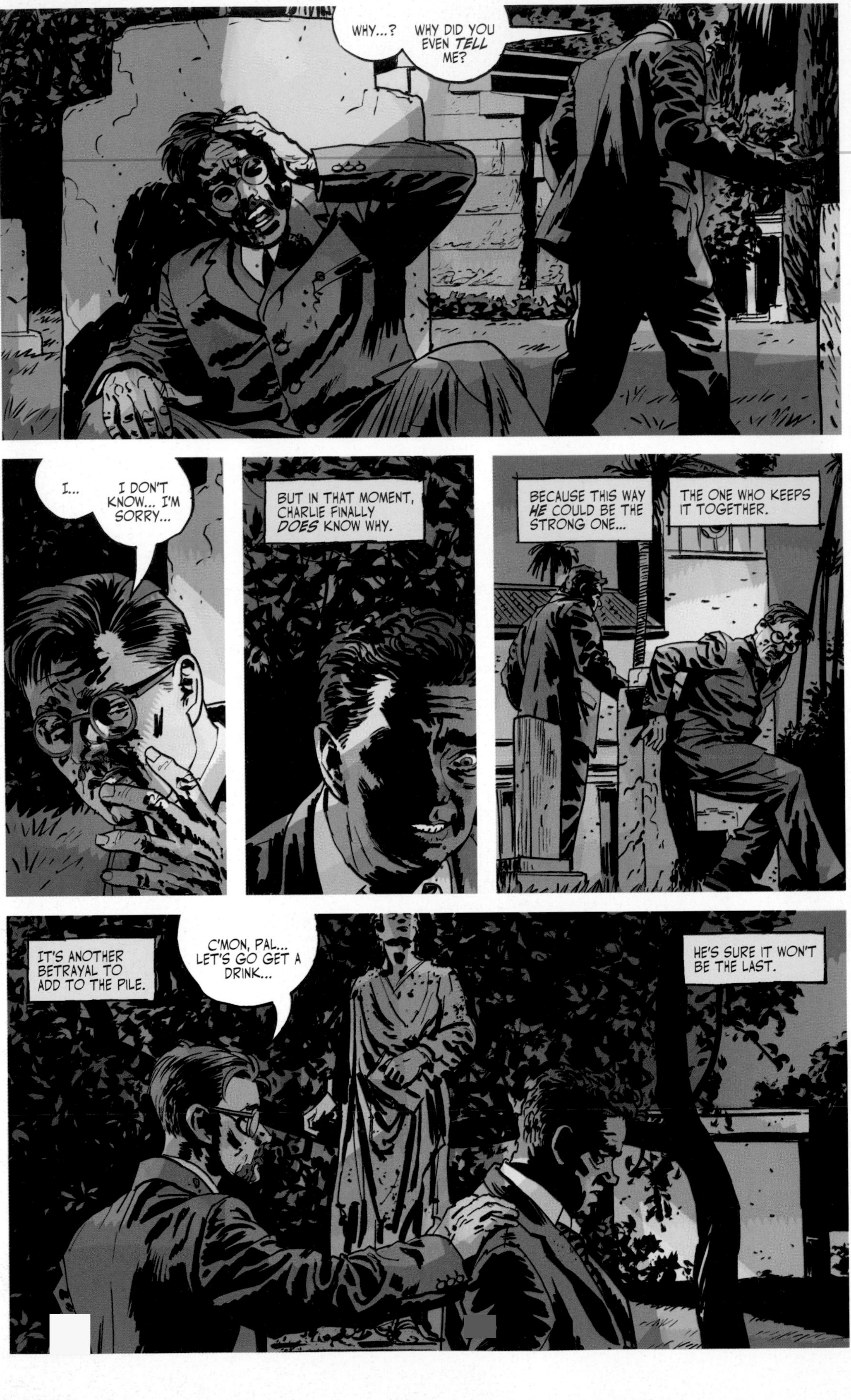
WHY...?
WHY DID YOU EVEN TELL ME?
I... I DON'T KNOW... I'M SORRY...
BUT IN THAT MOMENT, CHARLIE FINALLY DOES KNOW WHY.
BECAUSE THIS WAY HE COULD BE THE STRONG ONE...
THE ONE WHO KEEPS IT TOGETHER.
IT'S ANOTHER BETRAYAL TO ADD TO THE PILE.
C'MON, PAL... LET'S GO GET A DRINK...
HE'S SURE IT WON'T BE THE LAST.

The Replacement Blonde

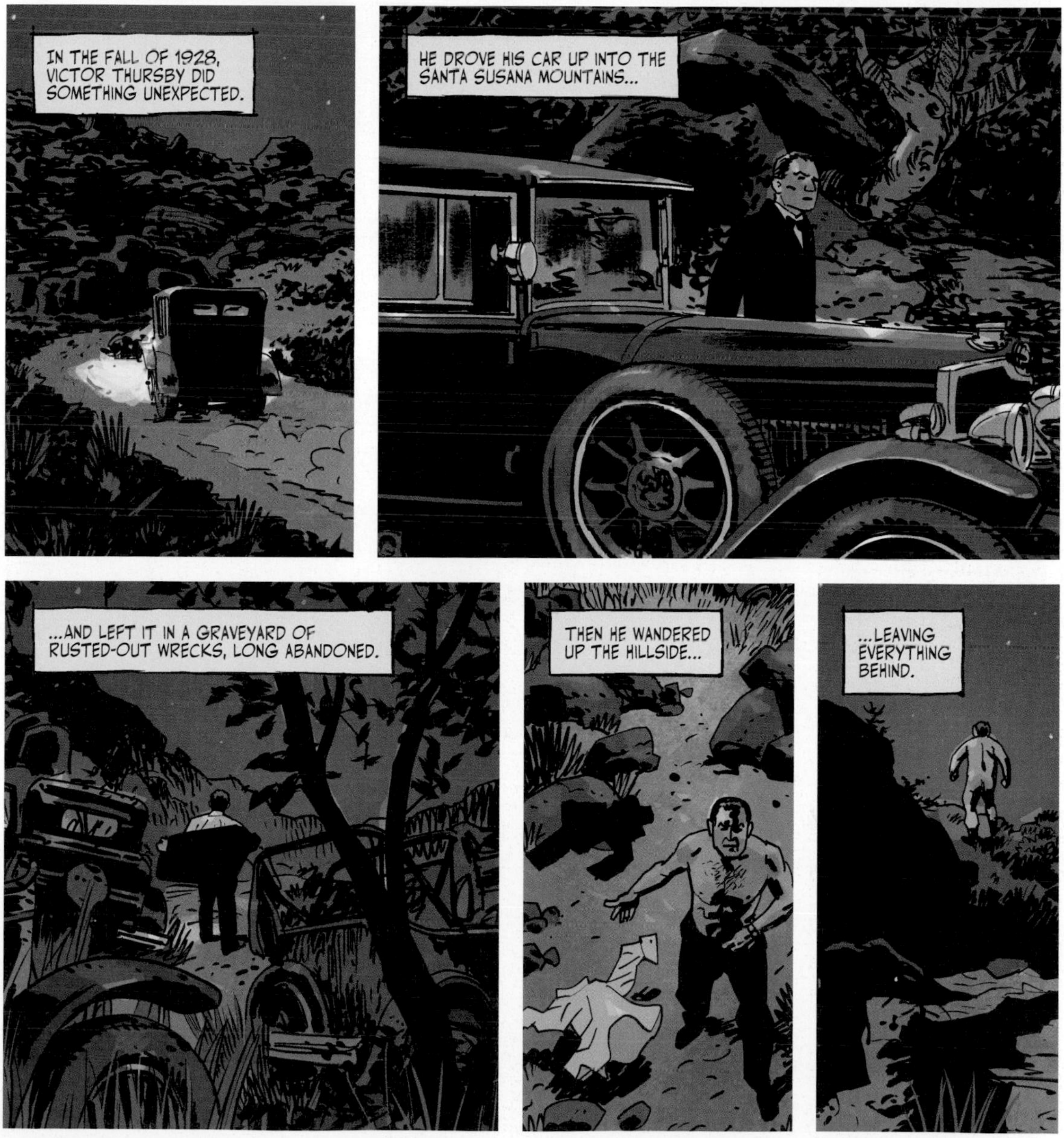
IN THE FALL OF 1928, VICTOR THURSBY DID SOMETHING UNEXPECTED.
HE DROVE HIS CAR UP INTO THE SANTA SUSANA MOUNTAINS...
...AND LEFT IT IN A GRAVEYARD OF RUSTED-OUT WRECKS, LONG ABANDONED.
THEN HE WANDERED UP THE HILLSIDE...
...LEAVING EVERYTHING BEHIND.

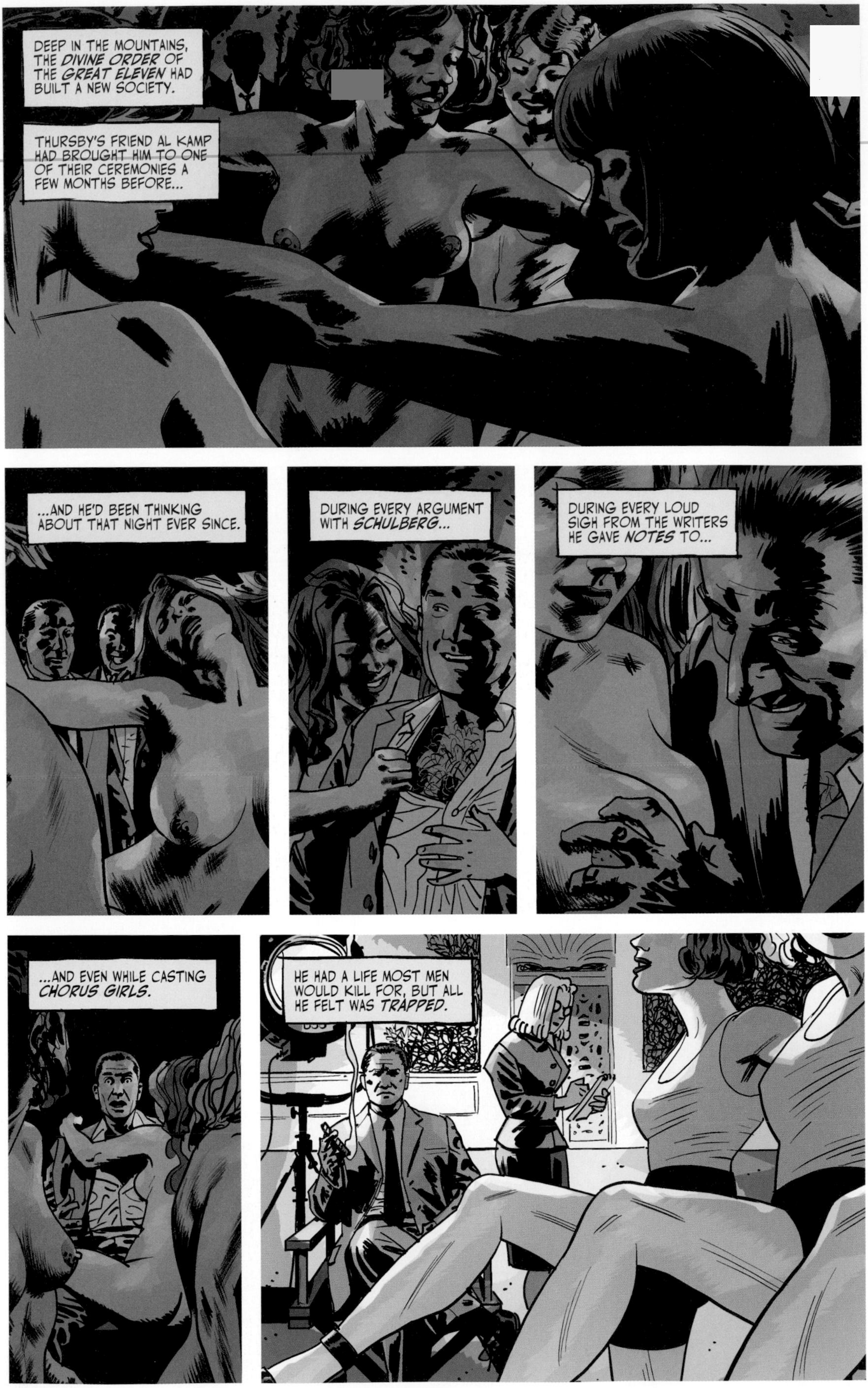
DEEP IN THE MOUNTAINS, THE *DIVINE ORDER* OF THE *GREAT ELEVEN* HAD BUILT A NEW SOCIETY.
THURSBY'S FRIEND AL KAMP HAD BROUGHT HIM TO ONE OF THEIR CEREMONIES A FEW MONTHS BEFORE...
...AND HE'D BEEN THINKING ABOUT THAT NIGHT EVER SINCE.
DURING EVERY ARGUMENT WITH *SCHULBERG*...
DURING EVERY LOUD SIGH FROM THE WRITERS HE GAVE *NOTES* TO...
...AND EVEN WHILE CASTING *CHORUS GIRLS*.
HE HAD A LIFE MOST MEN WOULD KILL FOR, BUT ALL HE FELT WAS *TRAPPED*.

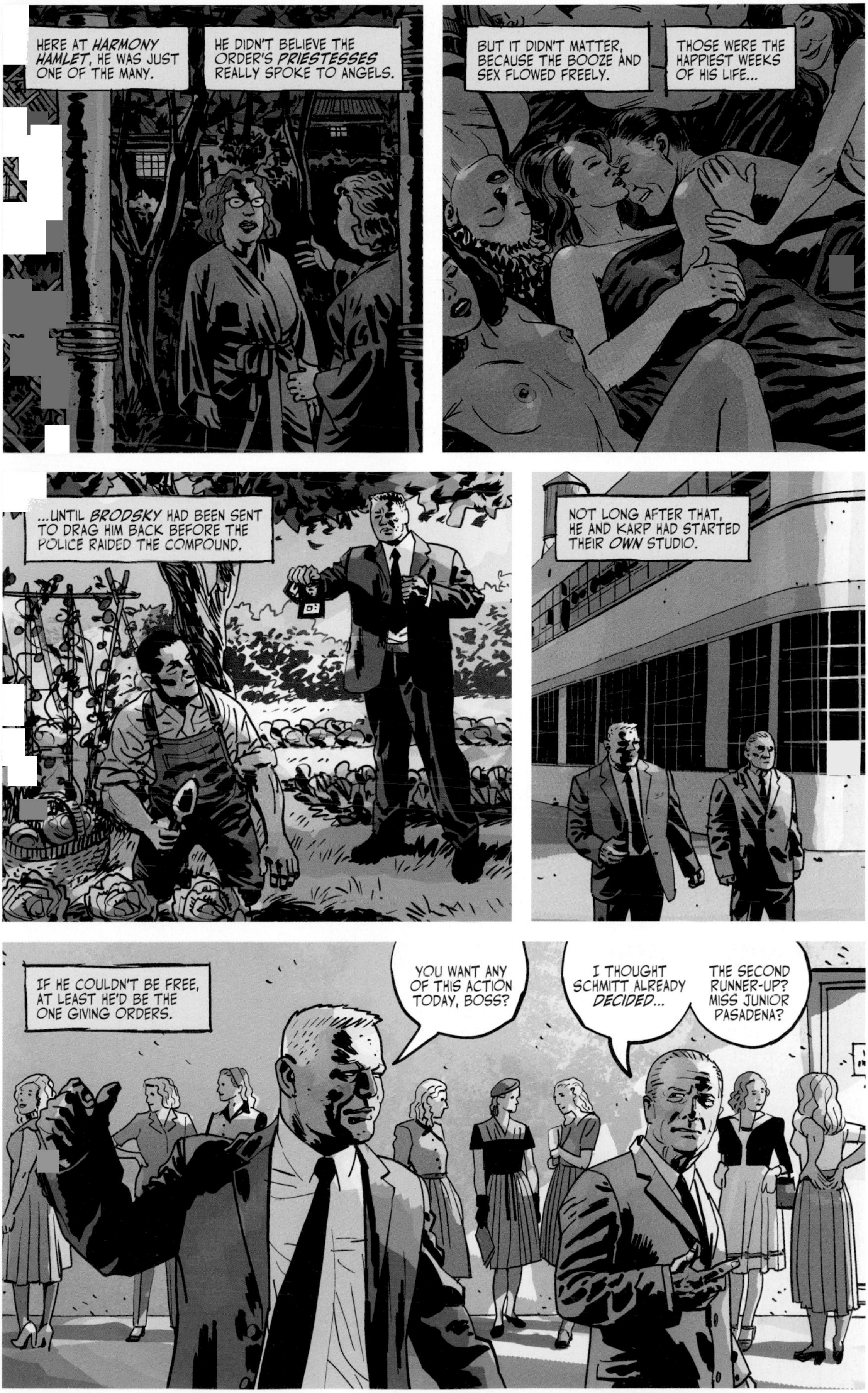
HERE AT *HARMONY HAMLET*, HE WAS JUST ONE OF THE MANY.
HE DIDN'T BELIEVE THE ORDER'S *PRIESTESSES* REALLY SPOKE TO ANGELS.
BUT IT DIDN'T MATTER, BECAUSE THE BOOZE AND SEX FLOWED FREELY.
THOSE WERE THE HAPPIEST WEEKS OF HIS LIFE...
...UNTIL *BRODSKY* HAD BEEN SENT TO DRAG HIM BACK BEFORE THE POLICE RAIDED THE COMPOUND.
NOT LONG AFTER THAT, HE AND KARP HAD STARTED THEIR *OWN* STUDIO.
IF HE COULDN'T BE FREE, AT LEAST HE'D BE THE ONE GIVING ORDERS.
YOU WANT ANY OF THIS ACTION TODAY, BOSS?
I THOUGHT SCHMITT ALREADY *DECIDED*...
THE SECOND RUNNER-UP? MISS JUNIOR PASADENA?

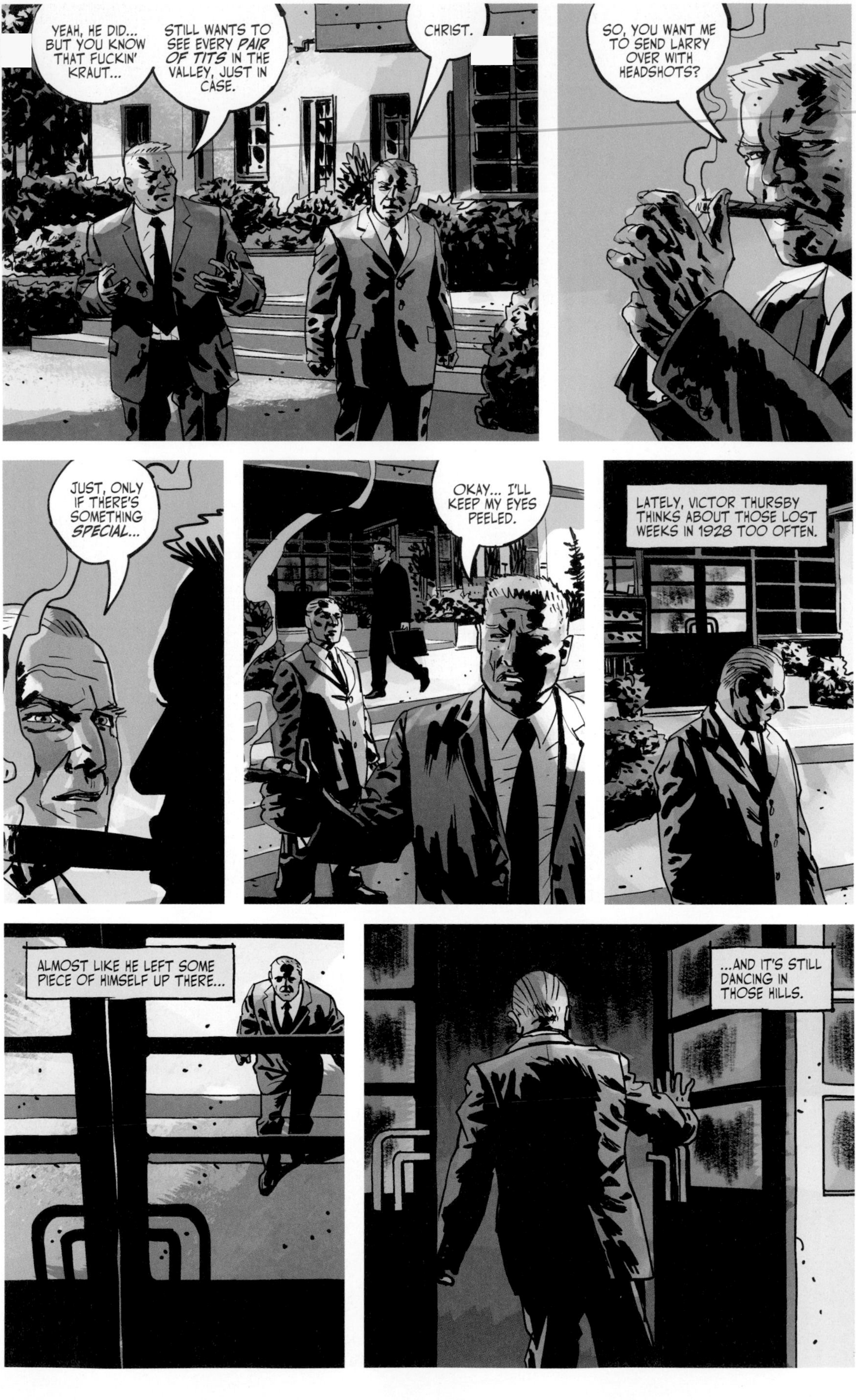
YEAH, HE DID... BUT YOU KNOW THAT FUCKIN' KRAUT...
STILL WANTS TO SEE EVERY *PAIR OF TITS* IN THE VALLEY, JUST IN CASE.
CHRIST.
SO, YOU WANT ME TO SEND LARRY OVER WITH HEADSHOTS?
JUST, ONLY IF THERE'S SOMETHING *SPECIAL*...
OKAY... I'LL KEEP MY EYES PEELED.
LATELY, VICTOR THURSBY THINKS ABOUT THOSE LOST WEEKS IN 1928 TOO OFTEN.
ALMOST LIKE HE LEFT SOME PIECE OF HIMSELF UP THERE...
...AND IT'S STILL DANCING IN THOSE HILLS.

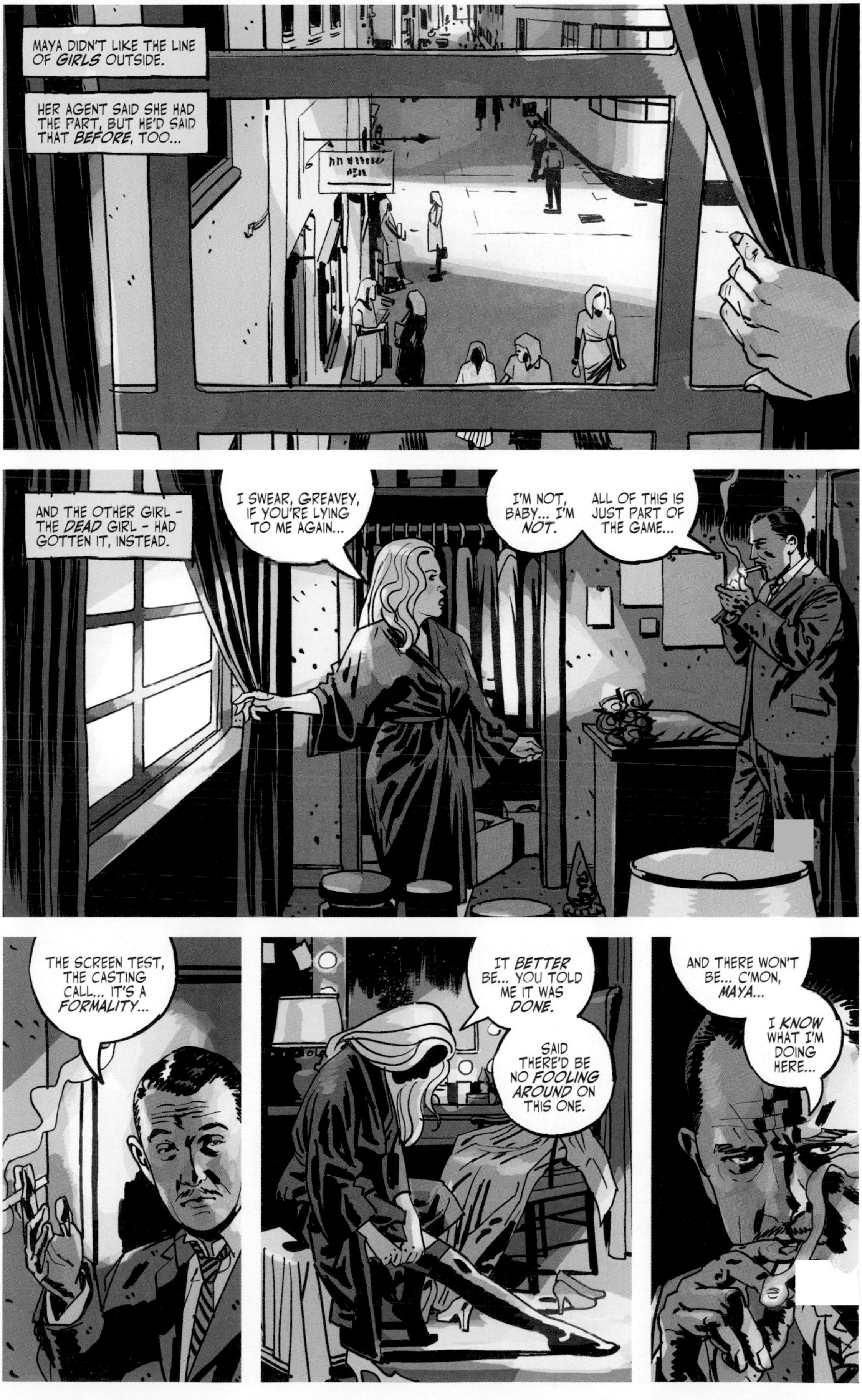
MAYA DIDN'T LIKE THE LINE OF *GIRLS* OUTSIDE.
HER AGENT SAID SHE HAD THE PART, BUT HE'D SAID THAT *BEFORE*, TOO...
AND THE OTHER GIRL - THE *DEAD* GIRL - HAD GOTTEN IT, INSTEAD.
I SWEAR, GREAVEY, IF YOU'RE LYING TO ME AGAIN...
I'M NOT, BABY... I'M *NOT*.
ALL OF THIS IS JUST PART OF THE GAME...
THE SCREEN TEST, THE CASTING CALL... IT'S A *FORMALITY*...
IT *BETTER* BE... YOU TOLD ME IT WAS *DONE*.
SAID THERE'D BE NO *FOOLING AROUND* ON THIS ONE.
AND THERE WON'T BE... C'MON, *MAYA*...
I *KNOW* WHAT I'M DOING HERE...

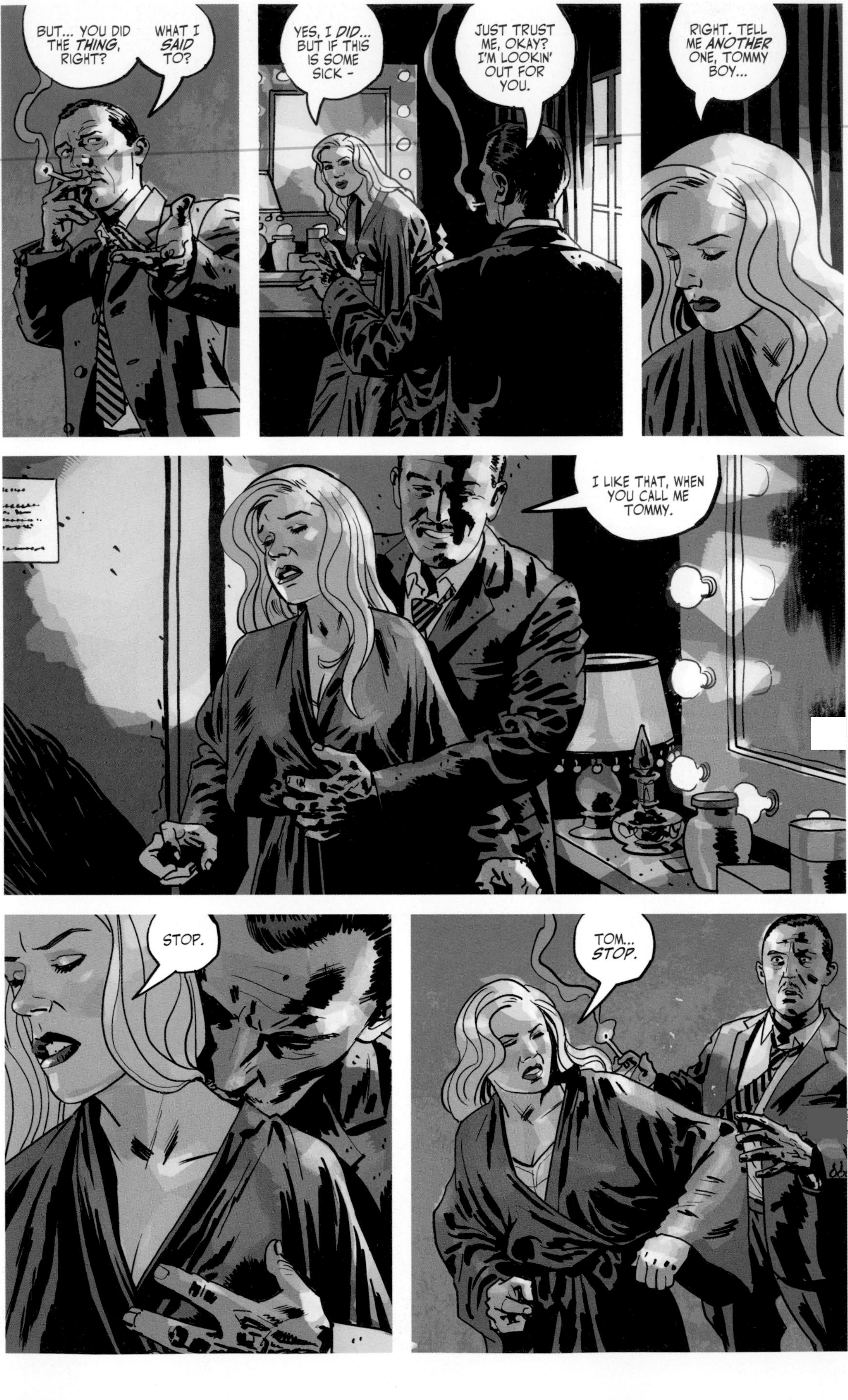
BUT... YOU DID THE THING, RIGHT?
WHAT I SAID TO?
YES, I DID... BUT IF THIS IS SOME SICK -
JUST TRUST ME, OKAY? I'M LOOKIN' OUT FOR YOU.
RIGHT. TELL ME ANOTHER ONE, TOMMY BOY...
I LIKE THAT, WHEN YOU CALL ME TOMMY.
STOP.
TOM... STOP.

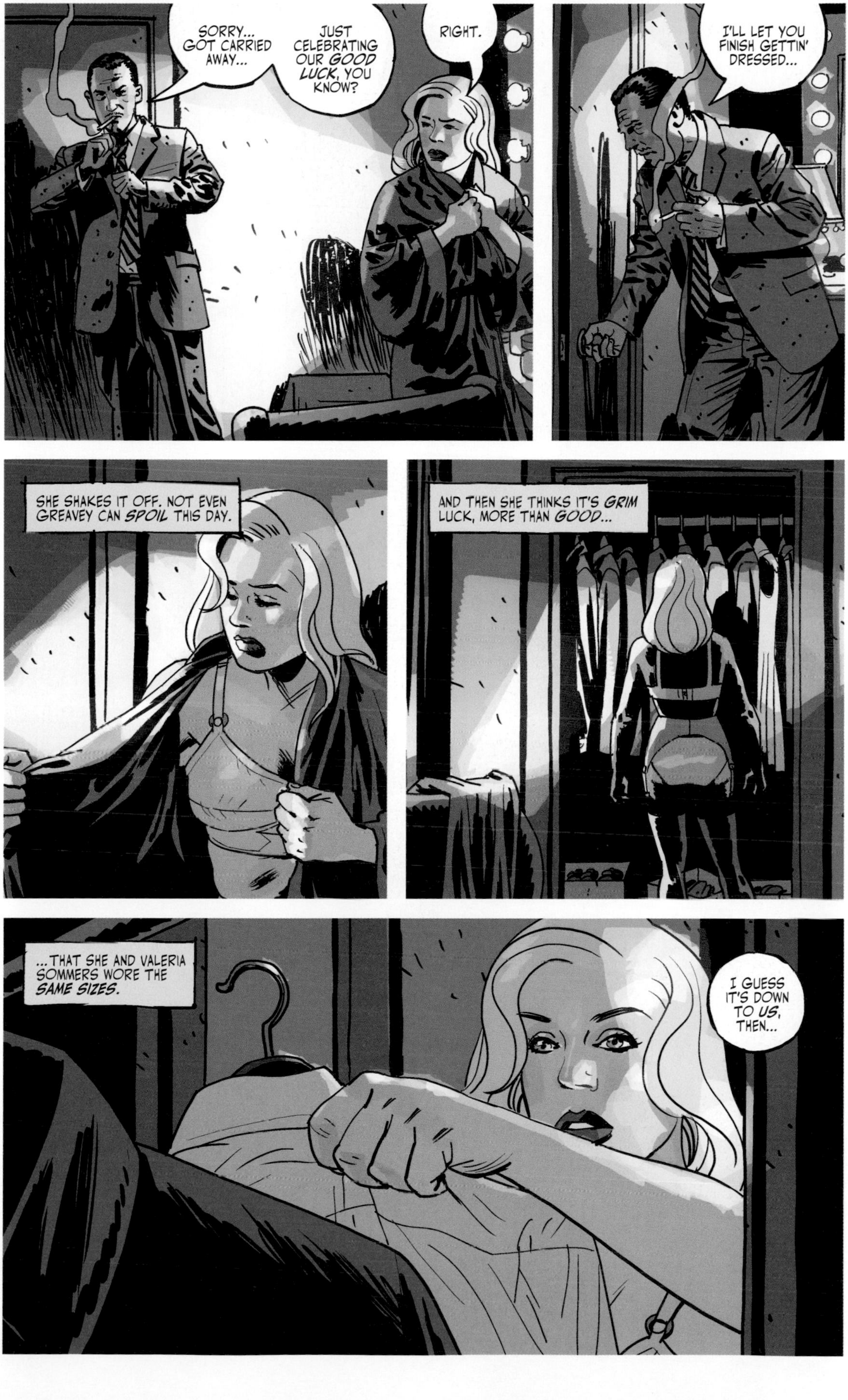
SORRY... GOT CARRIED AWAY...
JUST CELEBRATING OUR GOOD LUCK, YOU KNOW?
RIGHT.
I'LL LET YOU FINISH GETTIN' DRESSED...
SHE SHAKES IT OFF. NOT EVEN GREAVEY CAN SPOIL THIS DAY.
AND THEN SHE THINKS IT'S GRIM LUCK, MORE THAN GOOD...
...THAT SHE AND VALERIA SOMMERS WORE THE SAME SIZES.
I GUESS IT'S DOWN TO US, THEN...

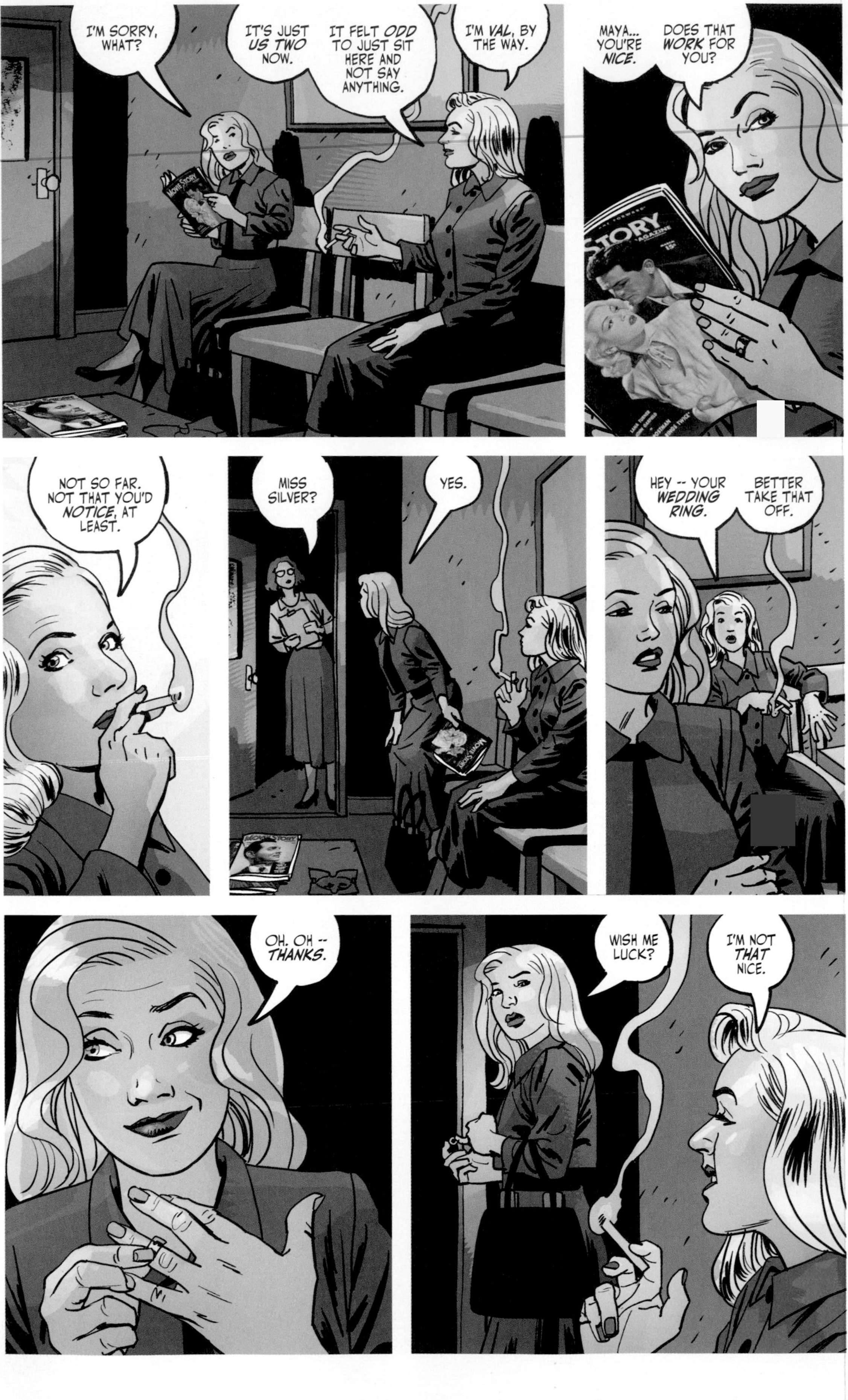
I'M SORRY, WHAT?
IT'S JUST US TWO NOW.
IT FELT ODD TO JUST SIT HERE AND NOT SAY ANYTHING.
I'M VAL, BY THE WAY.
MAYA... YOU'RE NICE.
DOES THAT WORK FOR YOU?
NOT SO FAR. NOT THAT YOU'D NOTICE, AT LEAST.
MISS SILVER?
YES.
HEY -- YOUR WEDDING RING.
BETTER TAKE THAT OFF.
OH. OH -- THANKS.
WISH ME LUCK?
I'M NOT THAT NICE.

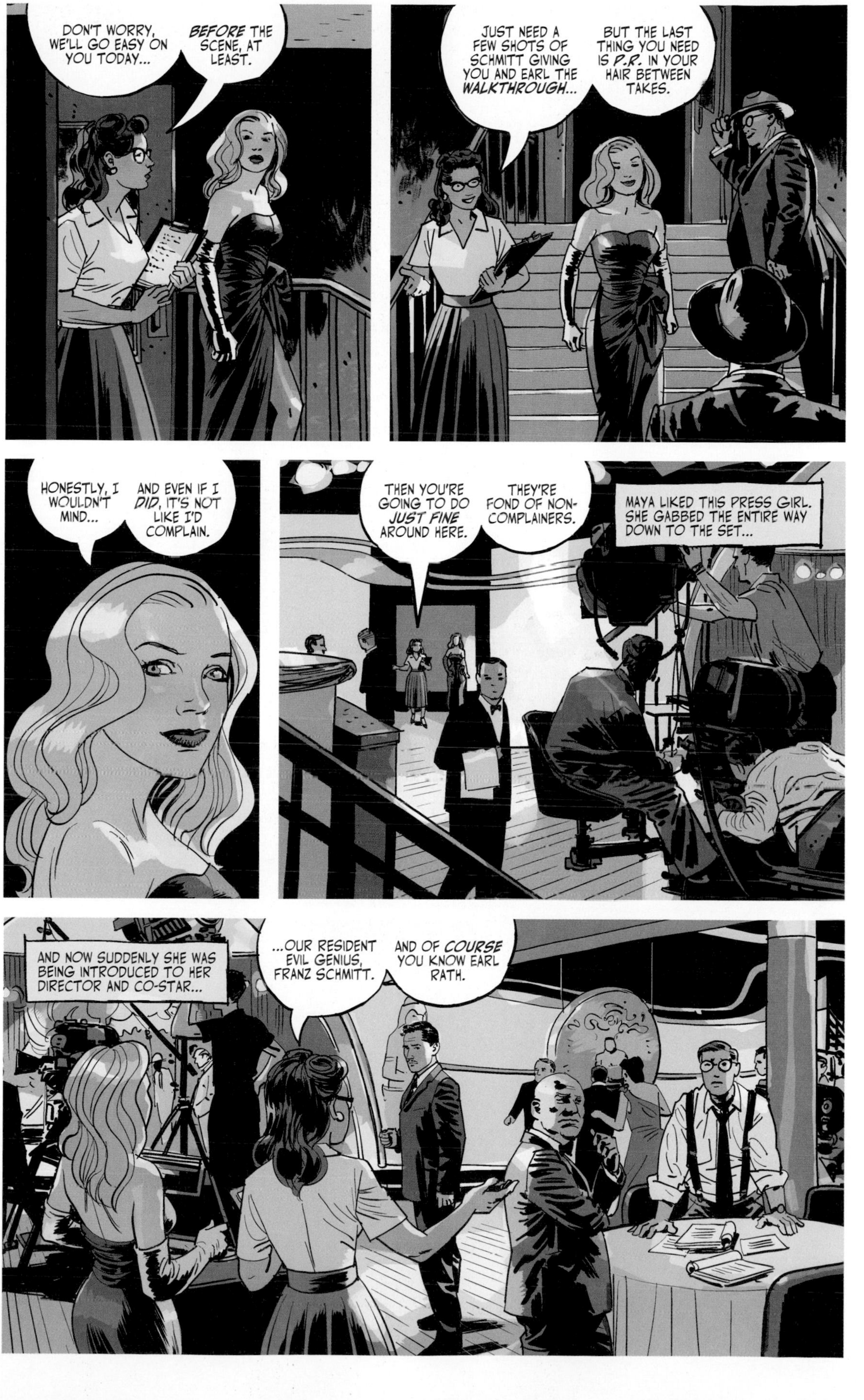

DON'T WORRY, WE'LL GO EASY ON YOU TODAY...
BEFORE THE SCENE, AT LEAST.
JUST NEED A FEW SHOTS OF SCHMITT GIVING YOU AND EARL THE WALKTHROUGH...
BUT THE LAST THING YOU NEED IS P.R. IN YOUR HAIR BETWEEN TAKES.
HONESTLY, I WOULDN'T MIND...
AND EVEN IF I DID, IT'S NOT LIKE I'D COMPLAIN.
THEN YOU'RE GOING TO DO JUST FINE AROUND HERE.
THEY'RE FOND OF NON-COMPLAINERS.
MAYA LIKED THIS PRESS GIRL. SHE GABBED THE ENTIRE WAY DOWN TO THE SET...
AND NOW SUDDENLY SHE WAS BEING INTRODUCED TO HER DIRECTOR AND CO-STAR...
...OUR RESIDENT EVIL GENIUS, FRANZ SCHMITT.
AND OF COURSE YOU KNOW EARL RATH.

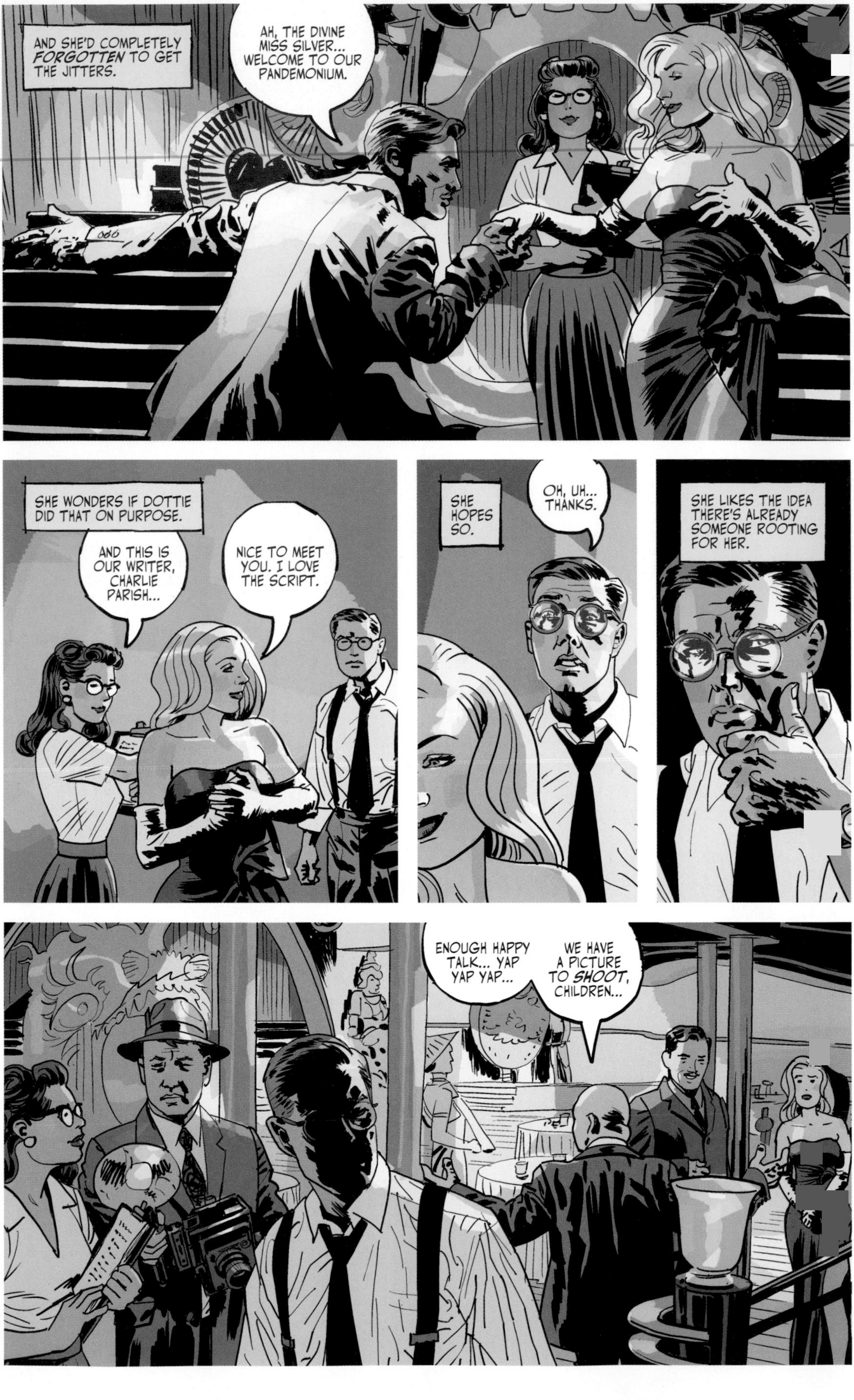

AND SHE'D COMPLETELY FORGOTTEN TO GET THE JITTERS.
AH, THE DIVINE MISS SILVER... WELCOME TO OUR PANDEMONIUM.
SHE WONDERS IF DOTTIE DID THAT ON PURPOSE.
AND THIS IS OUR WRITER, CHARLIE PARISH...
NICE TO MEET YOU. I LOVE THE SCRIPT.
SHE HOPES SO.
OH, UH... THANKS.
SHE LIKES THE IDEA THERE'S ALREADY SOMEONE ROOTING FOR HER.
ENOUGH HAPPY TALK... YAP YAP YAP...
WE HAVE A PICTURE TO SHOOT, CHILDREN...

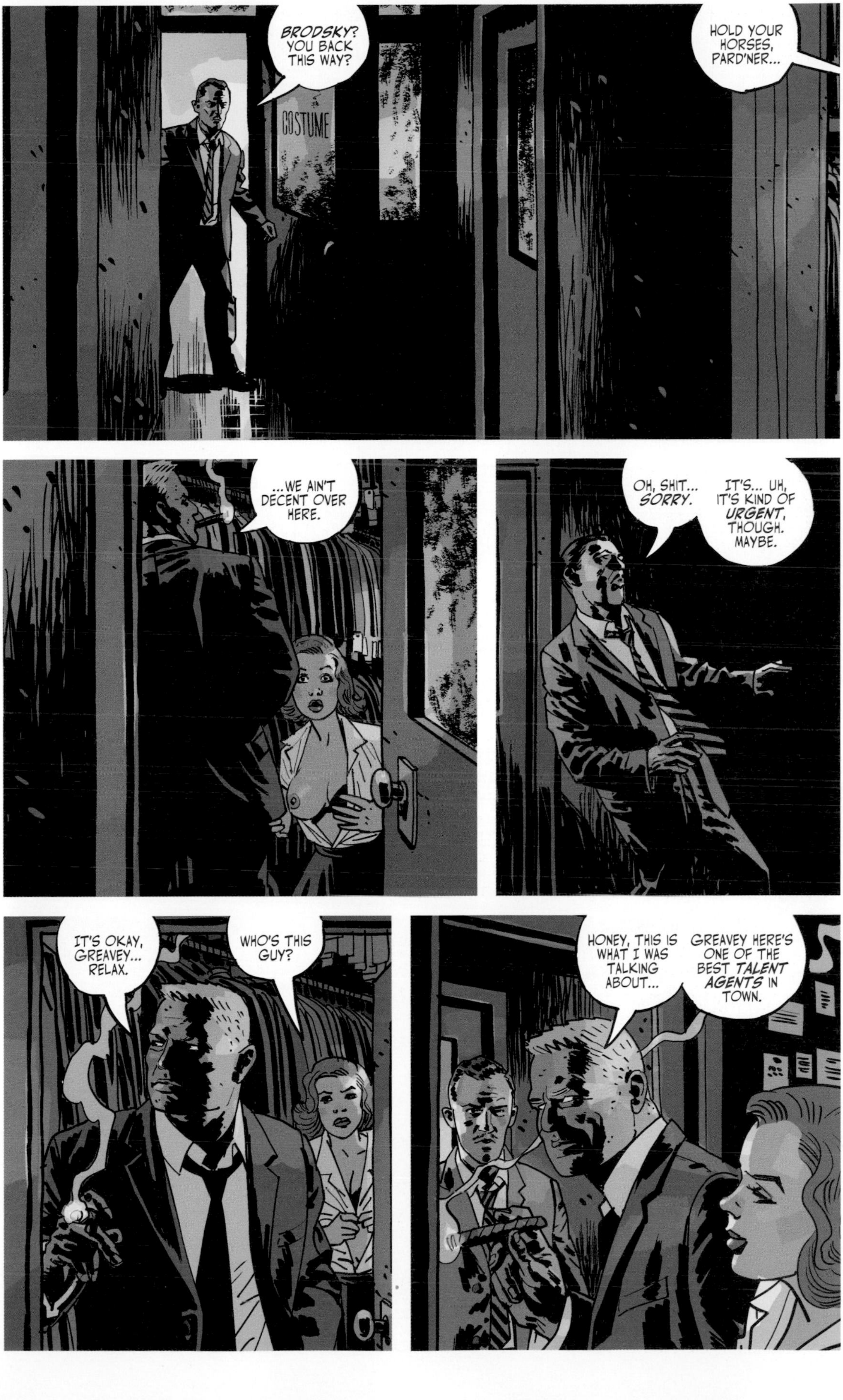
BRODSKY? YOU BACK THIS WAY?
COSTUME
HOLD YOUR HORSES, PARD'NER...
...WE AIN'T DECENT OVER HERE.
OH, SHIT... SORRY.
IT'S... UH, IT'S KIND OF URGENT, THOUGH. MAYBE.
IT'S OKAY, GREAVEY... RELAX.
WHO'S THIS GUY?
HONEY, THIS IS WHAT I WAS TALKING ABOUT...
GREAVEY HERE'S ONE OF THE BEST TALENT AGENTS IN TOWN.

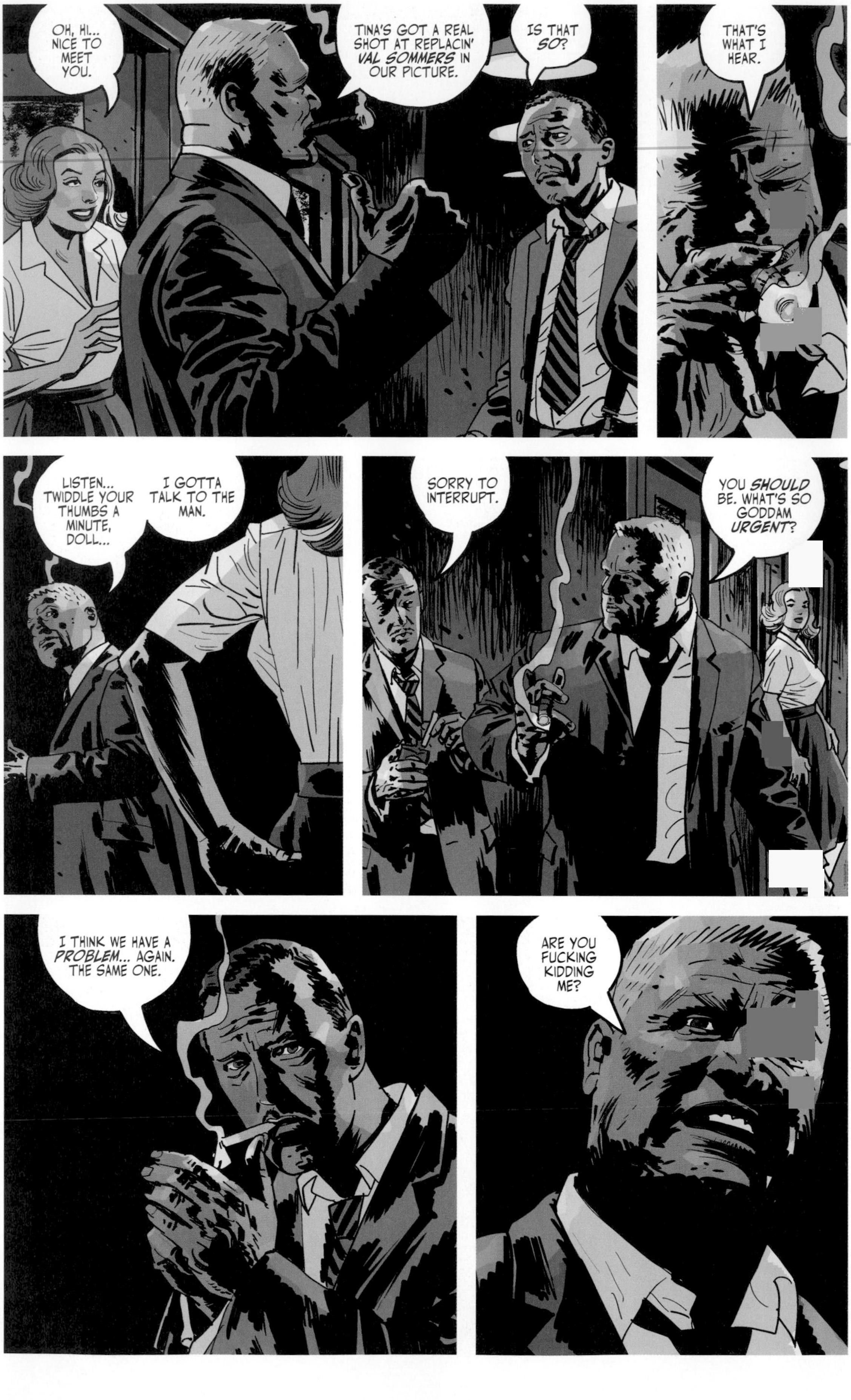

OH, HI... NICE TO MEET YOU.
TINA'S GOT A REAL SHOT AT REPLACIN' VAL SOMMERS IN OUR PICTURE.
IS THAT SO?
THAT'S WHAT I HEAR.
LISTEN... TWIDDLE YOUR THUMBS A MINUTE, DOLL...
I GOTTA TALK TO THE MAN.
SORRY TO INTERRUPT.
YOU SHOULD BE. WHAT'S SO GODDAM URGENT?
I THINK WE HAVE A PROBLEM... AGAIN. THE SAME ONE.
ARE YOU FUCKING KIDDING ME?

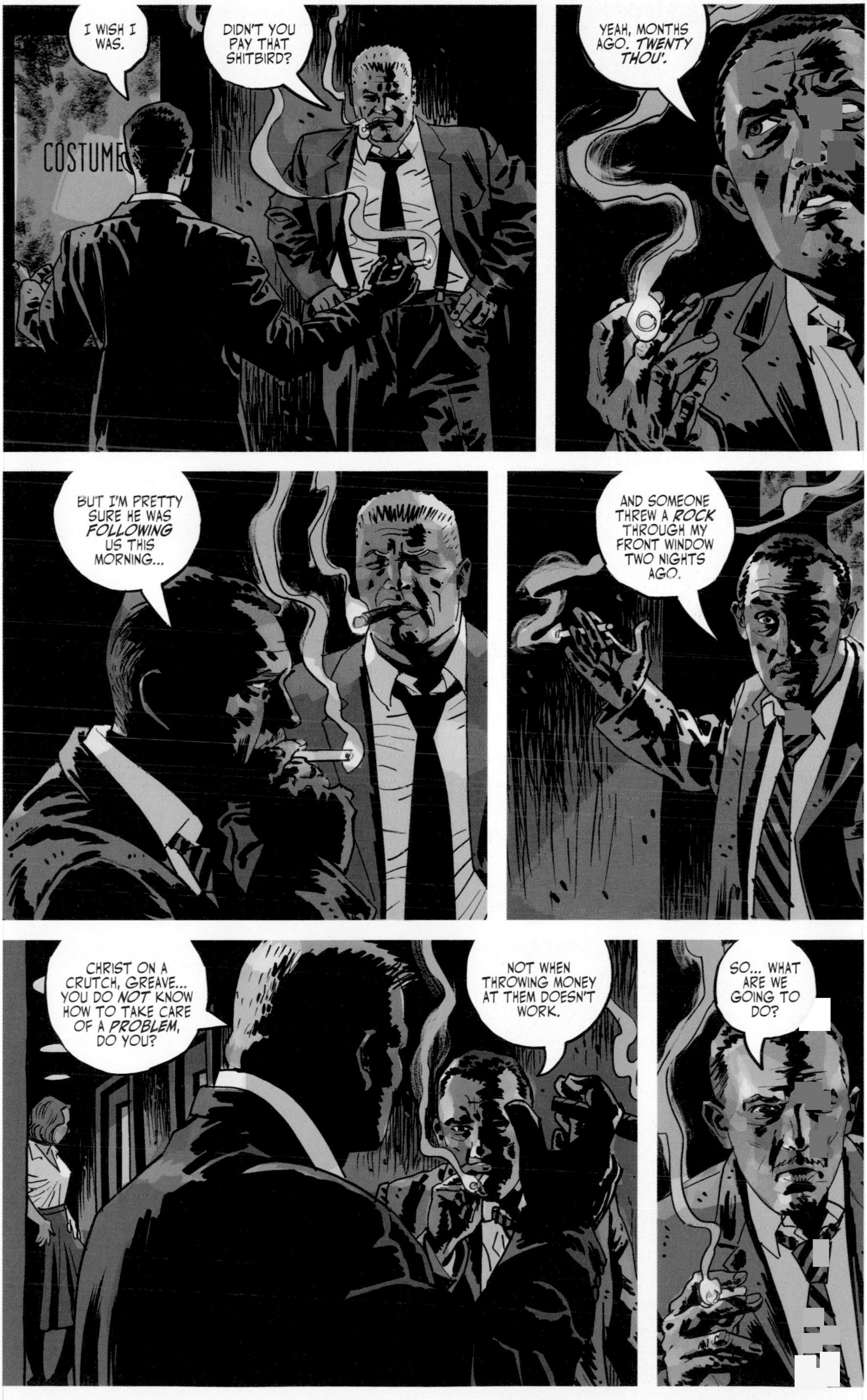
I WISH I WAS.
DIDN'T YOU PAY THAT SHITBIRD?
COSTUME
YEAH, MONTHS AGO. TWENTY THOU'.
BUT I'M PRETTY SURE HE WAS FOLLOWING US THIS MORNING...
AND SOMEONE THREW A ROCK THROUGH MY FRONT WINDOW TWO NIGHTS AGO.
CHRIST ON A CRUTCH, GREAVE... YOU DO NOT KNOW HOW TO TAKE CARE OF A PROBLEM, DO YOU?
NOT WHEN THROWING MONEY AT THEM DOESN'T WORK.
SO... WHAT ARE WE GOING TO DO?

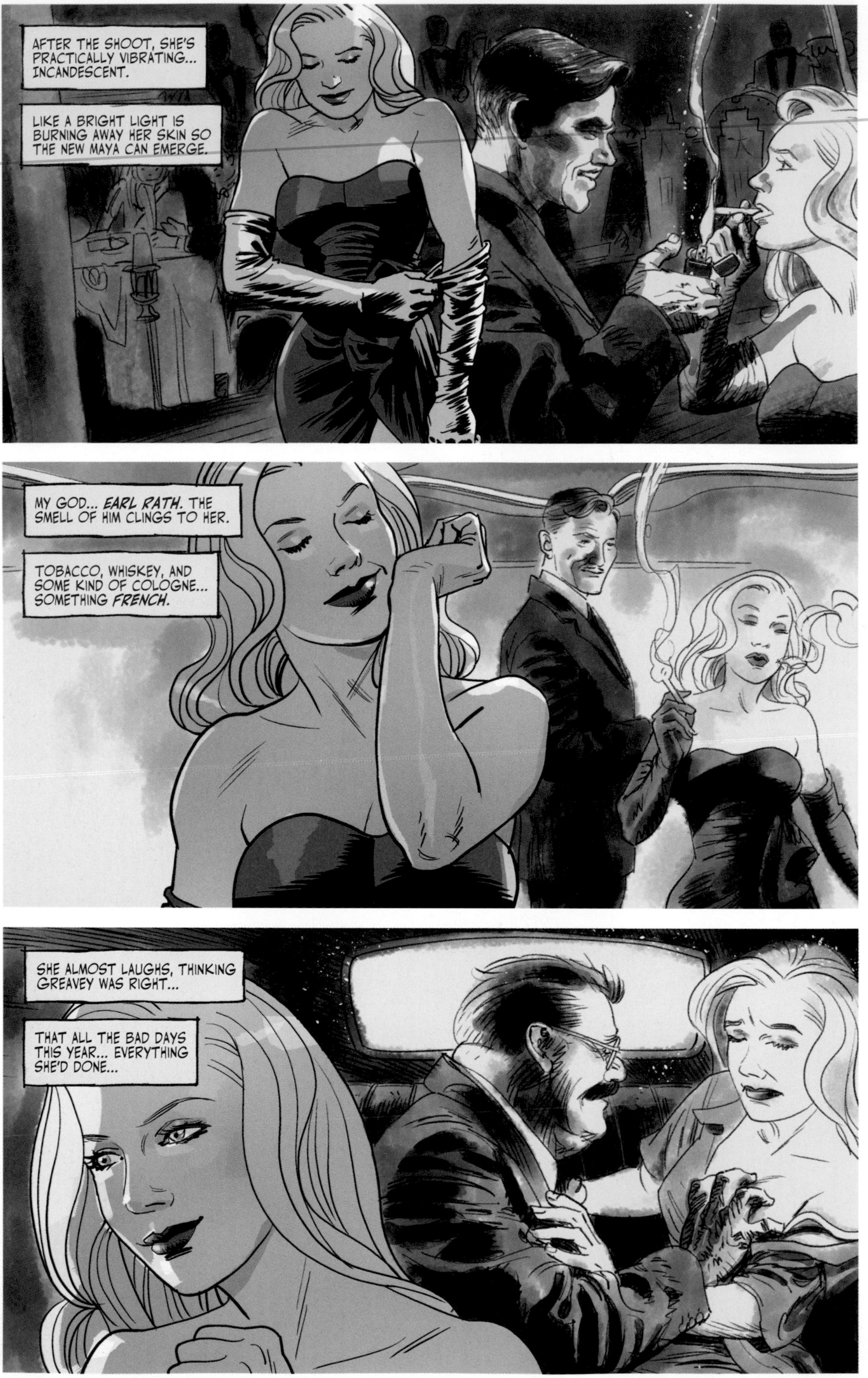
AFTER THE SHOOT, SHE'S PRACTICALLY VIBRATING... INCANDESCENT.
LIKE A BRIGHT LIGHT IS BURNING AWAY HER SKIN SO THE NEW MAYA CAN EMERGE.
MY GOD... *EARL RATH.* THE SMELL OF HIM CLINGS TO HER.
TOBACCO, WHISKEY, AND SOME KIND OF COLOGNE... SOMETHING *FRENCH.*
SHE ALMOST LAUGHS, THINKING GREAVEY WAS RIGHT...
THAT ALL THE BAD DAYS THIS YEAR... EVERYTHING SHE'D DONE...

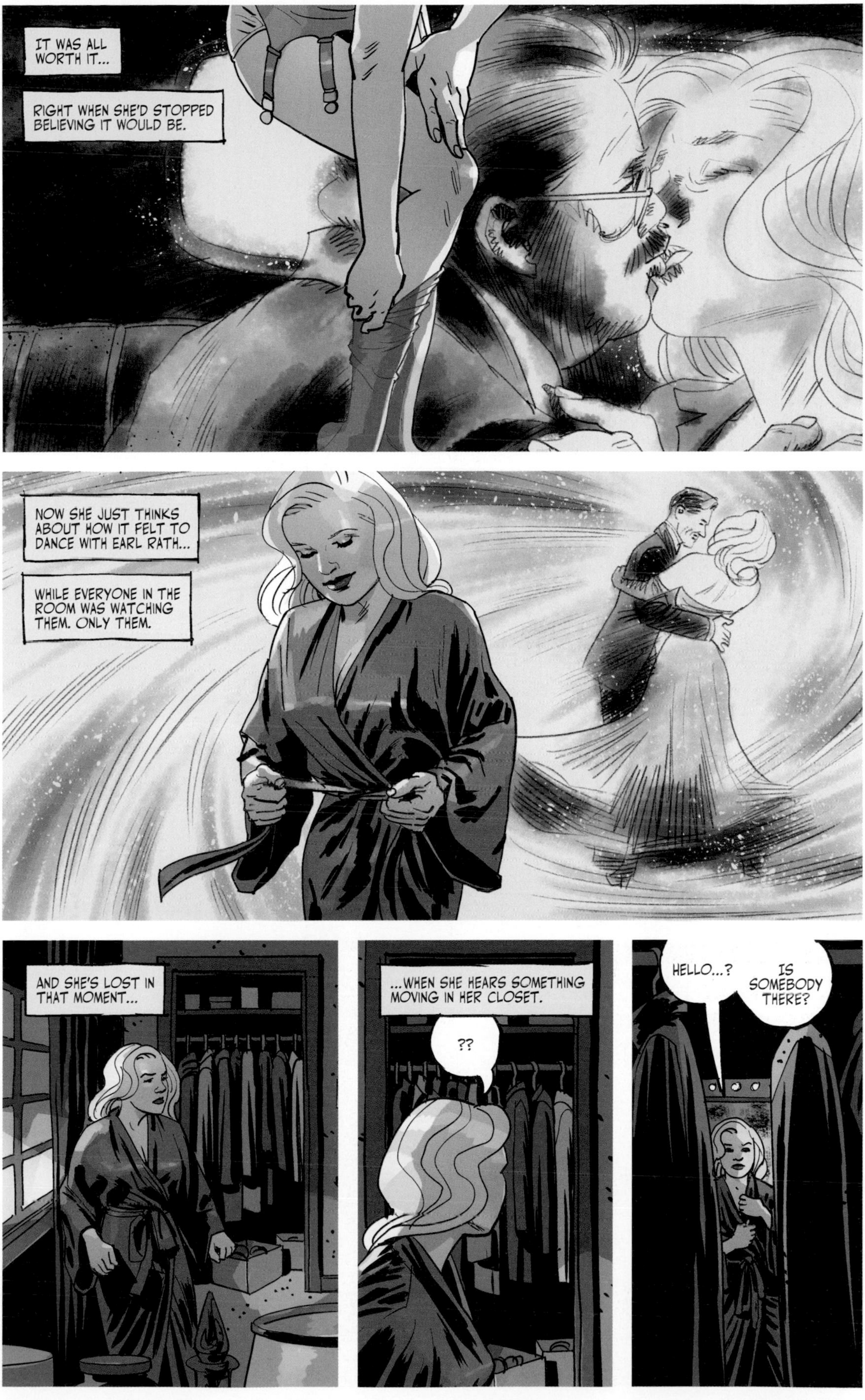
IT WAS ALL WORTH IT...
RIGHT WHEN SHE'D STOPPED BELIEVING IT WOULD BE.
NOW SHE JUST THINKS ABOUT HOW IT FELT TO DANCE WITH EARL RATH...
WHILE EVERYONE IN THE ROOM WAS WATCHING THEM. ONLY THEM.
AND SHE'S LOST IN THAT MOMENT...
...WHEN SHE HEARS SOMETHING MOVING IN HER CLOSET.
??
HELLO...?
IS SOMEBODY THERE?

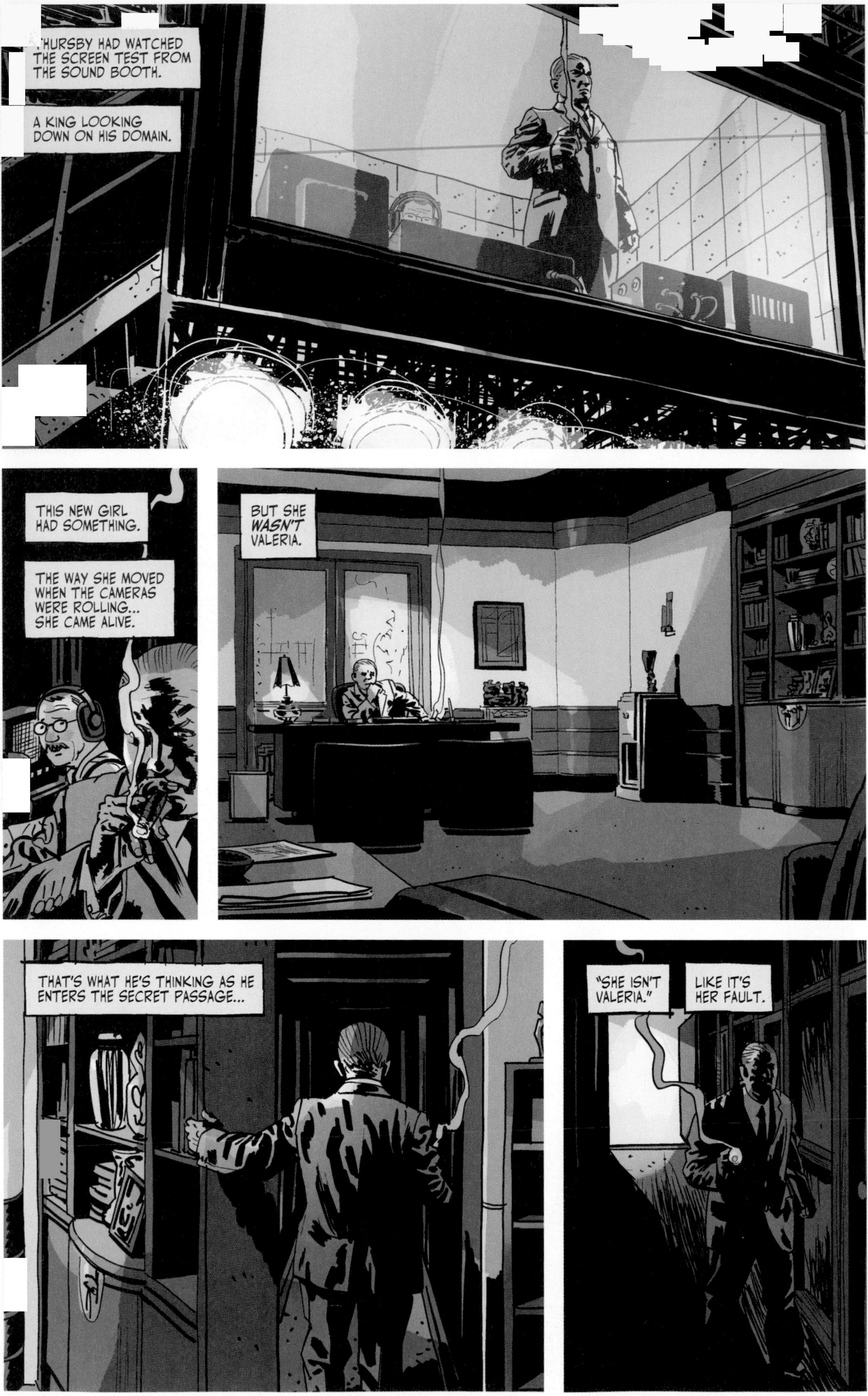
THURSBY HAD WATCHED THE SCREEN TEST FROM THE SOUND BOOTH.
A KING LOOKING DOWN ON HIS DOMAIN.
THIS NEW GIRL HAD SOMETHING.
THE WAY SHE MOVED WHEN THE CAMERAS WERE ROLLING... SHE CAME ALIVE.
BUT SHE *WASN'T* VALERIA.
THAT'S WHAT HE'S THINKING AS HE ENTERS THE SECRET PASSAGE...
"SHE ISN'T VALERIA."
LIKE IT'S HER FAULT.

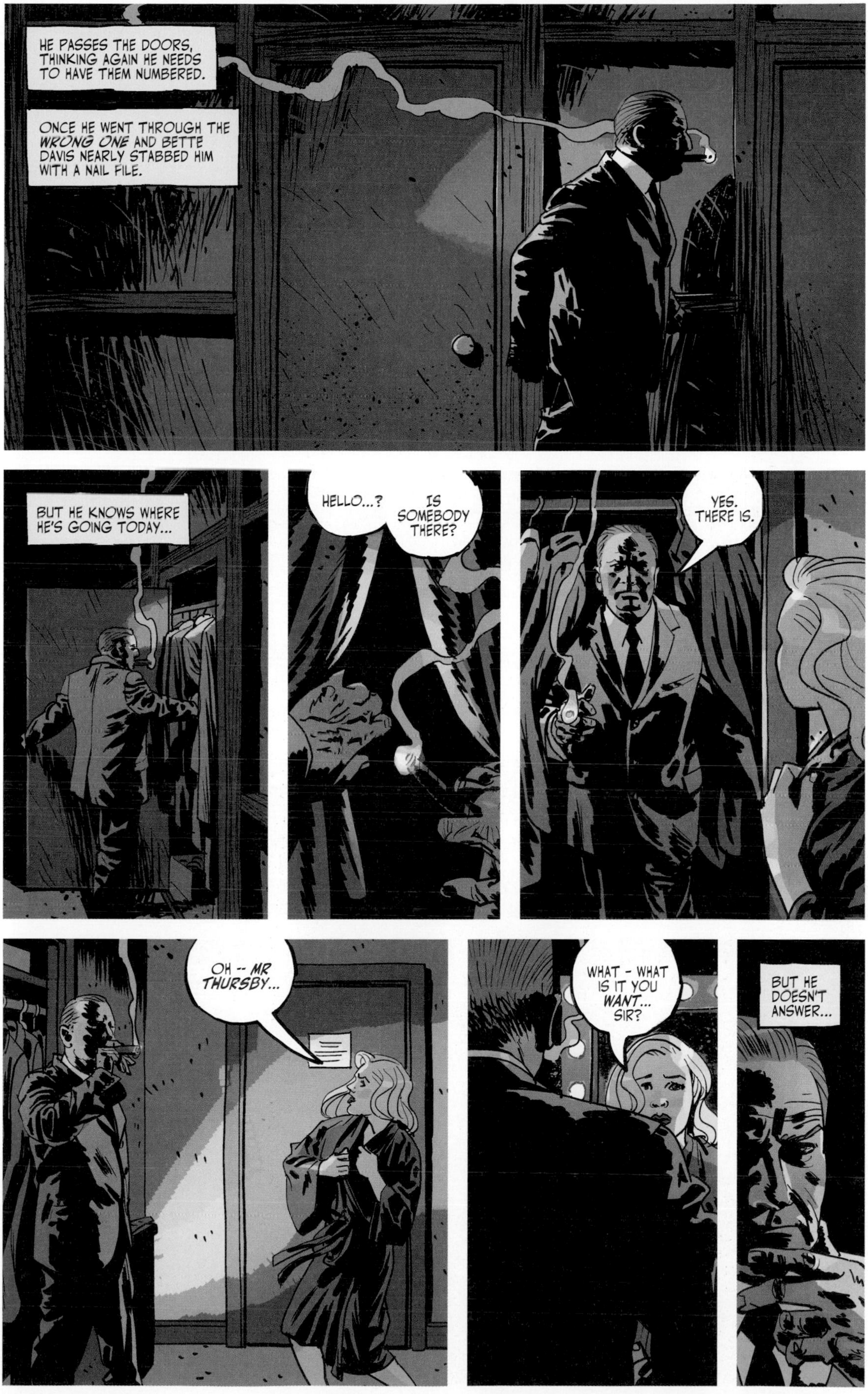
HE PASSES THE DOORS, THINKING AGAIN HE NEEDS TO HAVE THEM NUMBERED.
ONCE HE WENT THROUGH THE *WRONG ONE* AND BETTE DAVIS NEARLY STABBED HIM WITH A NAIL FILE.
BUT HE KNOWS WHERE HE'S GOING TODAY...
HELLO...?
IS SOMEBODY THERE?
YES. THERE IS.
OH -- *MR THURSBY*...
WHAT - WHAT IS IT YOU *WANT*... SIR?
BUT HE DOESN'T ANSWER...

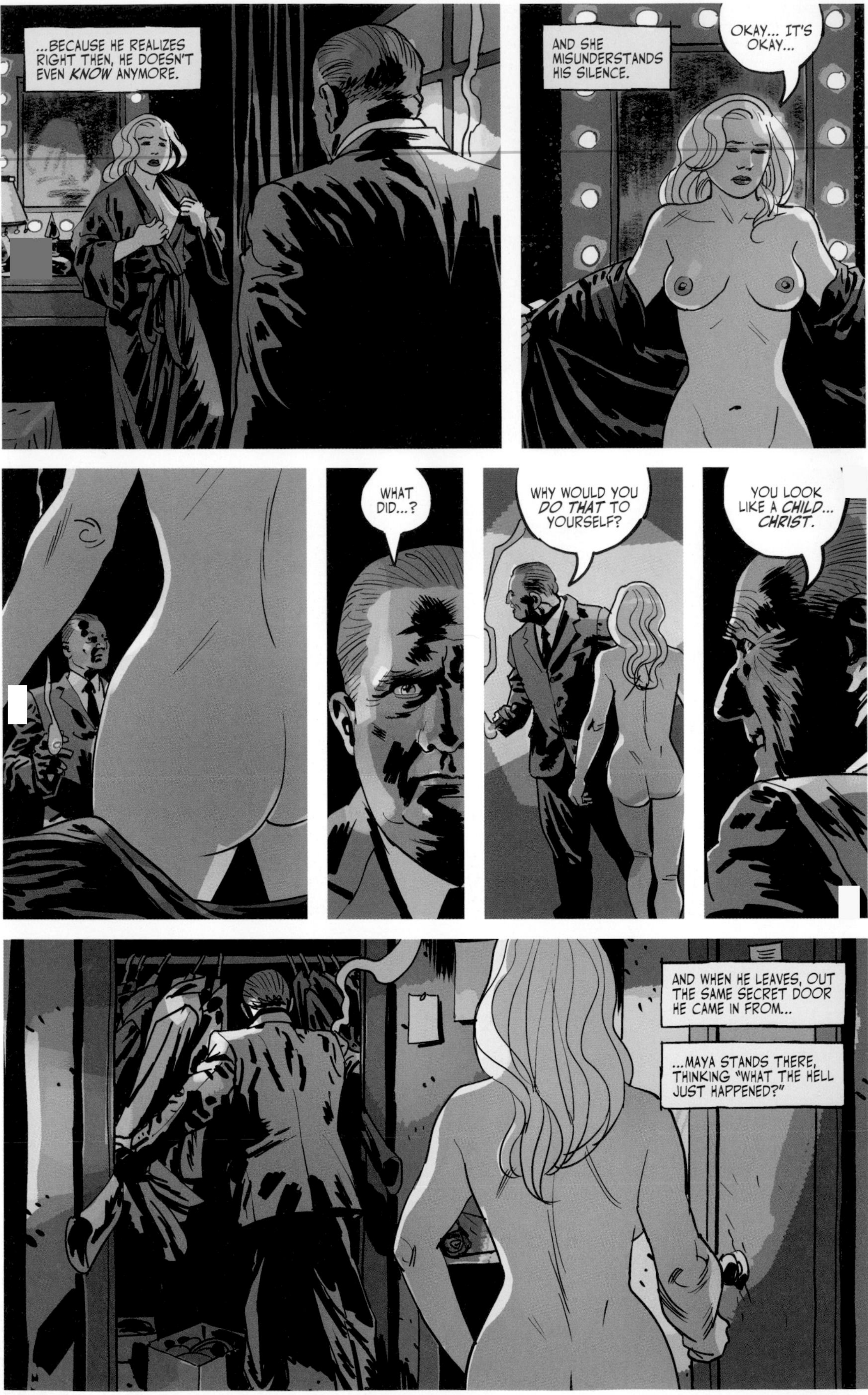
...BECAUSE HE REALIZES RIGHT THEN, HE DOESN'T EVEN KNOW ANYMORE.
AND SHE MISUNDERSTANDS HIS SILENCE.
OKAY... IT'S OKAY...
WHAT DID...?
WHY WOULD YOU DO THAT TO YOURSELF?
YOU LOOK LIKE A CHILD... CHRIST.
AND WHEN HE LEAVES, OUT THE SAME SECRET DOOR HE CAME IN FROM...
...MAYA STANDS THERE, THINKING "WHAT THE HELL JUST HAPPENED?"

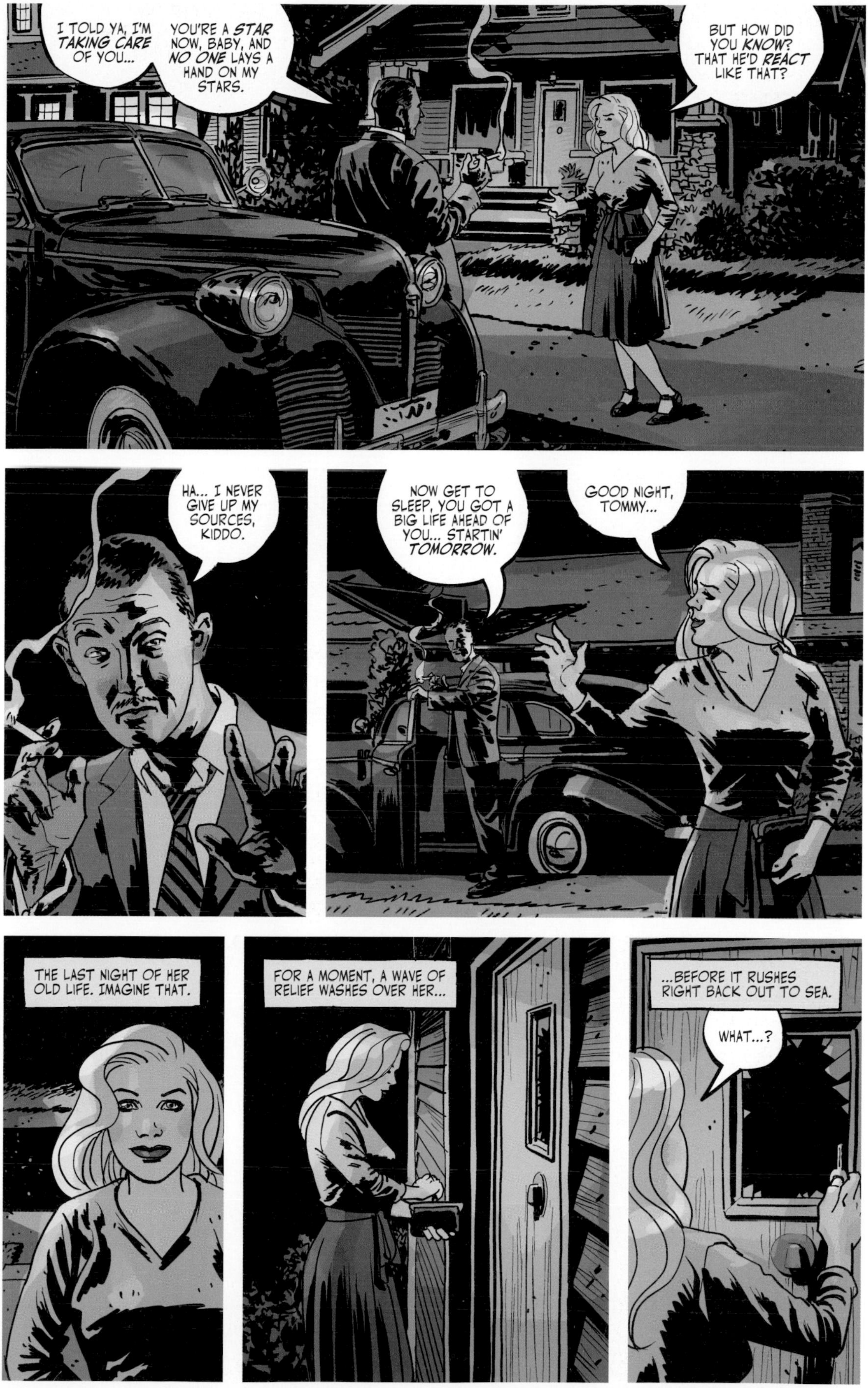
I TOLD YA, I'M TAKING CARE OF YOU...
YOU'RE A STAR NOW, BABY, AND NO ONE LAYS A HAND ON MY STARS.
BUT HOW DID YOU KNOW? THAT HE'D REACT LIKE THAT?
HA... I NEVER GIVE UP MY SOURCES, KIDDO.
NOW GET TO SLEEP, YOU GOT A BIG LIFE AHEAD OF YOU... STARTIN' TOMORROW.
GOOD NIGHT, TOMMY...
THE LAST NIGHT OF HER OLD LIFE. IMAGINE THAT.
FOR A MOMENT, A WAVE OF RELIEF WASHES OVER HER...
...BEFORE IT RUSHES RIGHT BACK OUT TO SEA.
WHAT...?

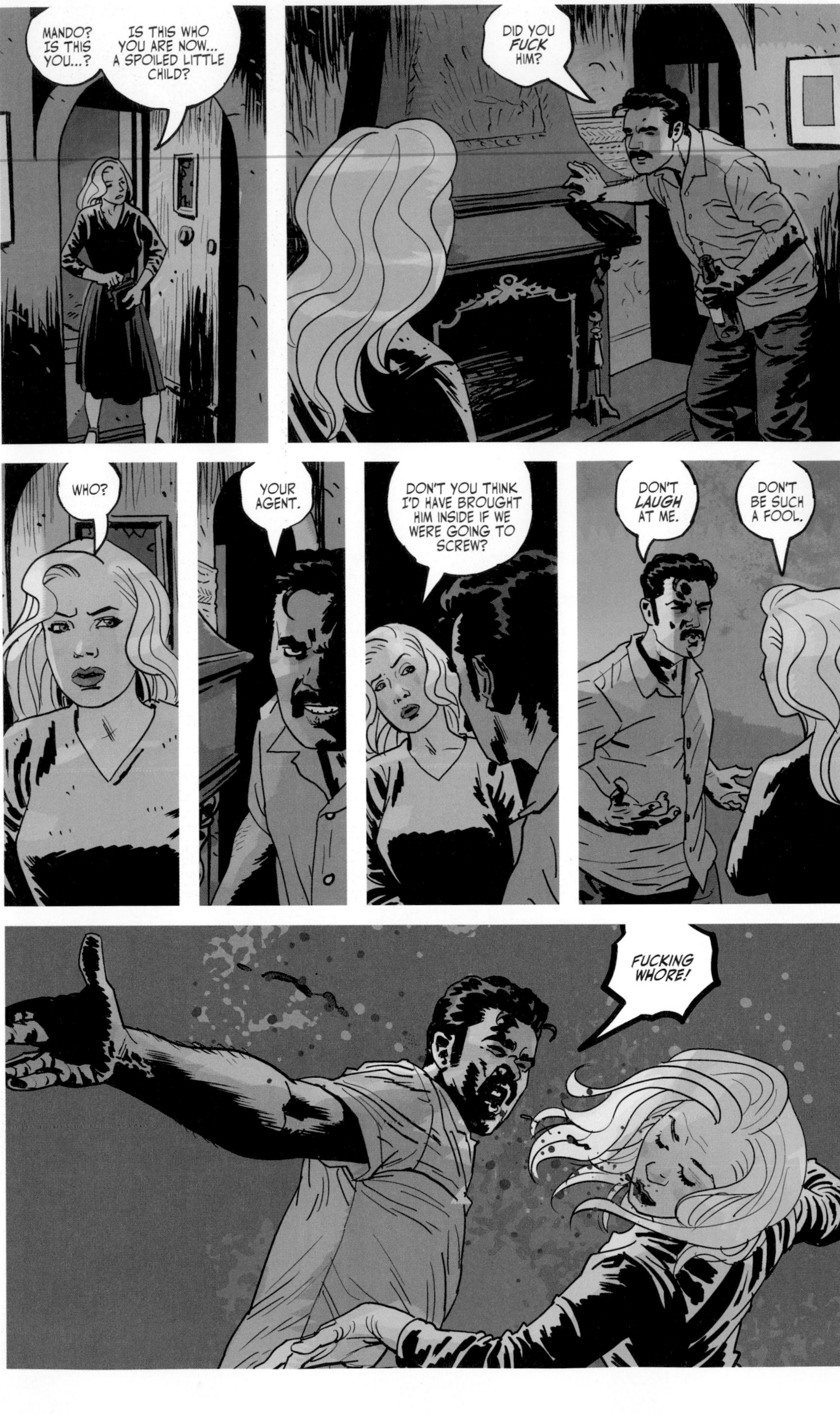
MANDO? IS THIS YOU...?
IS THIS WHO YOU ARE NOW... A SPOILED LITTLE CHILD?
DID YOU *FUCK* HIM?
WHO?
YOUR AGENT.
DON'T YOU THINK I'D HAVE BROUGHT HIM INSIDE IF WE WERE GOING TO SCREW?
DON'T *LAUGH* AT ME.
DON'T BE SUCH A FOOL.
FUCKING WHORE!

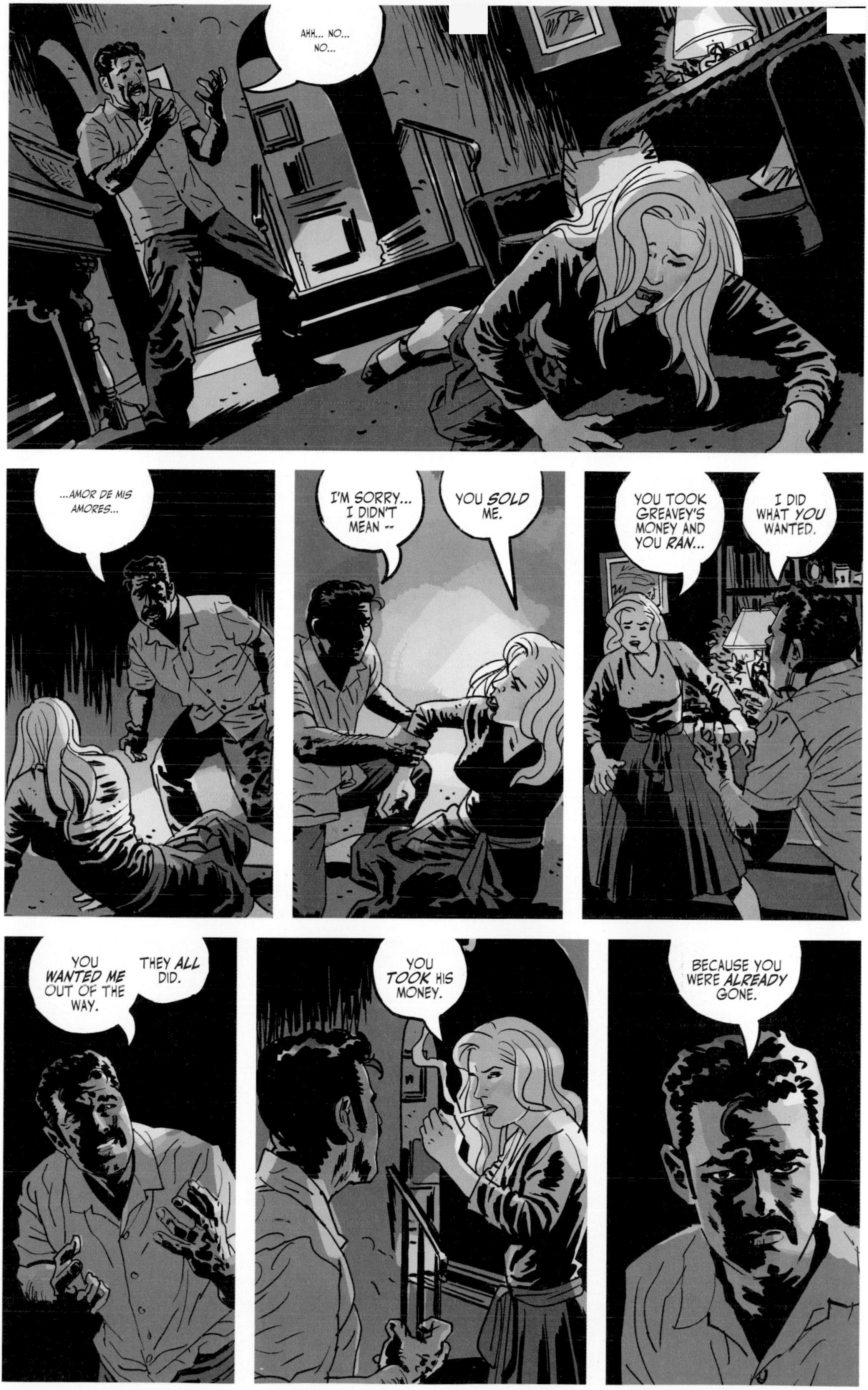
AHH... NO... NO...
...AMOR DE MIS AMORES...
I'M SORRY... I DIDN'T MEAN --
YOU SOLD ME.
YOU TOOK GREAVEY'S MONEY AND YOU RAN...
I DID WHAT YOU WANTED.
YOU WANTED ME OUT OF THE WAY.
THEY ALL DID.
YOU TOOK HIS MONEY.
BECAUSE YOU WERE ALREADY GONE.

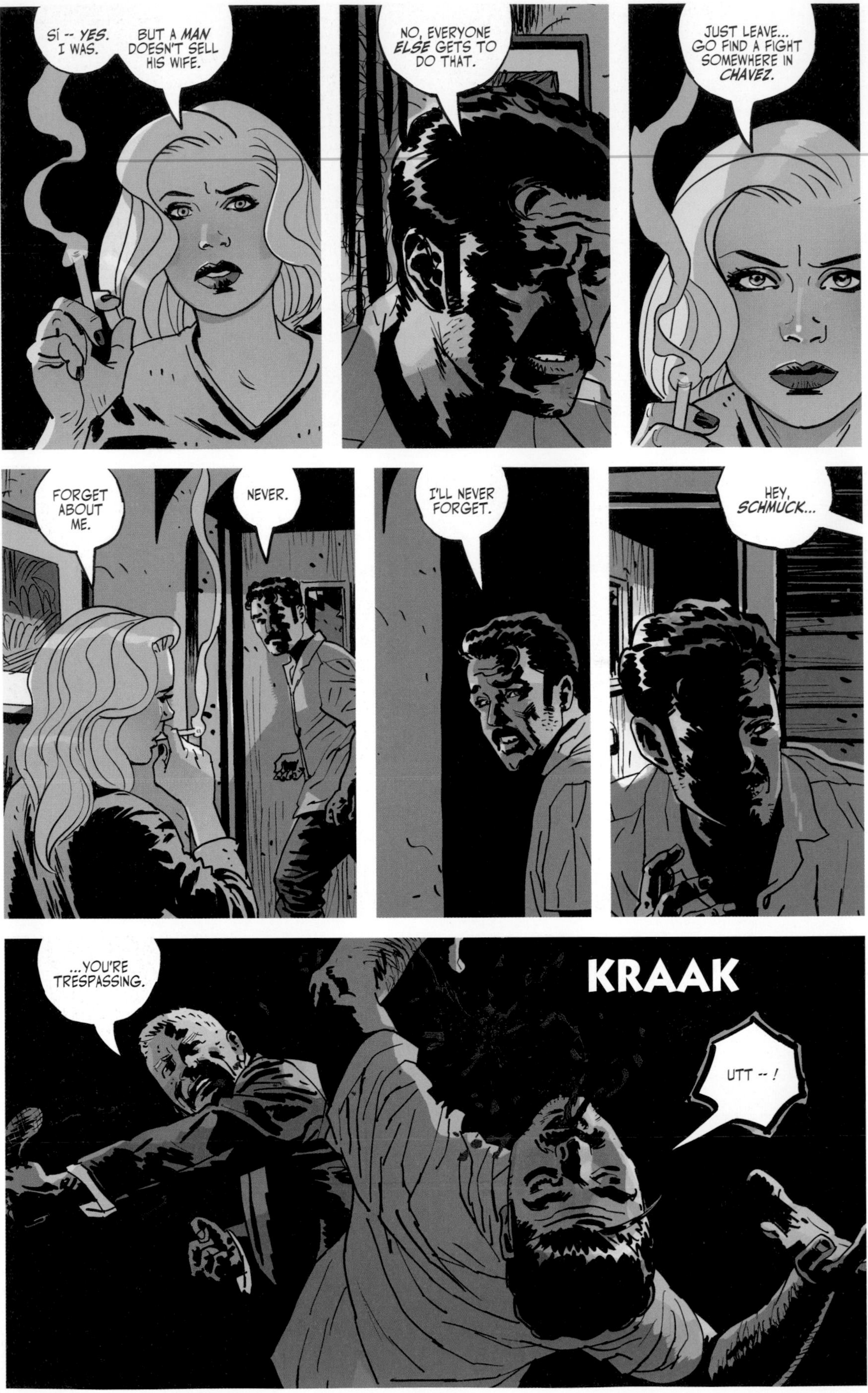
SÍ -- YES. I WAS.
BUT A MAN DOESN'T SELL HIS WIFE.
NO, EVERYONE ELSE GETS TO DO THAT.
JUST LEAVE... GO FIND A FIGHT SOMEWHERE IN CHAVEZ.
FORGET ABOUT ME.
NEVER.
I'LL NEVER FORGET.
HEY, SCHMUCK...
...YOU'RE TRESPASSING.
KRAAK
UTT -- !

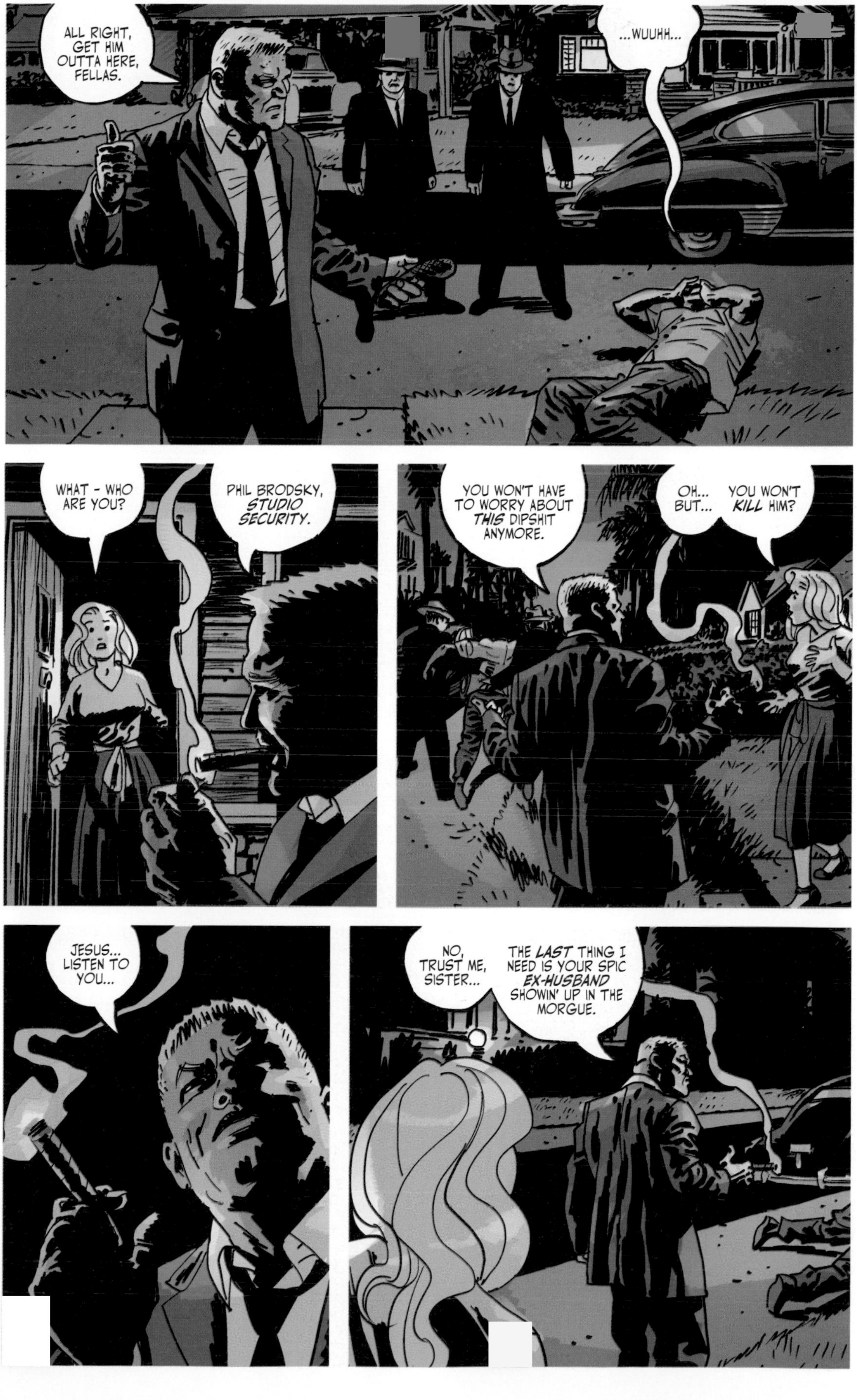
ALL RIGHT, GET HIM OUTTA HERE, FELLAS.
...WUUHH...
WHAT - WHO ARE YOU?
PHIL BRODSKY, *STUDIO SECURITY*.
YOU WON'T HAVE TO WORRY ABOUT *THIS* DIPSHIT ANYMORE.
OH... BUT...
YOU WON'T *KILL* HIM?
JESUS... LISTEN TO YOU...
NO, TRUST ME, SISTER...
THE *LAST* THING I NEED IS YOUR SPIC *EX-HUSBAND* SHOWIN' UP IN THE MORGUE.

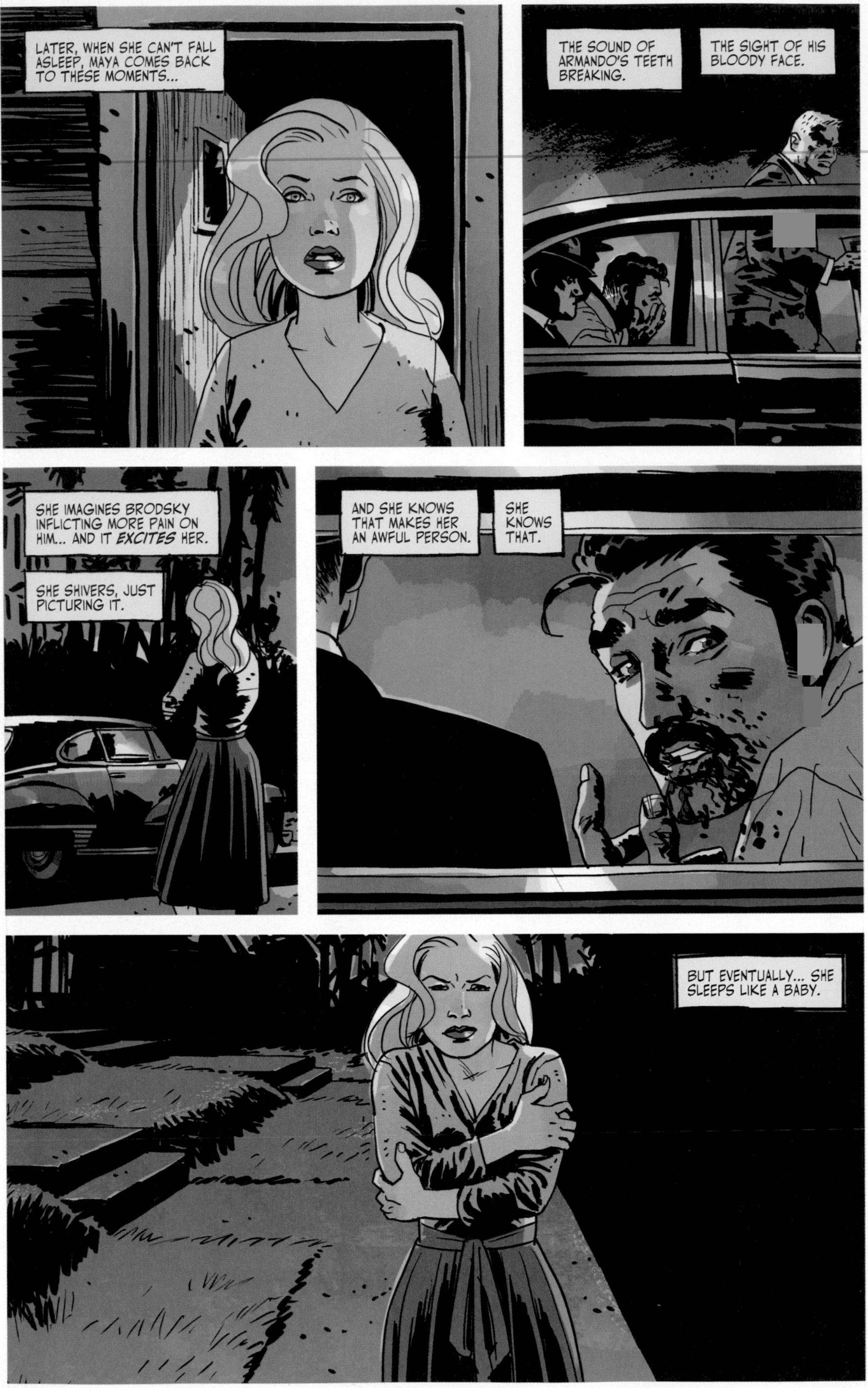
LATER, WHEN SHE CAN'T FALL ASLEEP, MAYA COMES BACK TO THESE MOMENTS...
THE SOUND OF ARMANDO'S TEETH BREAKING.
THE SIGHT OF HIS BLOODY FACE.
SHE IMAGINES BRODSKY INFLICTING MORE PAIN ON HIM... AND IT *EXCITES* HER.
SHE SHIVERS, JUST PICTURING IT.
AND SHE KNOWS THAT MAKES HER AN AWFUL PERSON.
SHE KNOWS THAT.
BUT EVENTUALLY... SHE SLEEPS LIKE A BABY.

The Word on the Street

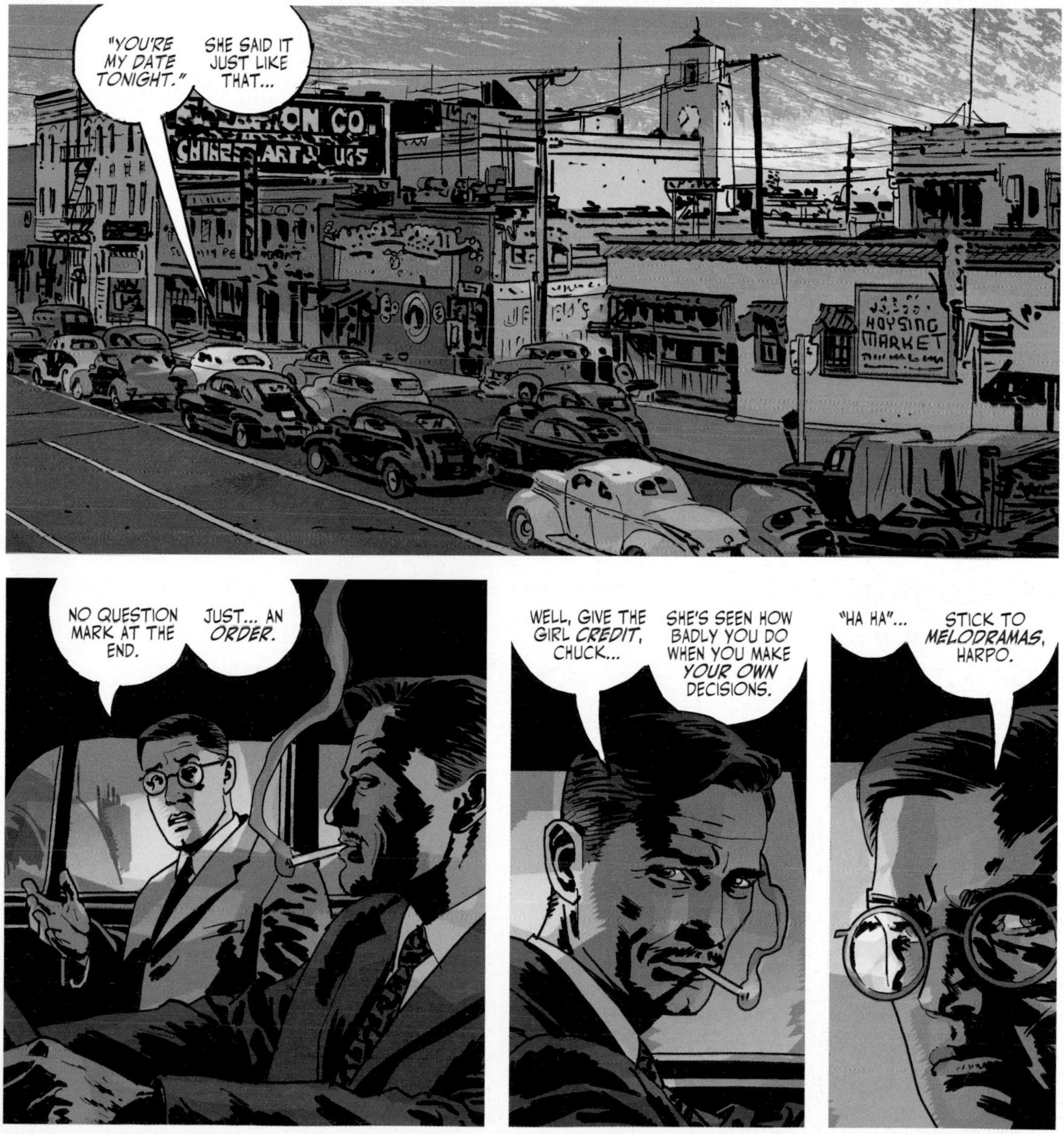
"YOU'RE MY DATE TONIGHT."
SHE SAID IT JUST LIKE THAT...
HOYSING MARKET
NO QUESTION MARK AT THE END.
JUST... AN *ORDER*.
WELL, GIVE THE GIRL *CREDIT*, CHUCK...
SHE'S SEEN HOW BADLY YOU DO WHEN YOU MAKE *YOUR OWN* DECISIONS.
"HA HA"...
STICK TO *MELODRAMAS*, HARPO.

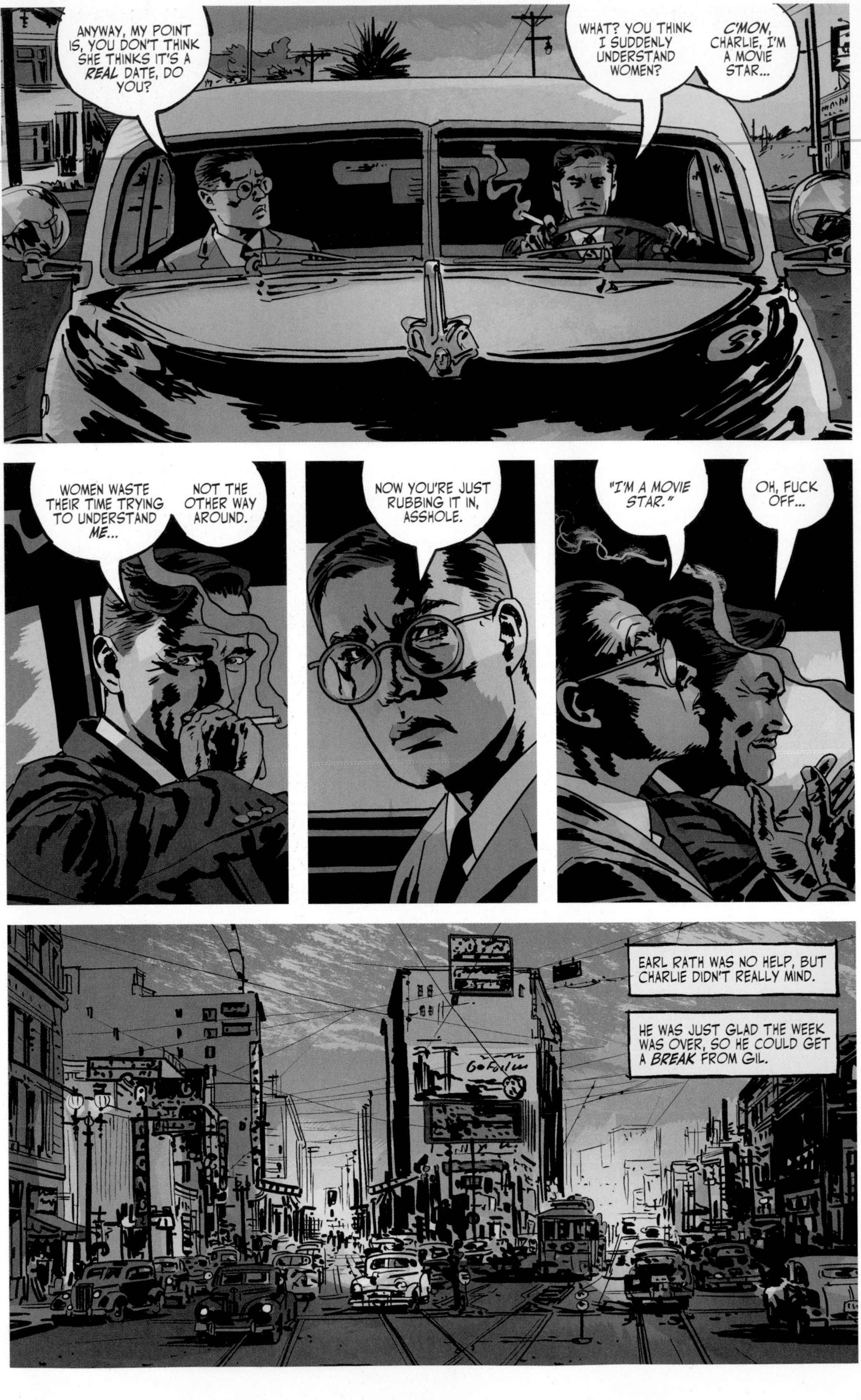
ANYWAY, MY POINT IS, YOU DON'T THINK SHE THINKS IT'S A REAL DATE, DO YOU?
WHAT? YOU THINK I SUDDENLY UNDERSTAND WOMEN?
C'MON, CHARLIE, I'M A MOVIE STAR...
WOMEN WASTE THEIR TIME TRYING TO UNDERSTAND ME...
NOT THE OTHER WAY AROUND.
NOW YOU'RE JUST RUBBING IT IN, ASSHOLE.
"I'M A MOVIE STAR."
OH, FUCK OFF...
EARL RATH WAS NO HELP, BUT CHARLIE DIDN'T REALLY MIND.
HE WAS JUST GLAD THE WEEK WAS OVER, SO HE COULD GET A BREAK FROM GIL.

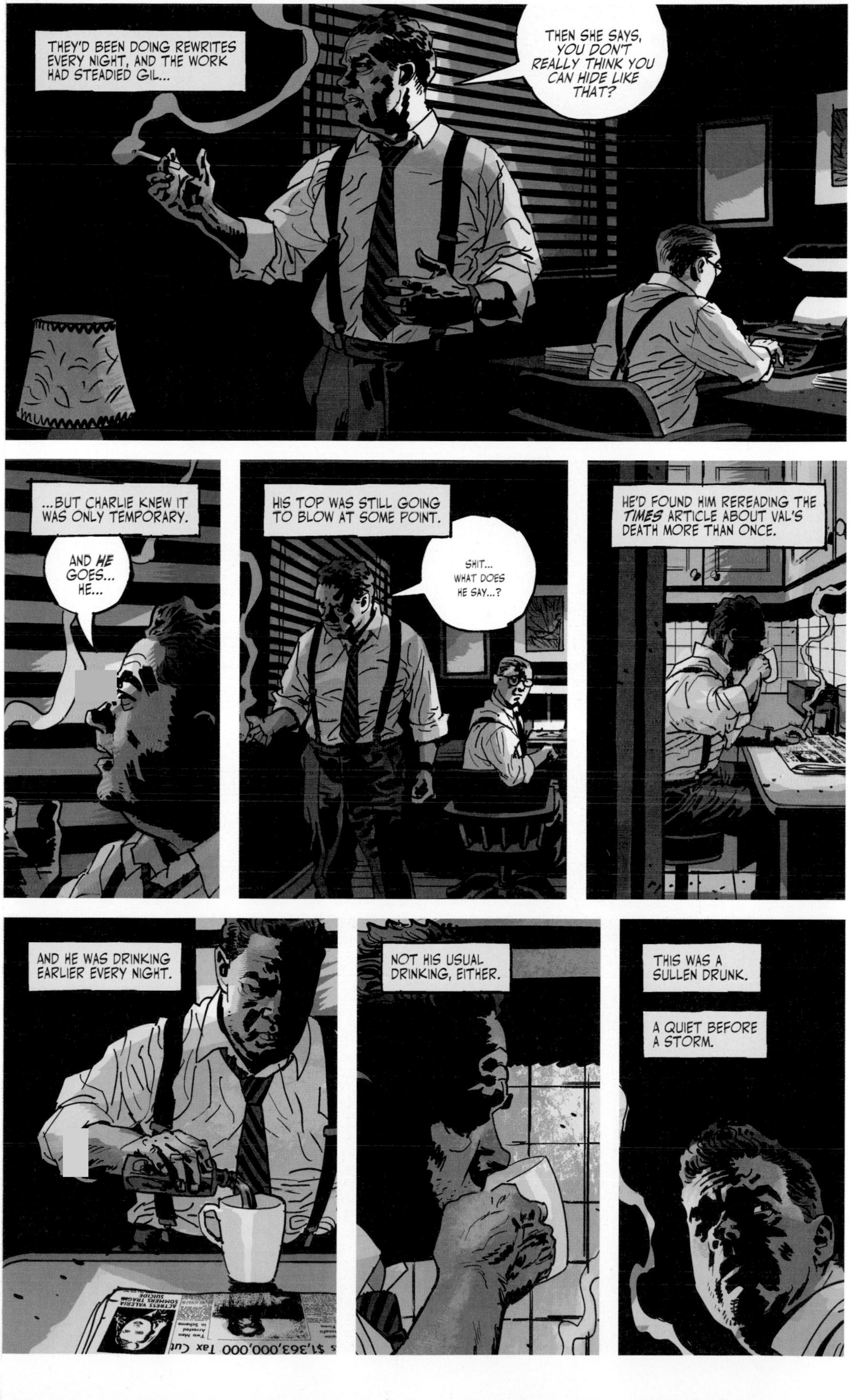

THEY'D BEEN DOING REWRITES EVERY NIGHT, AND THE WORK HAD STEADIED GIL...
THEN SHE SAYS, *YOU DON'T REALLY THINK YOU CAN HIDE LIKE THAT?*
...BUT CHARLIE KNEW IT WAS ONLY TEMPORARY.
AND *HE* GOES... HE...
HIS TOP WAS STILL GOING TO BLOW AT SOME POINT.
SHIT... WHAT DOES HE SAY...?
HE'D FOUND HIM REREADING THE *TIMES* ARTICLE ABOUT VAL'S DEATH MORE THAN ONCE.
AND HE WAS DRINKING EARLIER EVERY NIGHT.
ACTRESS VALERIA SOMMERS TRAGIC SUICIDE
$1,363,000,000 Tax Cut
NOT HIS USUAL DRINKING, EITHER.
THIS WAS A SULLEN DRUNK.
A QUIET BEFORE A STORM.

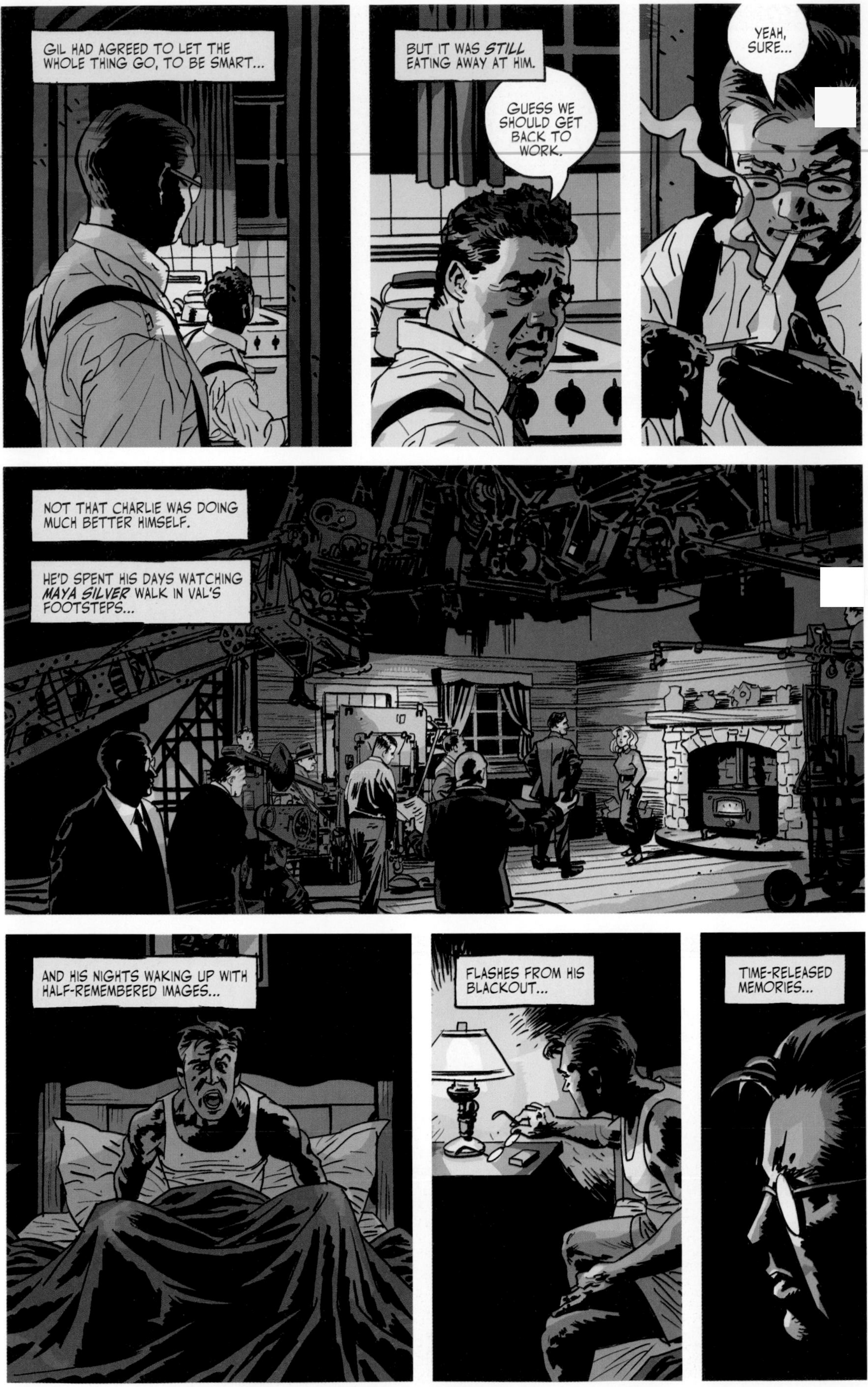
GIL HAD AGREED TO LET THE WHOLE THING GO, TO BE SMART...
BUT IT WAS STILL EATING AWAY AT HIM.
GUESS WE SHOULD GET BACK TO WORK.
YEAH, SURE...
NOT THAT CHARLIE WAS DOING MUCH BETTER HIMSELF.
HE'D SPENT HIS DAYS WATCHING MAYA SILVER WALK IN VAL'S FOOTSTEPS...
AND HIS NIGHTS WAKING UP WITH HALF-REMEMBERED IMAGES...
FLASHES FROM HIS BLACKOUT...
TIME-RELEASED MEMORIES...

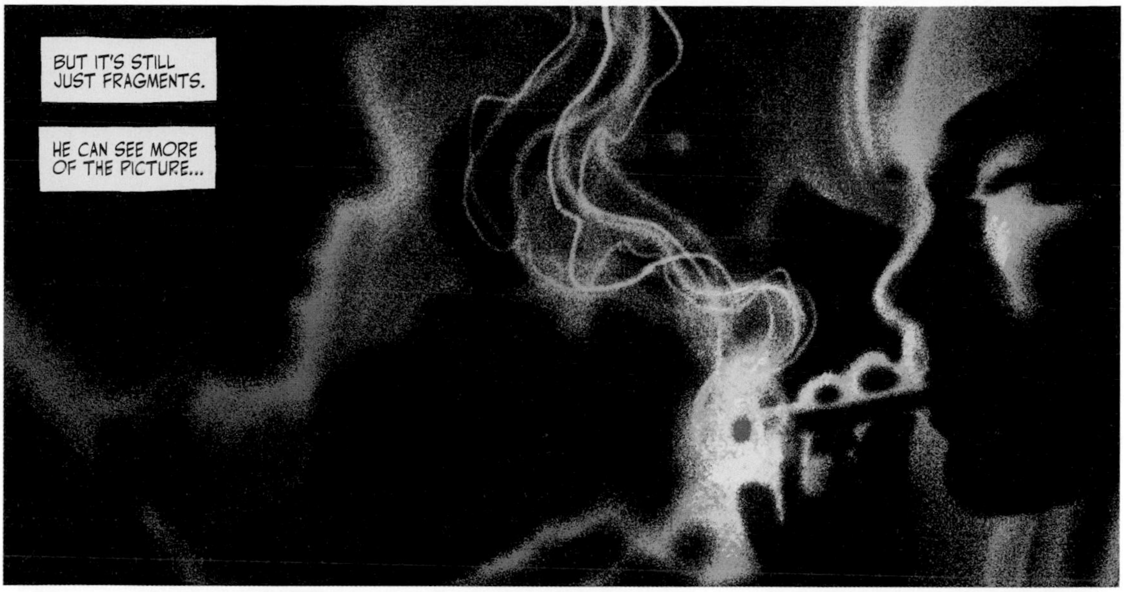
BUT IT'S STILL JUST FRAGMENTS.
HE CAN SEE MORE OF THE PICTURE...

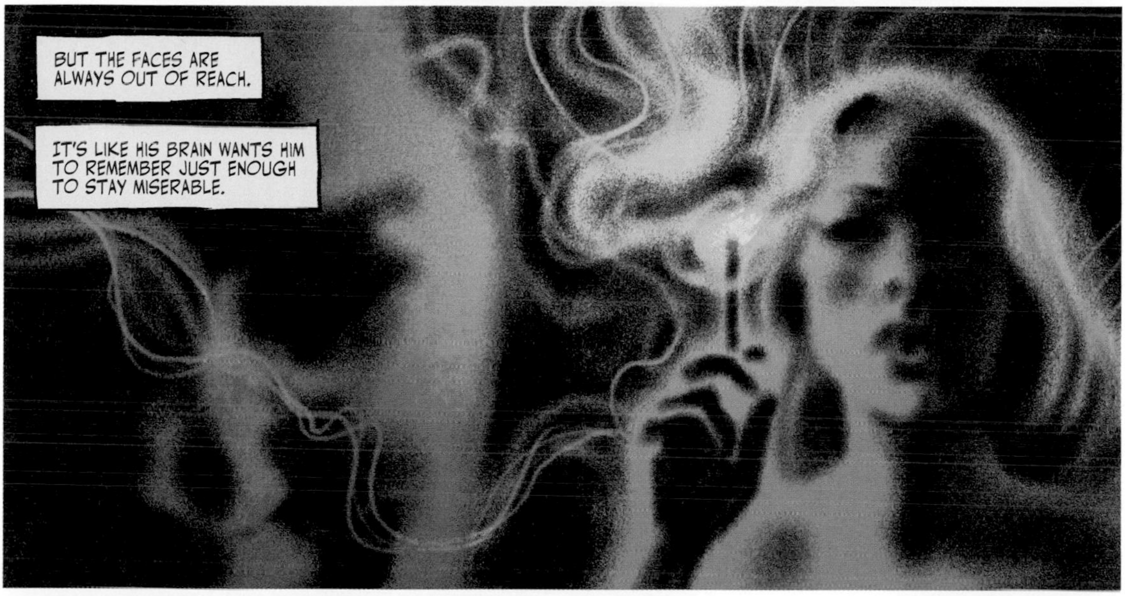
BUT THE FACES ARE ALWAYS OUT OF REACH.
IT'S LIKE HIS BRAIN WANTS HIM TO REMEMBER JUST ENOUGH TO STAY MISERABLE.

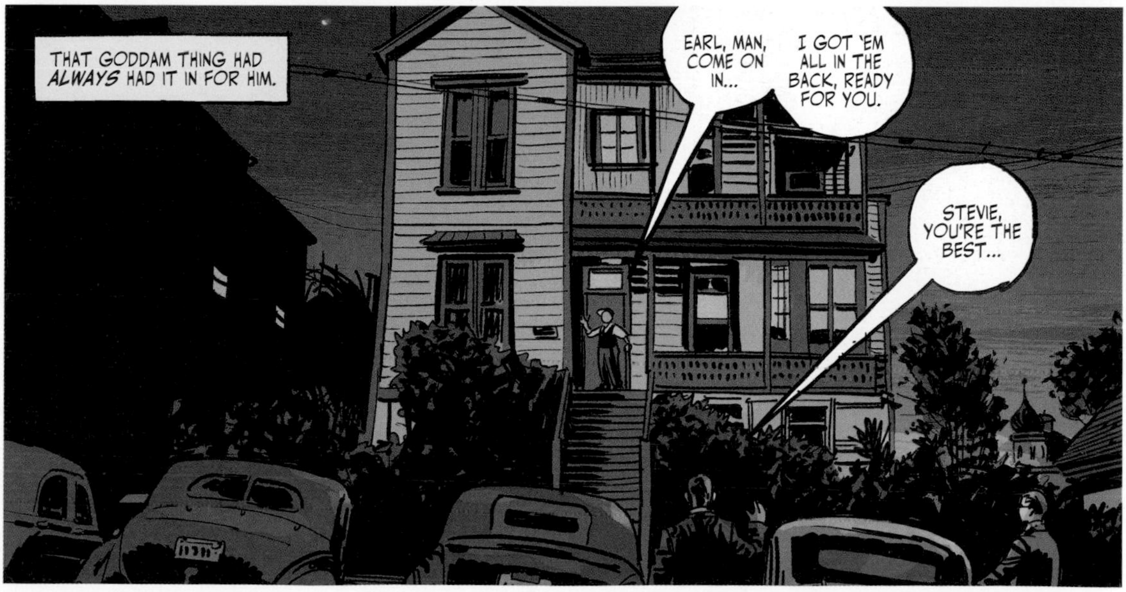
THAT GODDAM THING HAD *ALWAYS* HAD IT IN FOR HIM.
EARL, MAN, COME ON IN...
I GOT 'EM ALL IN THE BACK, READY FOR YOU.
STEVIE, YOU'RE THE BEST...

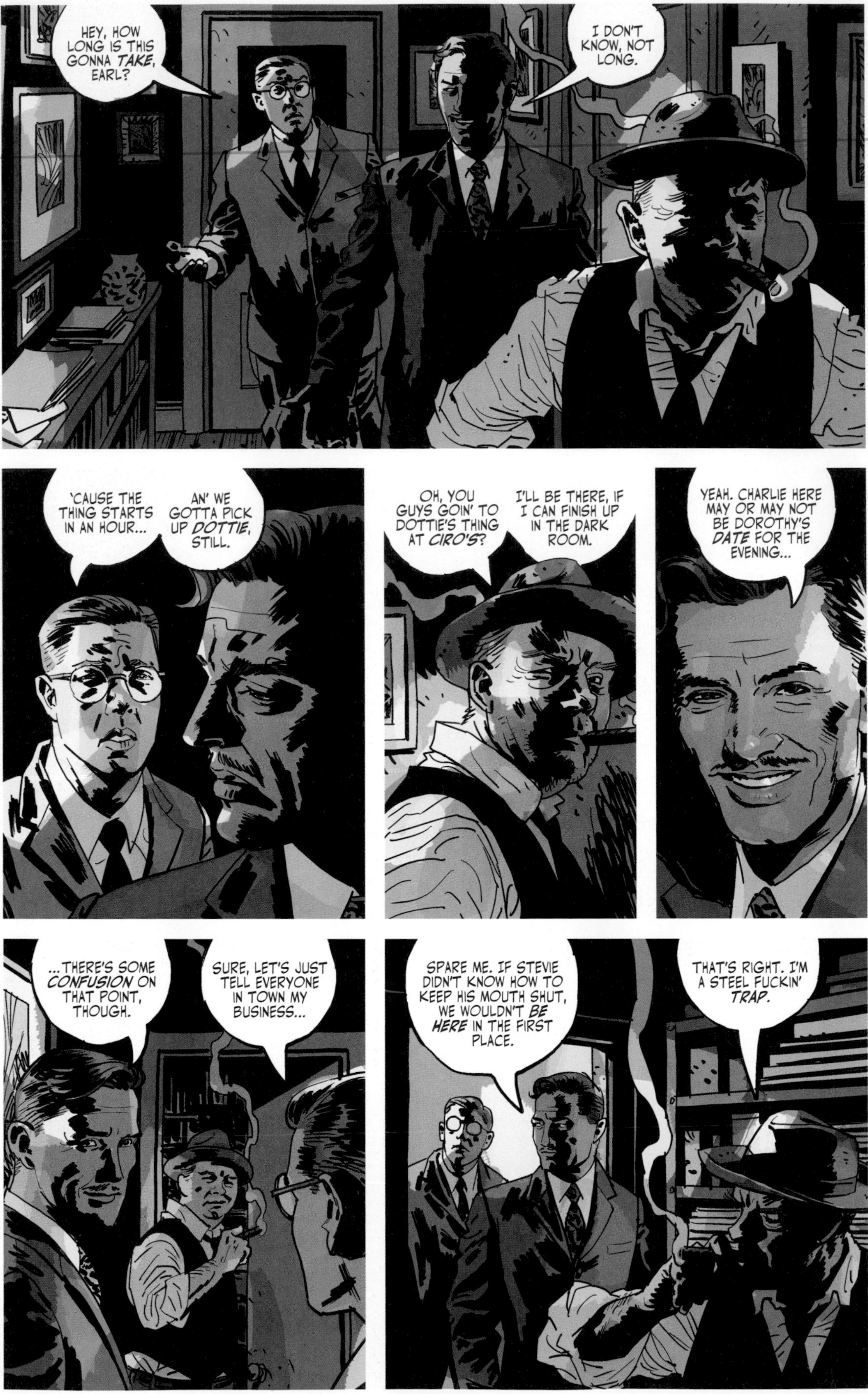
HEY, HOW LONG IS THIS GONNA *TAKE*, EARL?
I DON'T KNOW, NOT LONG.
'CAUSE THE THING STARTS IN AN HOUR...
AN' WE GOTTA PICK UP *DOTTIE*, STILL.
OH, YOU GUYS GOIN' TO DOTTIE'S THING AT *CIRO'S*?
I'LL BE THERE, IF I CAN FINISH UP IN THE DARK ROOM.
YEAH. CHARLIE HERE MAY OR MAY NOT BE DOROTHY'S *DATE* FOR THE EVENING...
...THERE'S SOME *CONFUSION* ON THAT POINT, THOUGH.
SURE, LET'S JUST TELL EVERYONE IN TOWN MY BUSINESS...
SPARE ME. IF STEVIE DIDN'T KNOW HOW TO KEEP HIS MOUTH SHUT, WE WOULDN'T *BE HERE* IN THE FIRST PLACE.
THAT'S RIGHT. I'M A STEEL FUCKIN' *TRAP*.

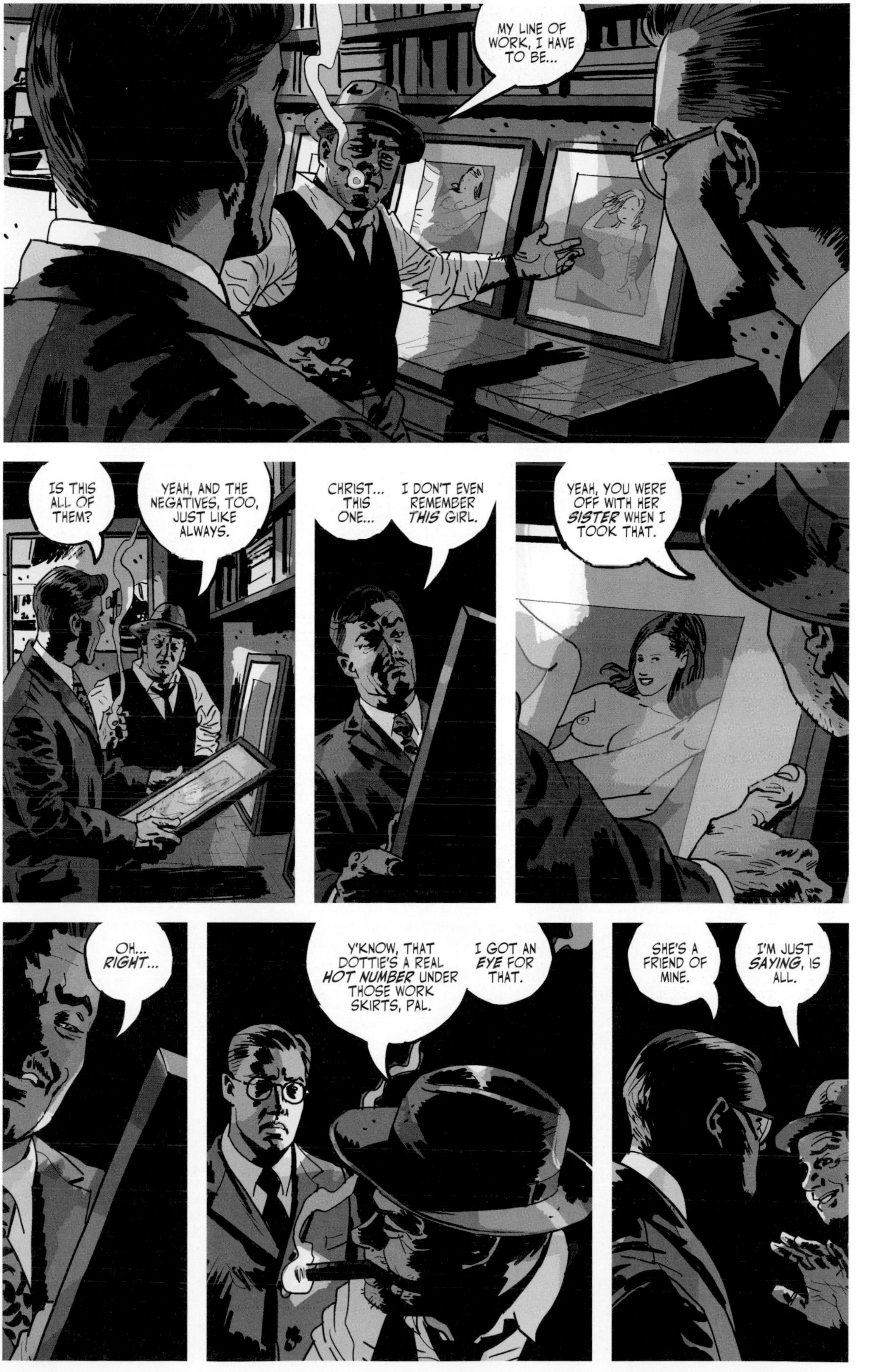
MY LINE OF WORK, I HAVE TO BE...
IS THIS ALL OF THEM?
YEAH, AND THE NEGATIVES, TOO, JUST LIKE ALWAYS.
CHRIST... THIS ONE...
I DON'T EVEN REMEMBER *THIS* GIRL.
YEAH, YOU WERE OFF WITH HER *SISTER* WHEN I TOOK THAT.
OH... *RIGHT*...
Y'KNOW, THAT DOTTIE'S A REAL *HOT NUMBER* UNDER THOSE WORK SKIRTS, PAL.
I GOT AN *EYE* FOR THAT.
SHE'S A FRIEND OF MINE.
I'M JUST *SAYING*, IS ALL.

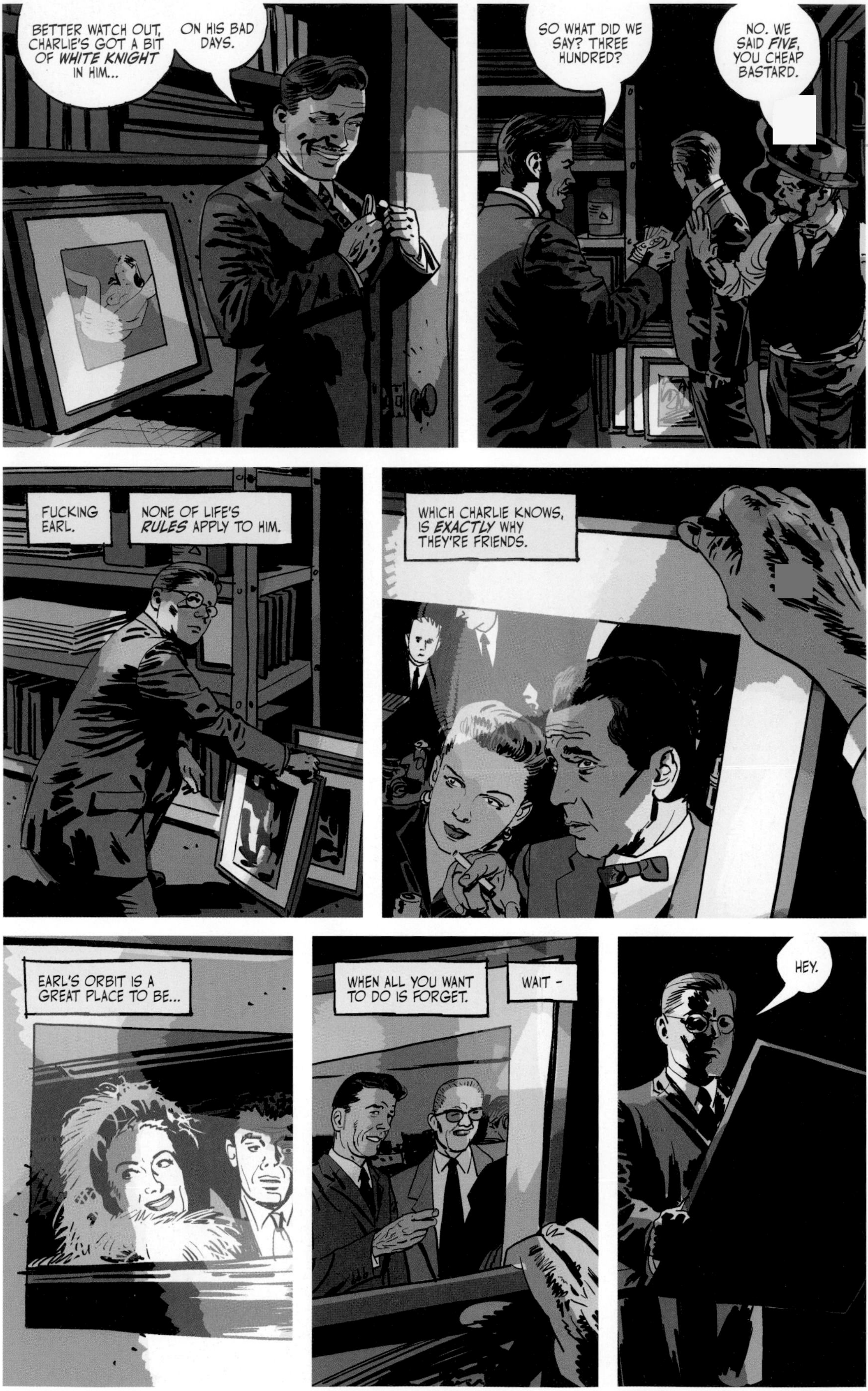
BETTER WATCH OUT, CHARLIE'S GOT A BIT OF *WHITE KNIGHT* IN HIM...
ON HIS BAD DAYS.
SO WHAT DID WE SAY? THREE HUNDRED?
NO. WE SAID *FIVE*, YOU CHEAP BASTARD.
FUCKING EARL.
NONE OF LIFE'S *RULES* APPLY TO HIM.
WHICH CHARLIE KNOWS, IS *EXACTLY* WHY THEY'RE FRIENDS.
EARL'S ORBIT IS A GREAT PLACE TO BE...
WHEN ALL YOU WANT TO DO IS FORGET.
WAIT -
HEY.

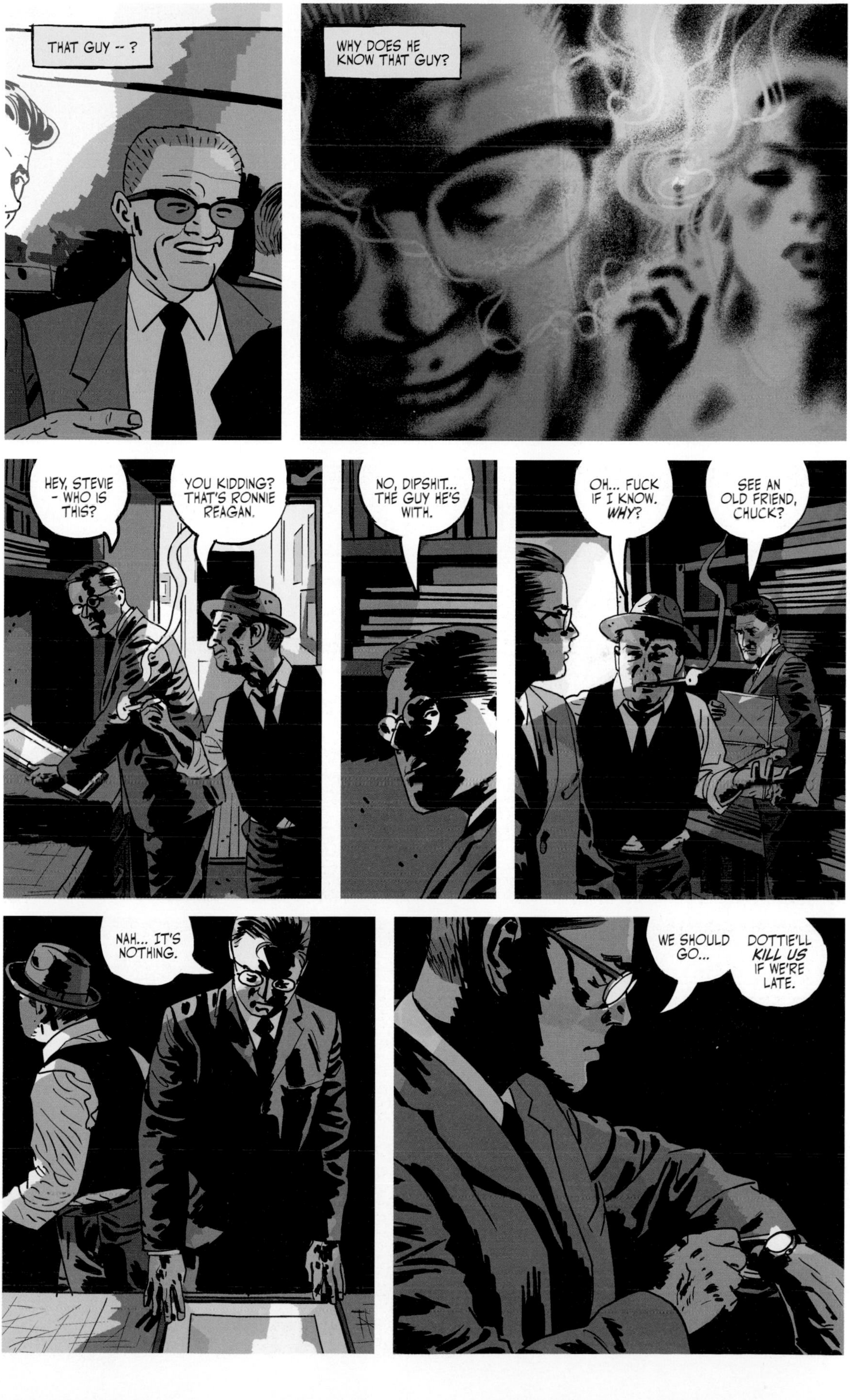
THAT GUY -- ?
WHY DOES HE KNOW THAT GUY?
HEY, STEVIE - WHO IS THIS?
YOU KIDDING? THAT'S RONNIE REAGAN.
NO, DIPSHIT... THE GUY HE'S WITH.
OH... FUCK IF I KNOW. WHY?
SEE AN OLD FRIEND, CHUCK?
NAH... IT'S NOTHING.
WE SHOULD GO...
DOTTIE'LL KILL US IF WE'RE LATE.

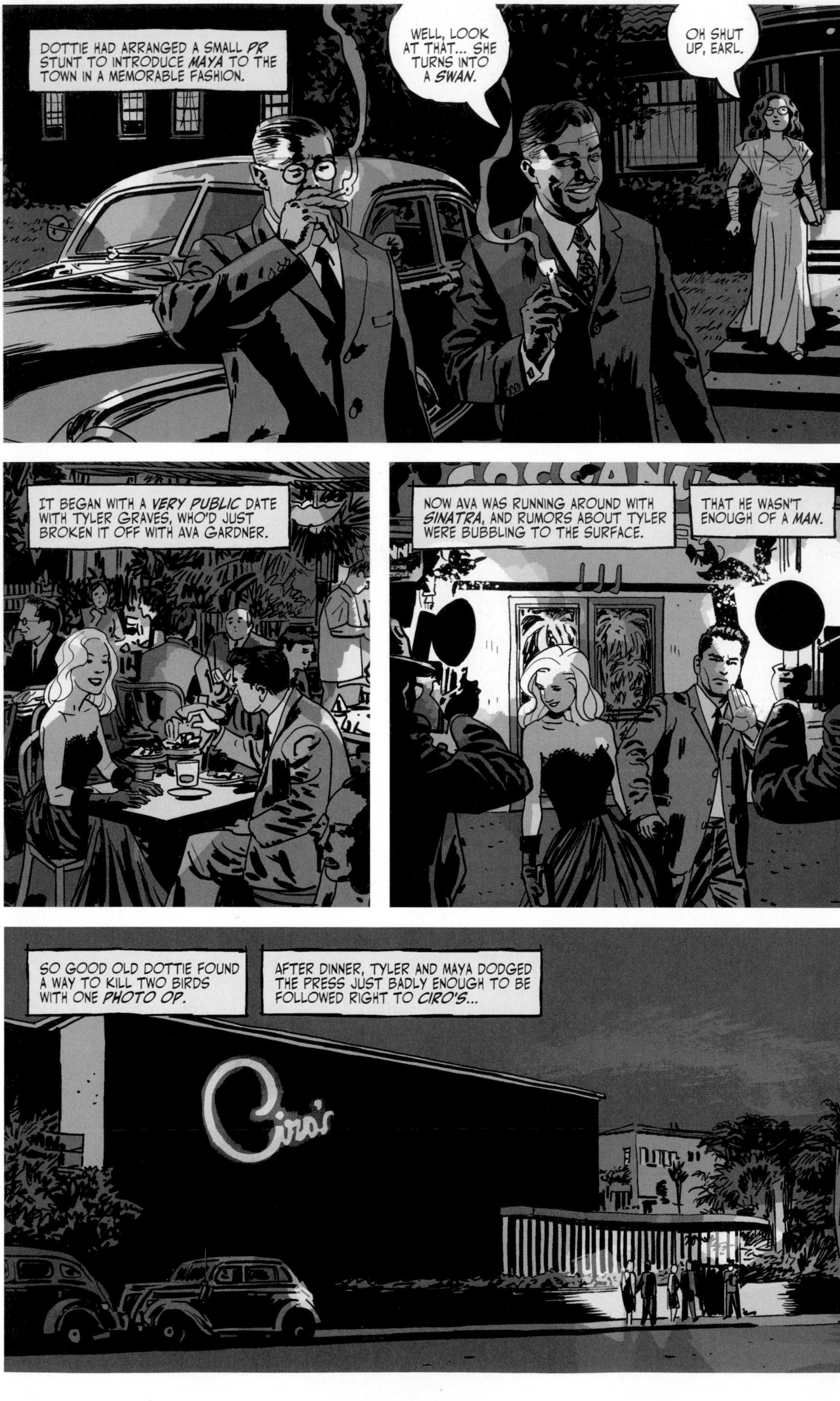

DOTTIE HAD ARRANGED A SMALL *PR* STUNT TO INTRODUCE *MAYA* TO THE TOWN IN A MEMORABLE FASHION.
WELL, LOOK AT THAT... SHE TURNS INTO A *SWAN*.
OH SHUT UP, EARL.
IT BEGAN WITH A *VERY PUBLIC* DATE WITH TYLER GRAVES, WHO'D JUST BROKEN IT OFF WITH AVA GARDNER.
NOW AVA WAS RUNNING AROUND WITH *SINATRA*, AND RUMORS ABOUT TYLER WERE BUBBLING TO THE SURFACE.
THAT HE WASN'T ENOUGH OF A *MAN*.
SO GOOD OLD DOTTIE FOUND A WAY TO KILL TWO BIRDS WITH ONE *PHOTO OP*.
AFTER DINNER, TYLER AND MAYA DODGED THE PRESS JUST BADLY ENOUGH TO BE FOLLOWED RIGHT TO *CIRO'S*...
Ciro's

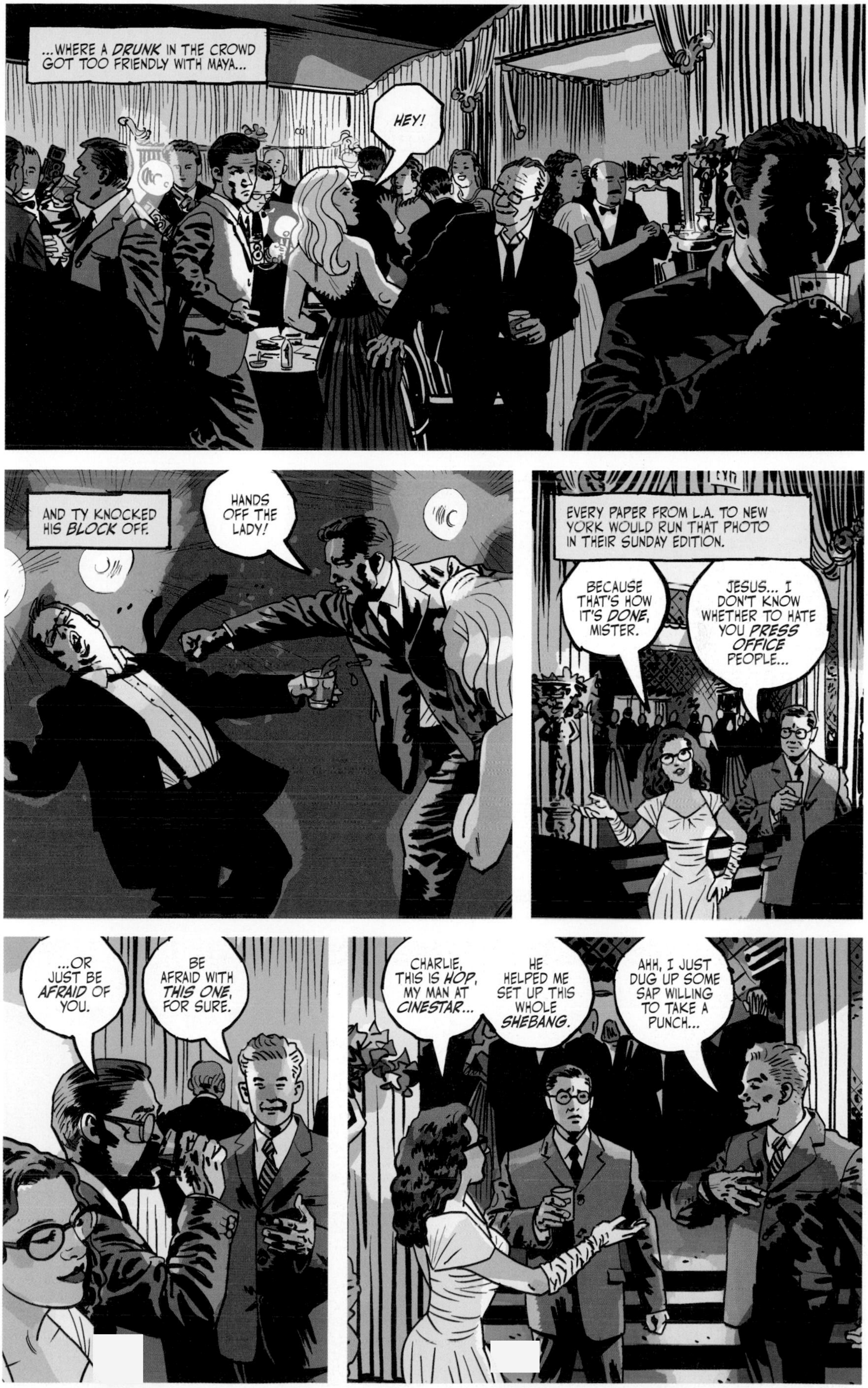
...WHERE A DRUNK IN THE CROWD GOT TOO FRIENDLY WITH MAYA...
HEY!
AND TY KNOCKED HIS BLOCK OFF.
HANDS OFF THE LADY!
EVERY PAPER FROM L.A. TO NEW YORK WOULD RUN THAT PHOTO IN THEIR SUNDAY EDITION.
JESUS... I DON'T KNOW WHETHER TO HATE YOU PRESS OFFICE PEOPLE...
BECAUSE THAT'S HOW IT'S DONE, MISTER.
...OR JUST BE AFRAID OF YOU.
BE AFRAID WITH THIS ONE, FOR SURE.
CHARLIE, THIS IS HOP, MY MAN AT CINESTAR...
HE HELPED ME SET UP THIS WHOLE SHEBANG.
AHH, I JUST DUG UP SOME SAP WILLING TO TAKE A PUNCH...

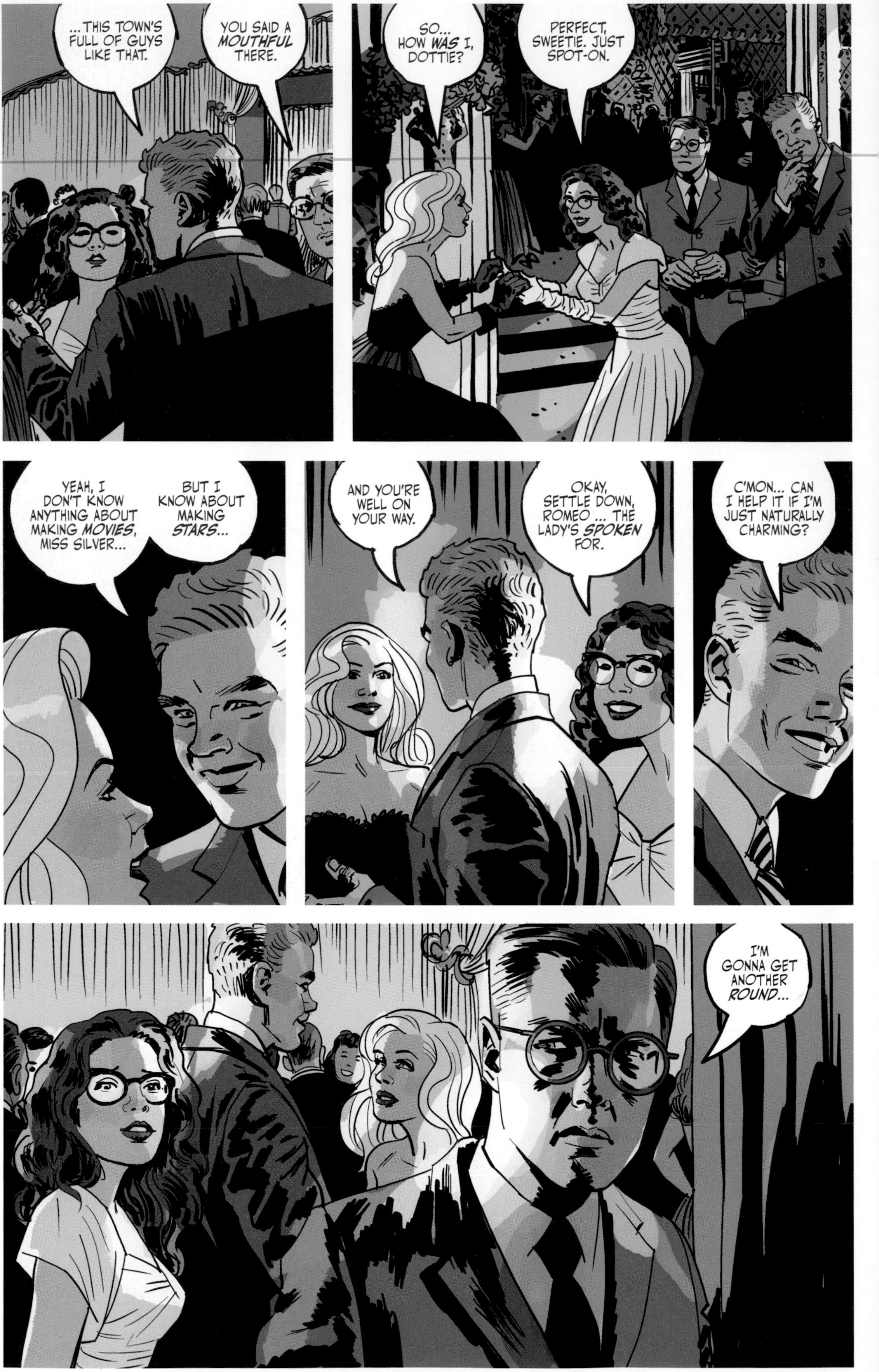
...THIS TOWN'S FULL OF GUYS LIKE THAT.
YOU SAID A *MOUTHFUL* THERE.
SO... HOW *WAS* I, DOTTIE?
PERFECT, SWEETIE. JUST SPOT-ON.
YEAH, I DON'T KNOW ANYTHING ABOUT MAKING *MOVIES*, MISS SILVER...
BUT I KNOW ABOUT MAKING *STARS*...
AND YOU'RE WELL ON YOUR WAY.
OKAY, SETTLE DOWN, ROMEO ... THE LADY'S *SPOKEN* FOR.
C'MON... CAN I HELP IT IF I'M JUST NATURALLY CHARMING?
I'M GONNA GET ANOTHER *ROUND*...

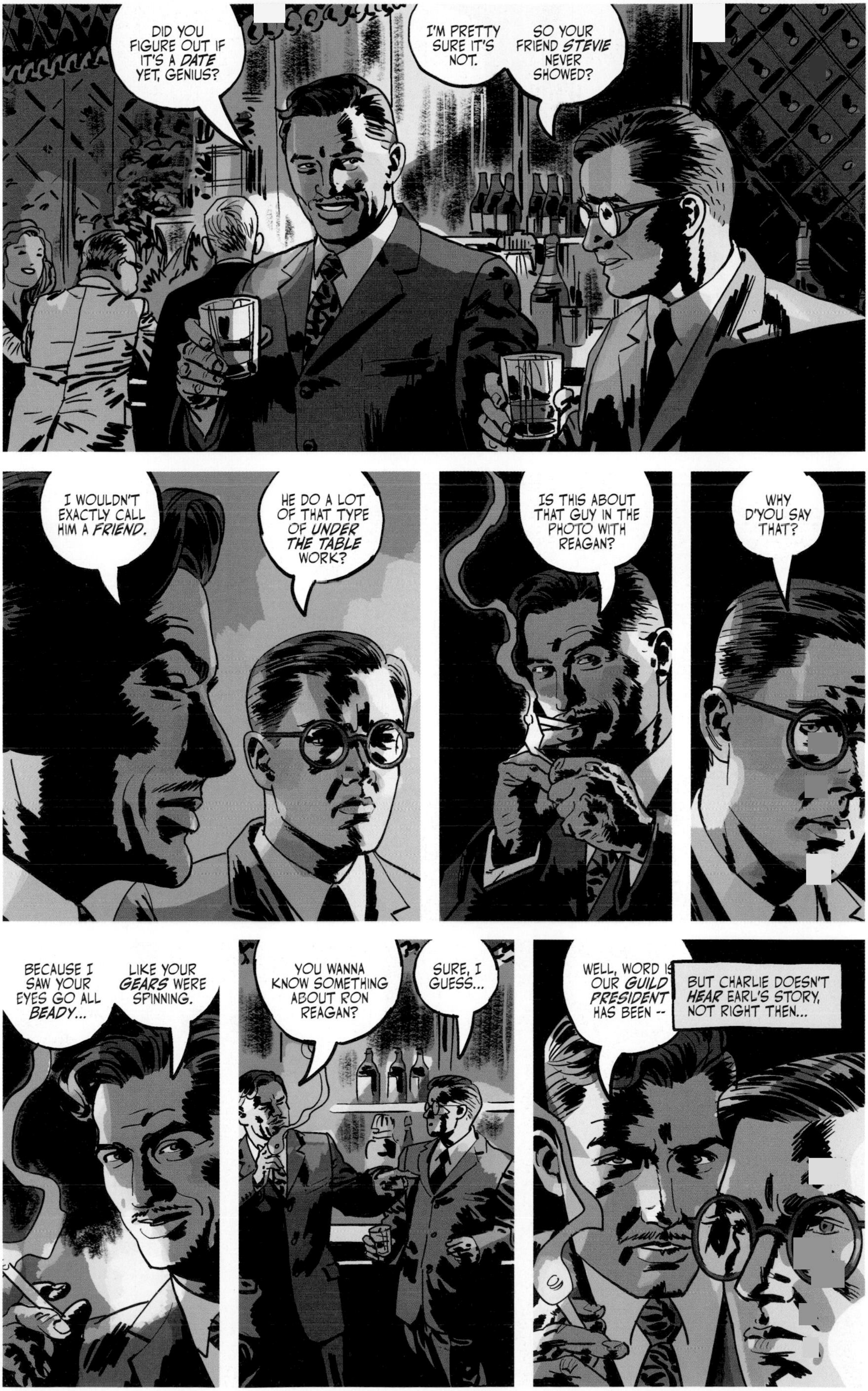
DID YOU FIGURE OUT IF IT'S A DATE YET, GENIUS?
I'M PRETTY SURE IT'S NOT.
SO YOUR FRIEND STEVIE NEVER SHOWED?
I WOULDN'T EXACTLY CALL HIM A FRIEND.
HE DO A LOT OF THAT TYPE OF UNDER THE TABLE WORK?
IS THIS ABOUT THAT GUY IN THE PHOTO WITH REAGAN?
WHY D'YOU SAY THAT?
BECAUSE I SAW YOUR EYES GO ALL BEADY...
LIKE YOUR GEARS WERE SPINNING.
YOU WANNA KNOW SOMETHING ABOUT RON REAGAN?
SURE, I GUESS...
WELL, WORD IS OUR GUILD PRESIDENT HAS BEEN --
BUT CHARLIE DOESN'T HEAR EARL'S STORY, NOT RIGHT THEN...

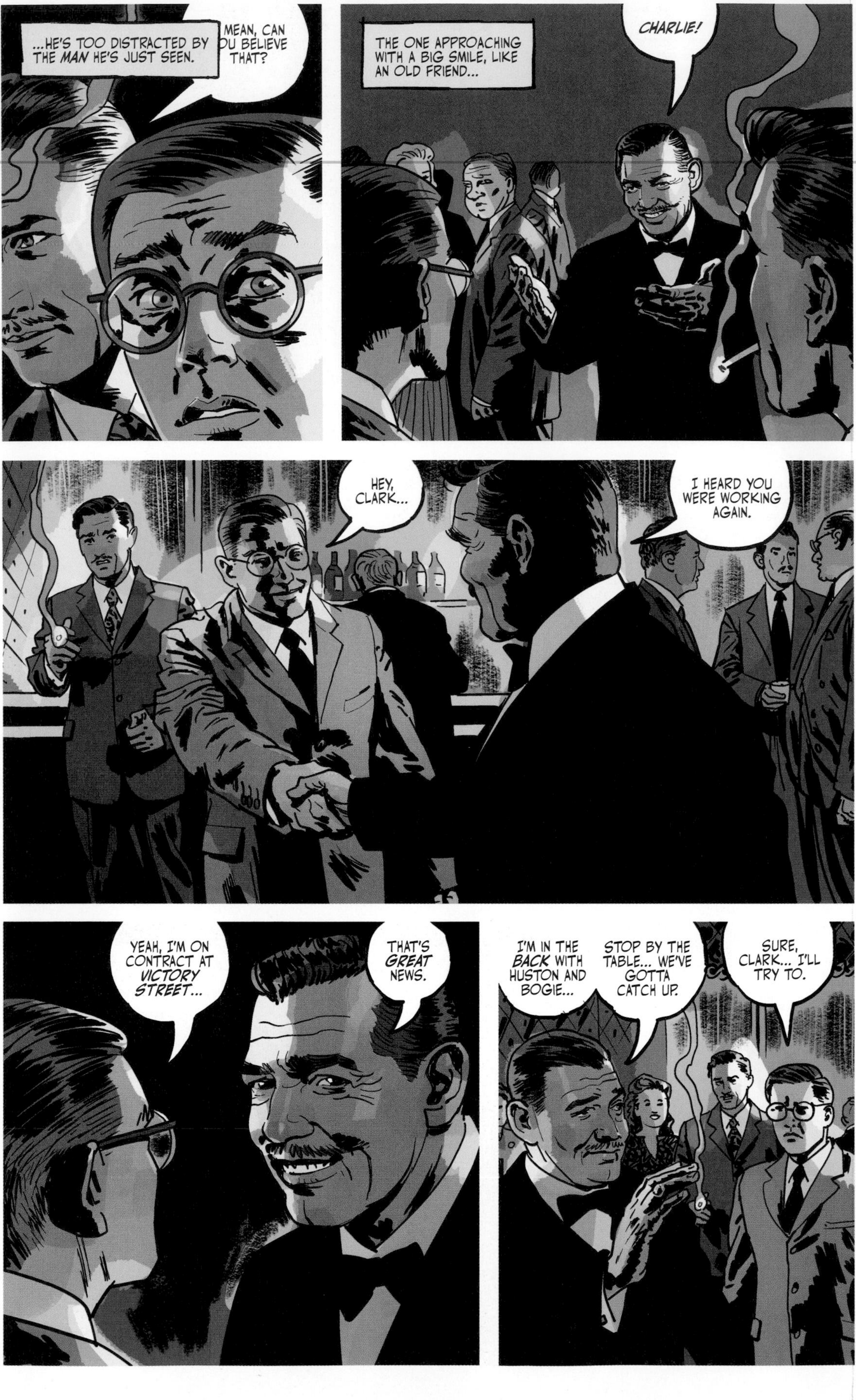
...HE'S TOO DISTRACTED BY THE MAN HE'S JUST SEEN.
MEAN, CAN OU BELIEVE THAT?
THE ONE APPROACHING WITH A BIG SMILE, LIKE AN OLD FRIEND...
CHARLIE!
HEY, CLARK...
I HEARD YOU WERE WORKING AGAIN.
YEAH, I'M ON CONTRACT AT VICTORY STREET...
THAT'S GREAT NEWS.
I'M IN THE BACK WITH HUSTON AND BOGIE...
STOP BY THE TABLE... WE'VE GOTTA CATCH UP.
SURE, CLARK... I'LL TRY TO.

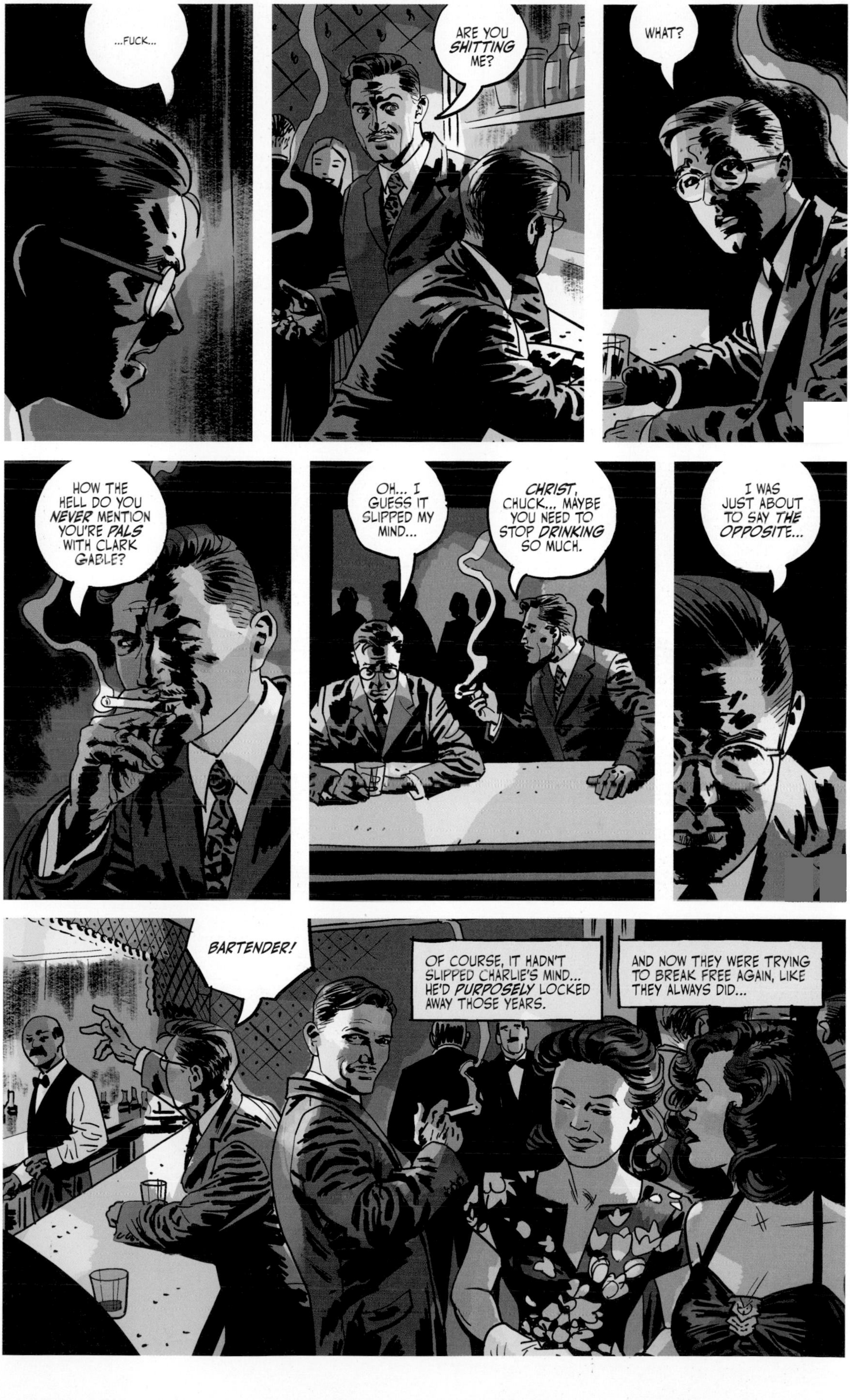

...FUCK...
ARE YOU *SHITTING* ME?
WHAT?
HOW THE HELL DO YOU *NEVER* MENTION YOU'RE *PALS* WITH CLARK GABLE?
OH... I GUESS IT SLIPPED MY MIND...
CHRIST, CHUCK... MAYBE YOU NEED TO STOP *DRINKING* SO MUCH.
I WAS JUST ABOUT TO SAY *THE OPPOSITE*...
BARTENDER!
OF COURSE, IT HADN'T SLIPPED CHARLIE'S MIND... HE'D *PURPOSELY* LOCKED AWAY THOSE YEARS.
AND NOW THEY WERE TRYING TO BREAK FREE AGAIN, LIKE THEY ALWAYS DID...

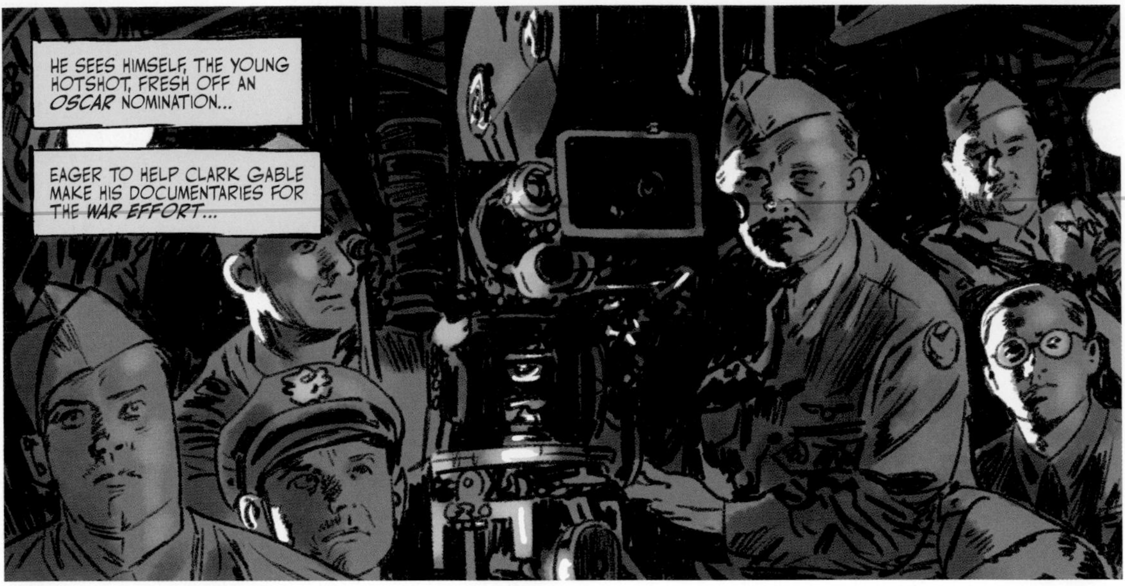
HE SEES HIMSELF, THE YOUNG HOTSHOT, FRESH OFF AN OSCAR NOMINATION...
EAGER TO HELP CLARK GABLE MAKE HIS DOCUMENTARIES FOR THE WAR EFFORT...

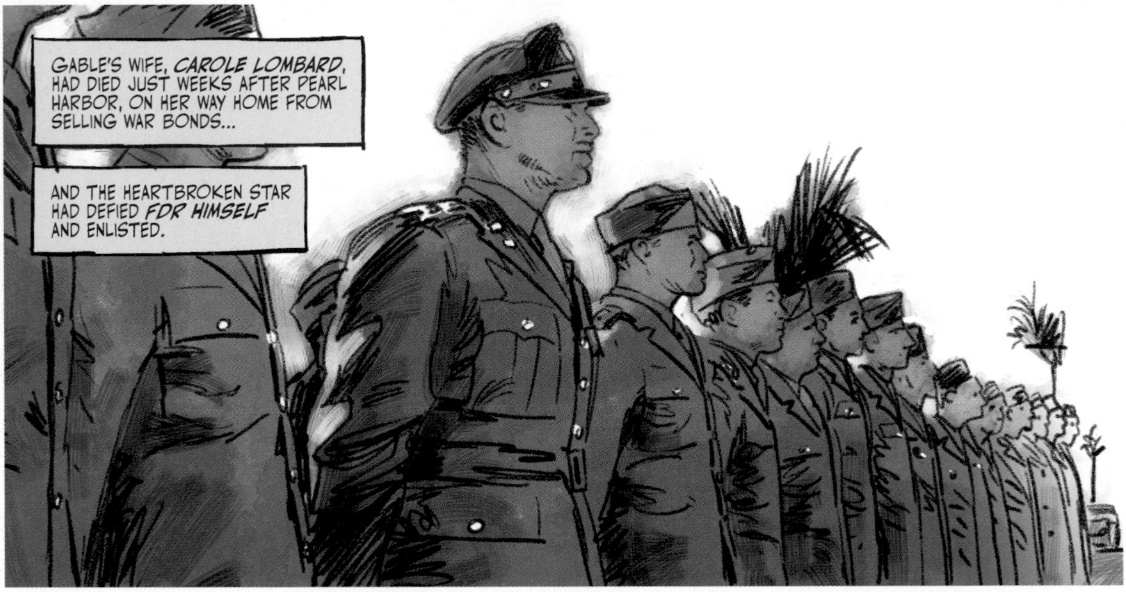
GABLE'S WIFE, CAROLE LOMBARD, HAD DIED JUST WEEKS AFTER PEARL HARBOR, ON HER WAY HOME FROM SELLING WAR BONDS...
AND THE HEARTBROKEN STAR HAD DEFIED FDR HIMSELF AND ENLISTED.

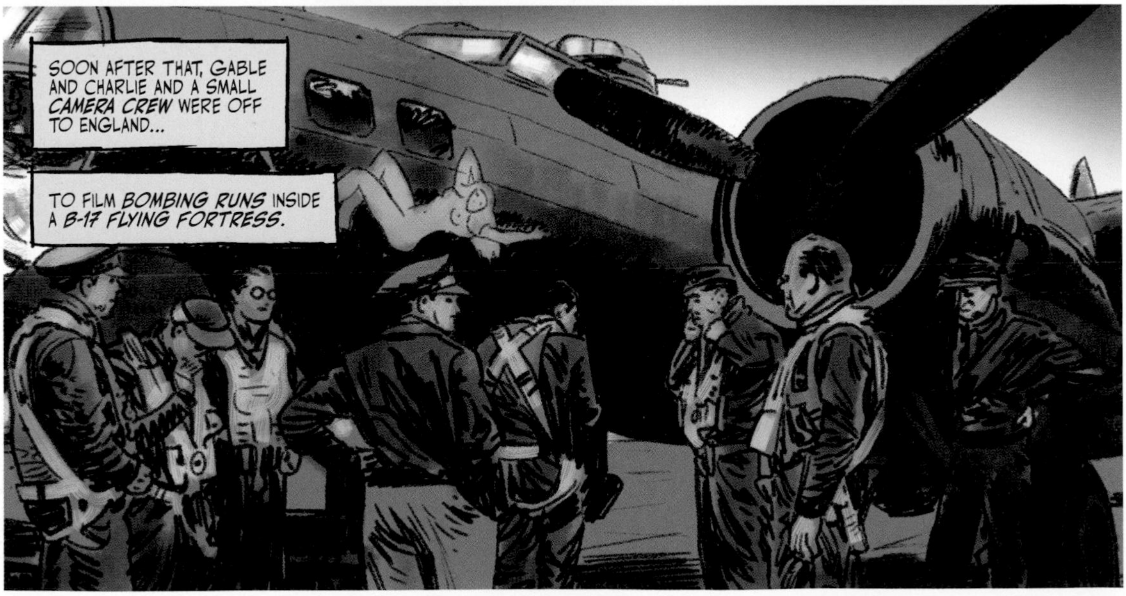
SOON AFTER THAT, GABLE AND CHARLIE AND A SMALL CAMERA CREW WERE OFF TO ENGLAND...
TO FILM BOMBING RUNS INSIDE A B-17 FLYING FORTRESS.

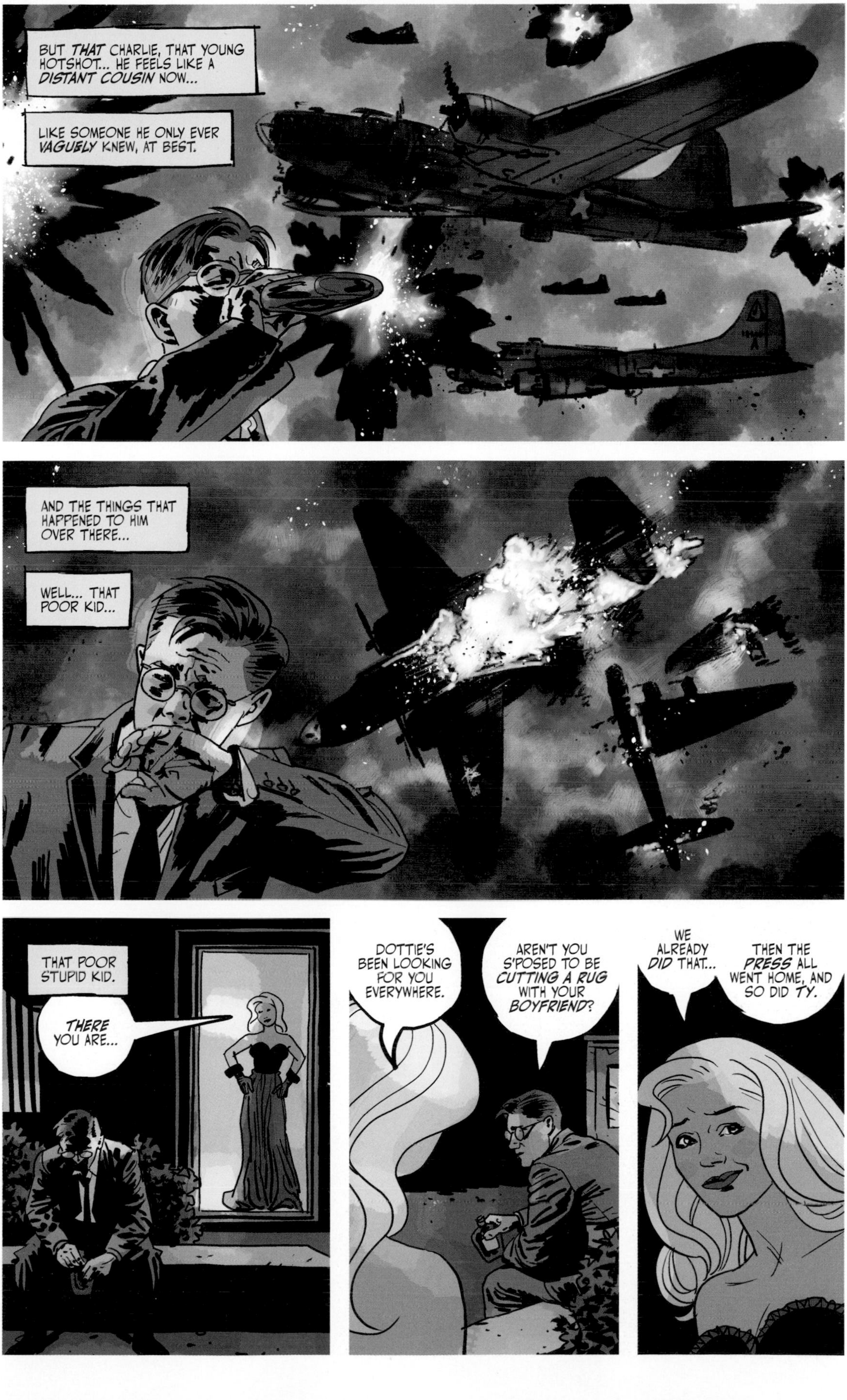
BUT THAT CHARLIE, THAT YOUNG HOTSHOT... HE FEELS LIKE A DISTANT COUSIN NOW...
LIKE SOMEONE HE ONLY EVER VAGUELY KNEW, AT BEST.
AND THE THINGS THAT HAPPENED TO HIM OVER THERE...
WELL... THAT POOR KID...
THAT POOR STUPID KID.
THERE YOU ARE...
DOTTIE'S BEEN LOOKING FOR YOU EVERYWHERE.
AREN'T YOU S'POSED TO BE CUTTING A RUG WITH YOUR BOYFRIEND?
WE ALREADY DID THAT...
THEN THE PRESS ALL WENT HOME, AND SO DID TY.

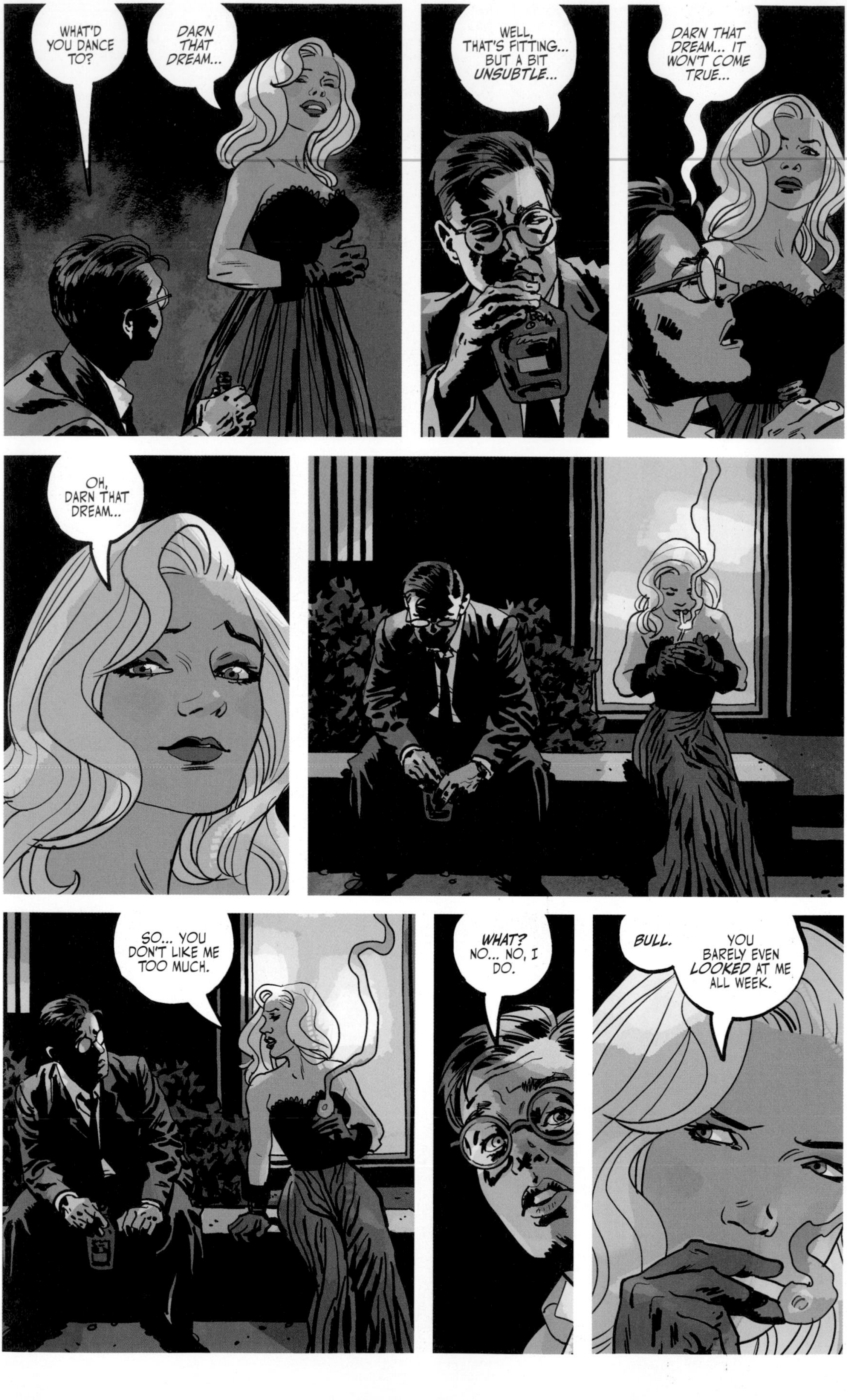
WHAT'D YOU DANCE TO?
DARN THAT DREAM...
WELL, THAT'S FITTING... BUT A BIT UNSUBTLE...
DARN THAT DREAM... IT WON'T COME TRUE...
OH, DARN THAT DREAM...
SO... YOU DON'T LIKE ME TOO MUCH.
WHAT? NO... NO, I DO.
BULL.
YOU BARELY EVEN LOOKED AT ME ALL WEEK.

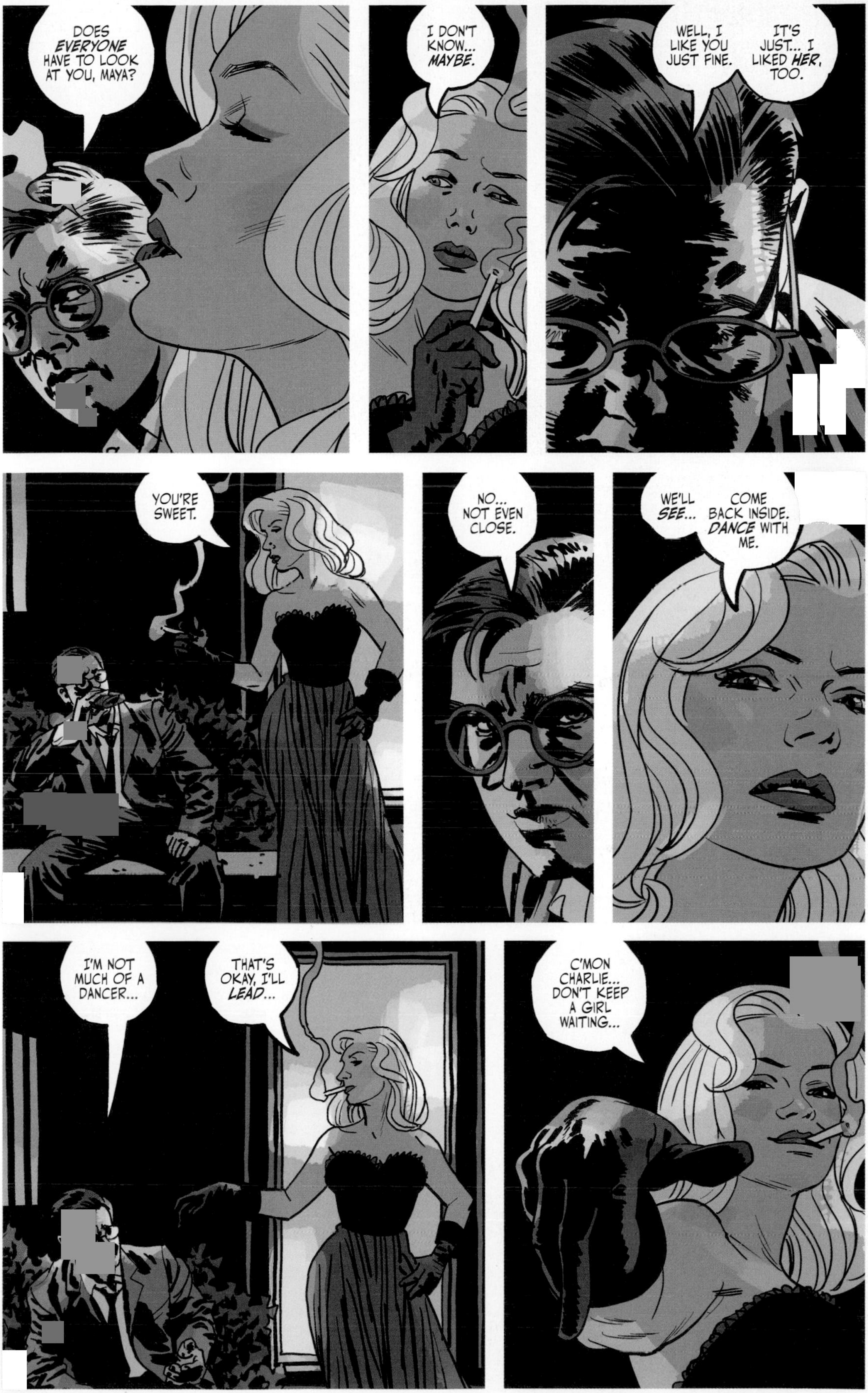
DOES EVERYONE HAVE TO LOOK AT YOU, MAYA?
I DON'T KNOW... MAYBE.
WELL, I LIKE YOU JUST FINE.
IT'S JUST... I LIKED HER, TOO.
YOU'RE SWEET.
NO... NOT EVEN CLOSE.
WE'LL SEE...
COME BACK INSIDE. DANCE WITH ME.
I'M NOT MUCH OF A DANCER...
THAT'S OKAY, I'LL LEAD...
C'MON CHARLIE... DON'T KEEP A GIRL WAITING...

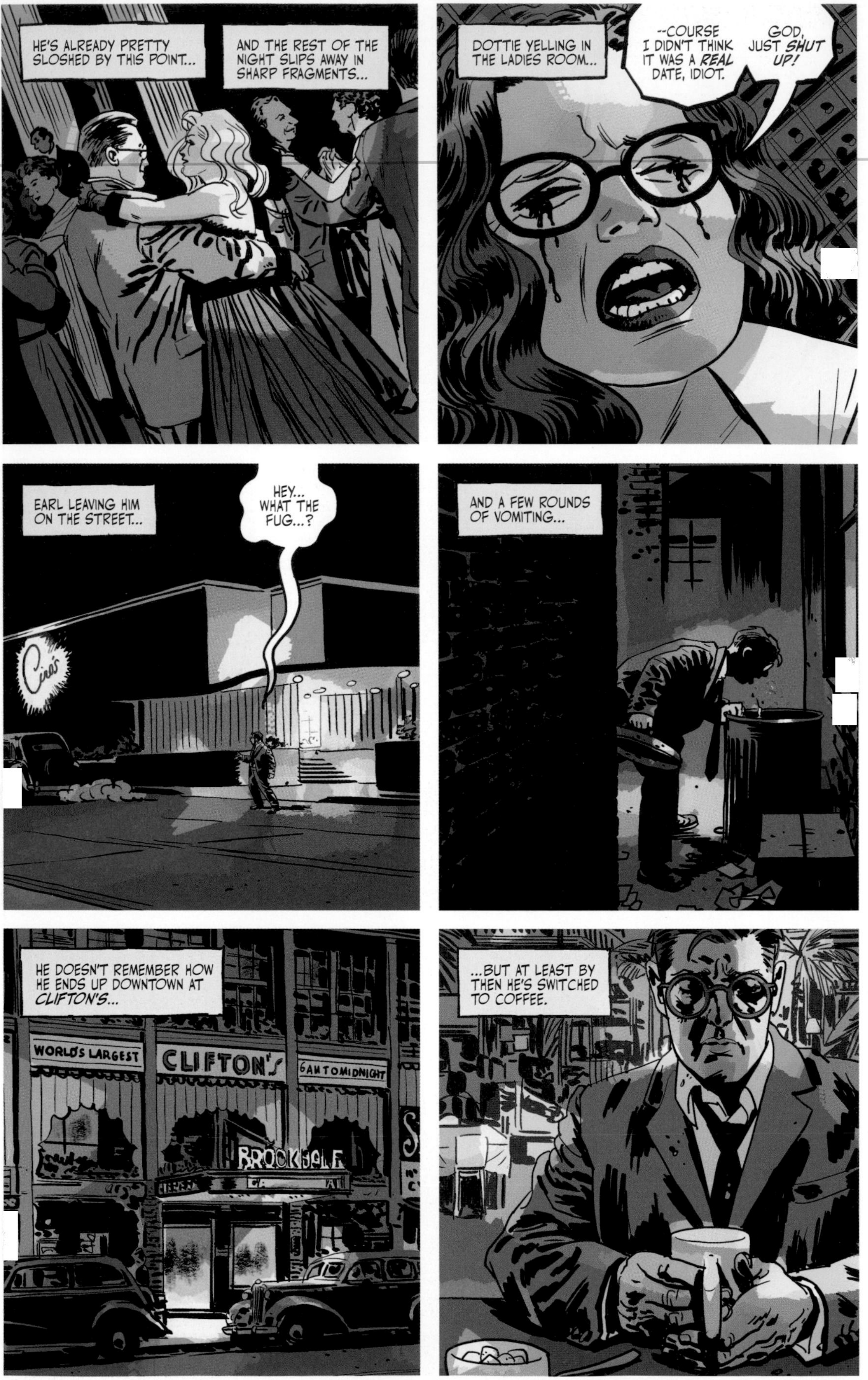

HE'S ALREADY PRETTY SLOSHED BY THIS POINT...
AND THE REST OF THE NIGHT SLIPS AWAY IN SHARP FRAGMENTS...
DOTTIE YELLING IN THE LADIES ROOM...
--COURSE I DIDN'T THINK IT WAS A REAL DATE, IDIOT.
GOD, JUST SHUT UP!
EARL LEAVING HIM ON THE STREET...
HEY... WHAT THE FUG...?
AND A FEW ROUNDS OF VOMITING...
HE DOESN'T REMEMBER HOW HE ENDS UP DOWNTOWN AT CLIFTON'S...
WORLD'S LARGEST
CLIFTON'S
6AM TO MIDNIGHT
BROOKDALE
...BUT AT LEAST BY THEN HE'S SWITCHED TO COFFEE.

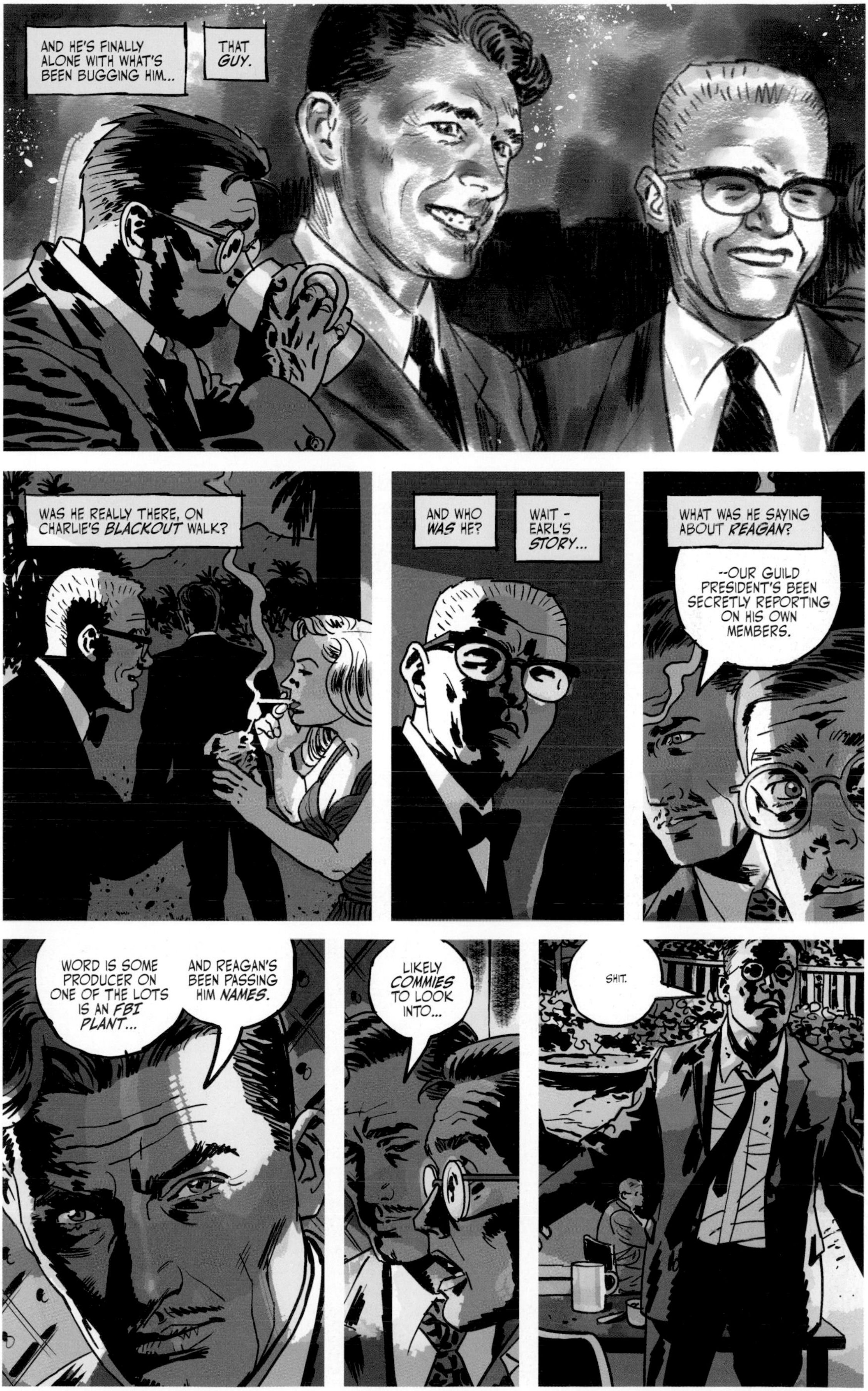
AND HE'S FINALLY ALONE WITH WHAT'S BEEN BUGGING HIM...
THAT *GUY*.
WAS HE REALLY THERE, ON CHARLIE'S *BLACKOUT* WALK?
AND WHO *WAS* HE?
WAIT - EARL'S *STORY*...
WHAT WAS HE SAYING ABOUT *REAGAN*?
--OUR GUILD PRESIDENT'S BEEN SECRETLY REPORTING ON HIS OWN MEMBERS.
WORD IS SOME PRODUCER ON ONE OF THE LOTS IS AN *FBI PLANT*...
AND REAGAN'S BEEN PASSING HIM *NAMES*.
LIKELY *COMMIES* TO LOOK INTO...
SHIT.

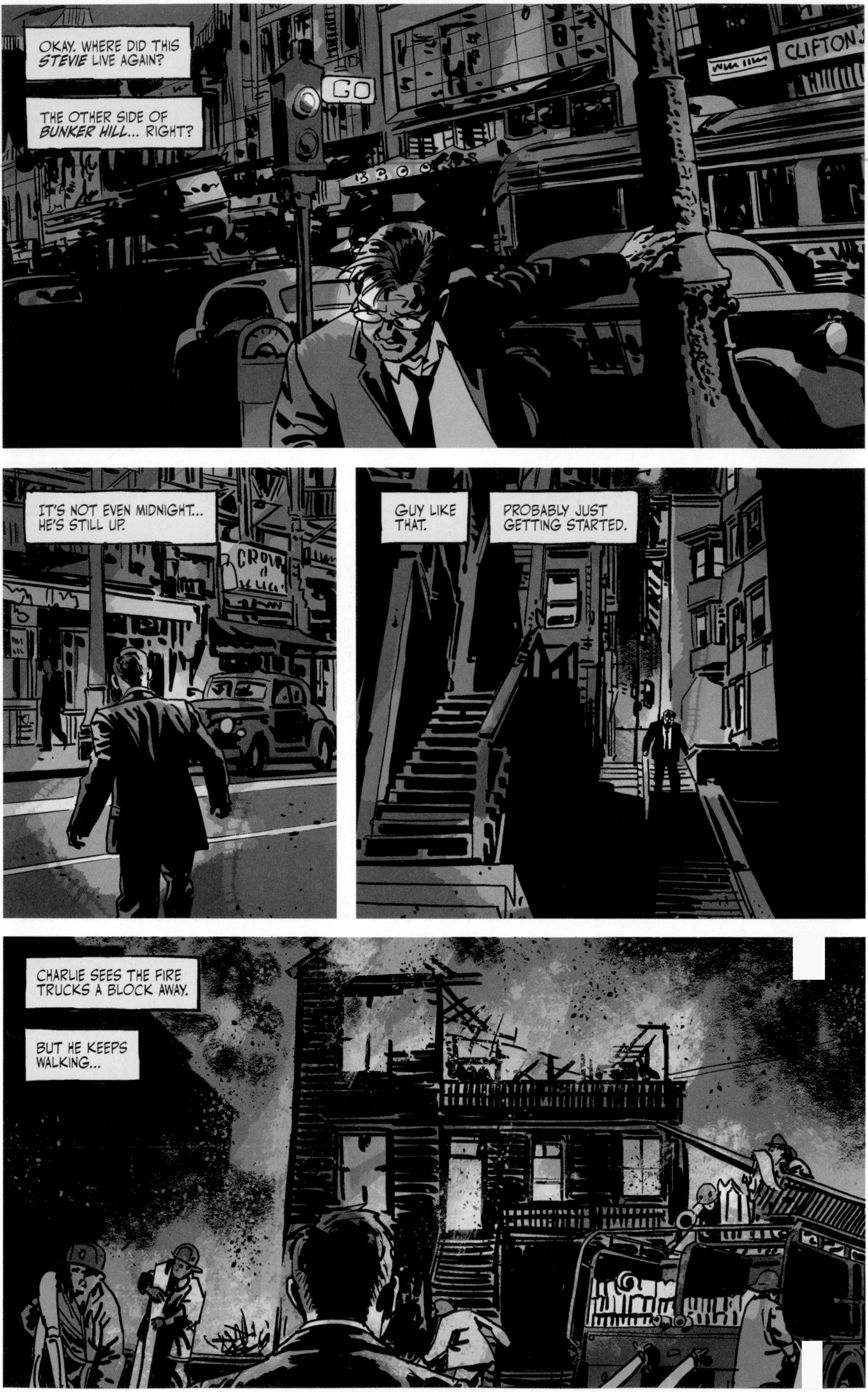
OKAY. WHERE DID THIS *STEVIE* LIVE AGAIN?
THE OTHER SIDE OF *BUNKER HILL*... RIGHT?
GO
CLIFTON'S
IT'S NOT EVEN MIDNIGHT... HE'S STILL UP.
GUY LIKE THAT.
PROBABLY JUST GETTING STARTED.
CHARLIE SEES THE FIRE TRUCKS A BLOCK AWAY.
BUT HE KEEPS WALKING...

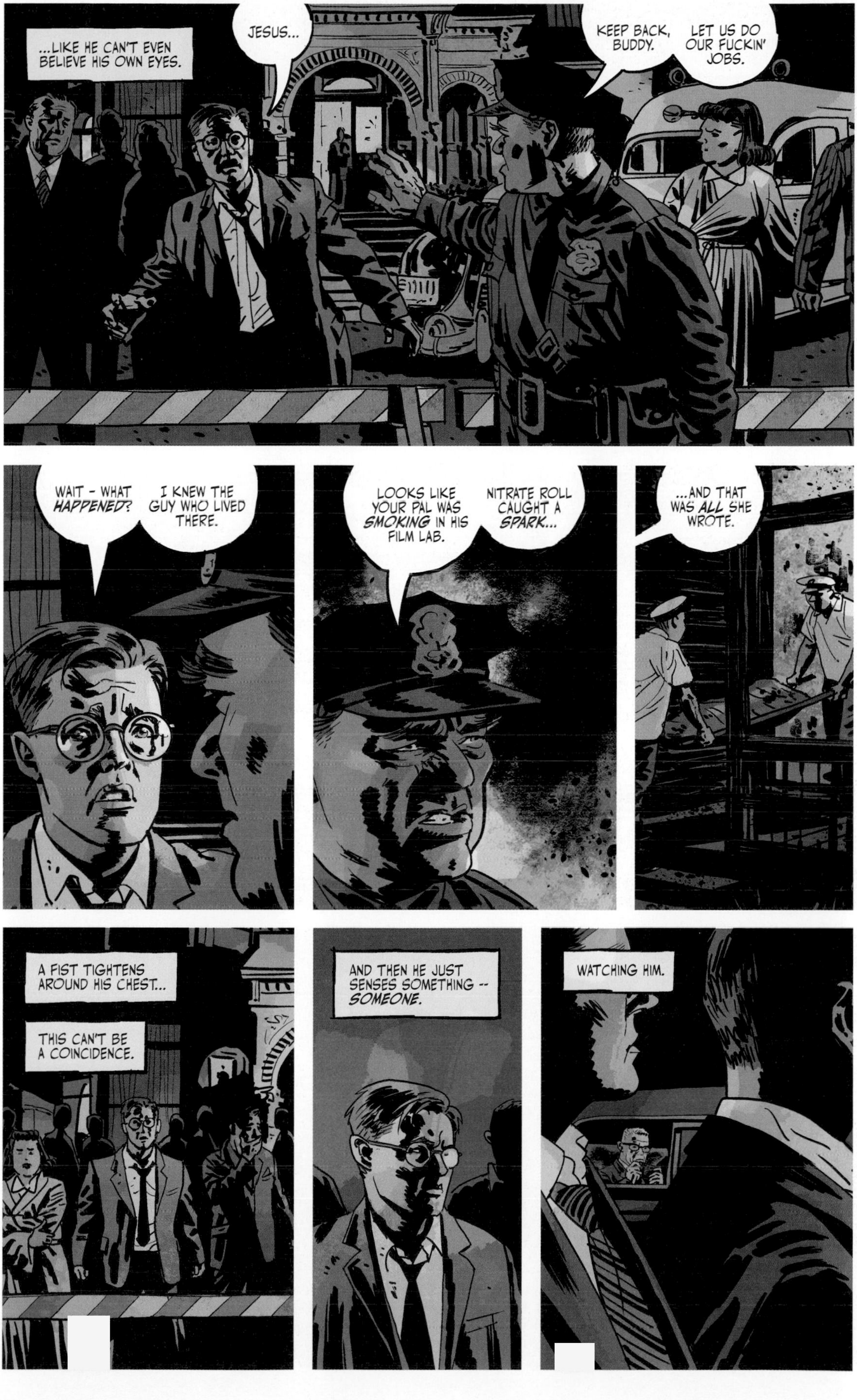
...LIKE HE CAN'T EVEN BELIEVE HIS OWN EYES.
JESUS...
KEEP BACK, BUDDY.
LET US DO OUR FUCKIN' JOBS.
WAIT - WHAT *HAPPENED*?
I KNEW THE GUY WHO LIVED THERE.
LOOKS LIKE YOUR PAL WAS *SMOKING* IN HIS FILM LAB.
NITRATE ROLL CAUGHT A *SPARK*...
...AND THAT WAS *ALL* SHE WROTE.
A FIST TIGHTENS AROUND HIS CHEST...
THIS CAN'T BE A COINCIDENCE.
AND THEN HE JUST SENSES SOMETHING -- *SOMEONE*.
WATCHING HIM.

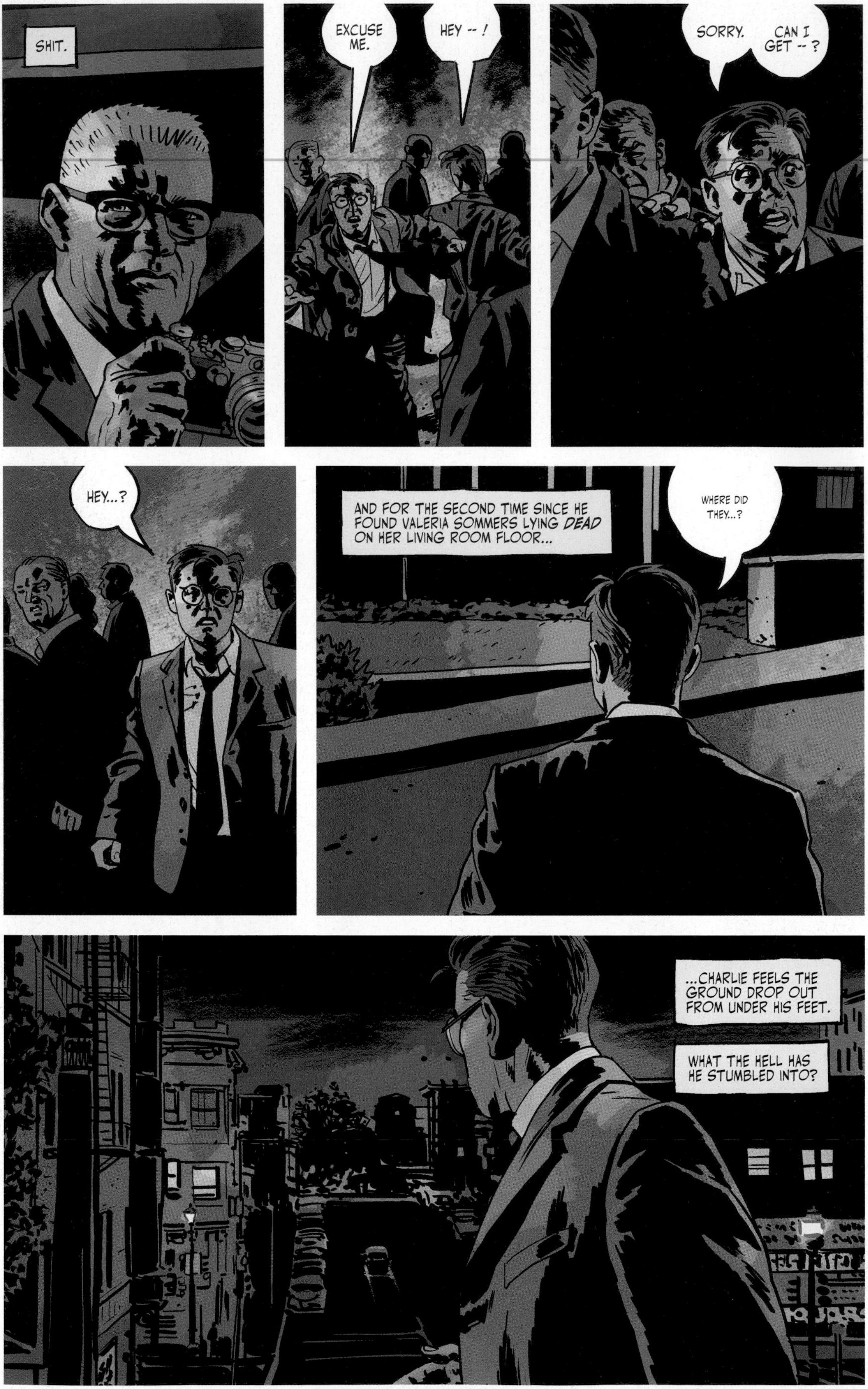
SHIT.
EXCUSE ME.
HEY -- !
SORRY.
CAN I GET -- ?
HEY...?
AND FOR THE SECOND TIME SINCE HE FOUND VALERIA SOMMERS LYING DEAD ON HER LIVING ROOM FLOOR...
WHERE DID THEY...?
...CHARLIE FEELS THE GROUND DROP OUT FROM UNDER HIS FEET.
WHAT THE HELL HAS HE STUMBLED INTO?

End of Act One

The covers from original serialization

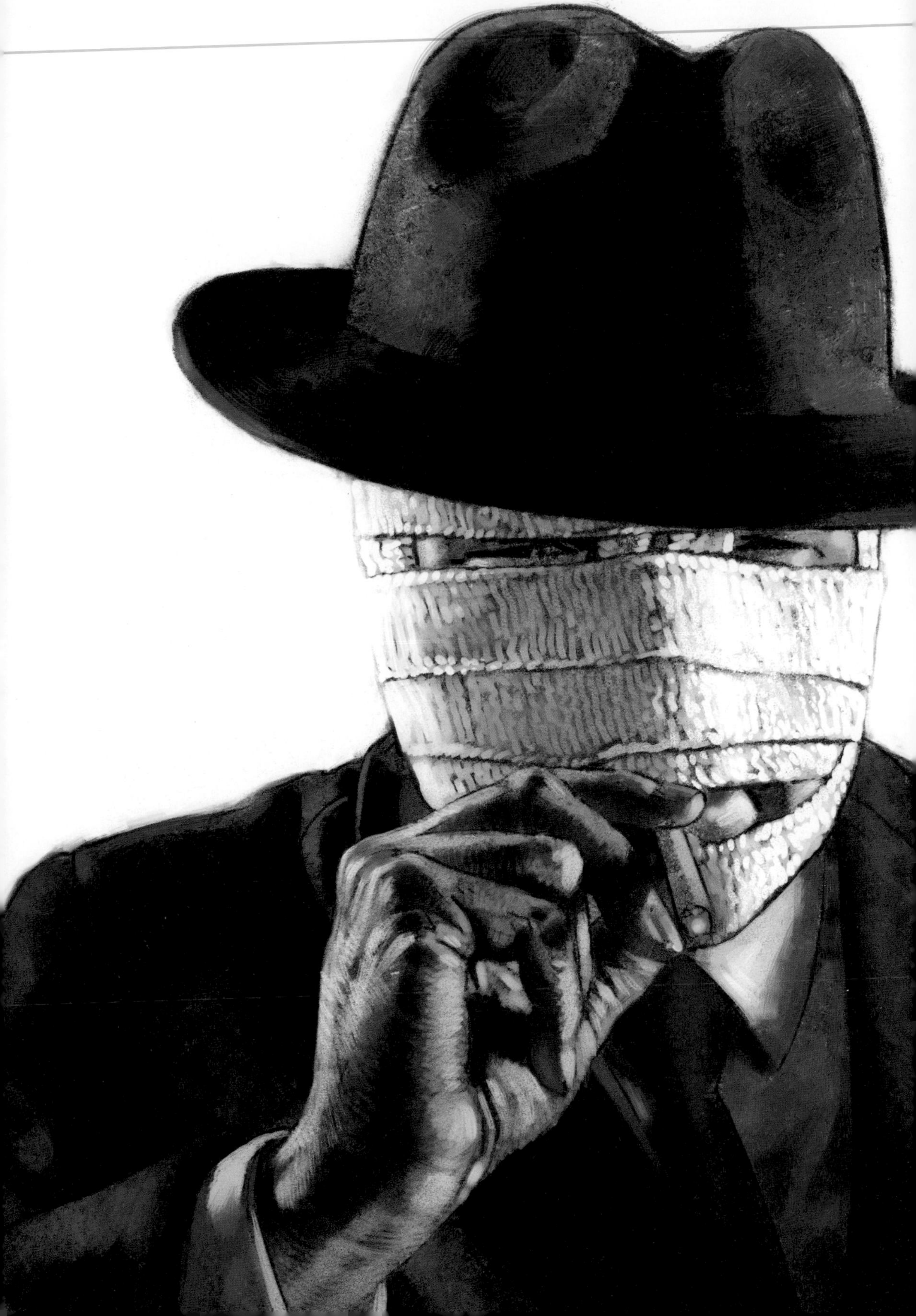

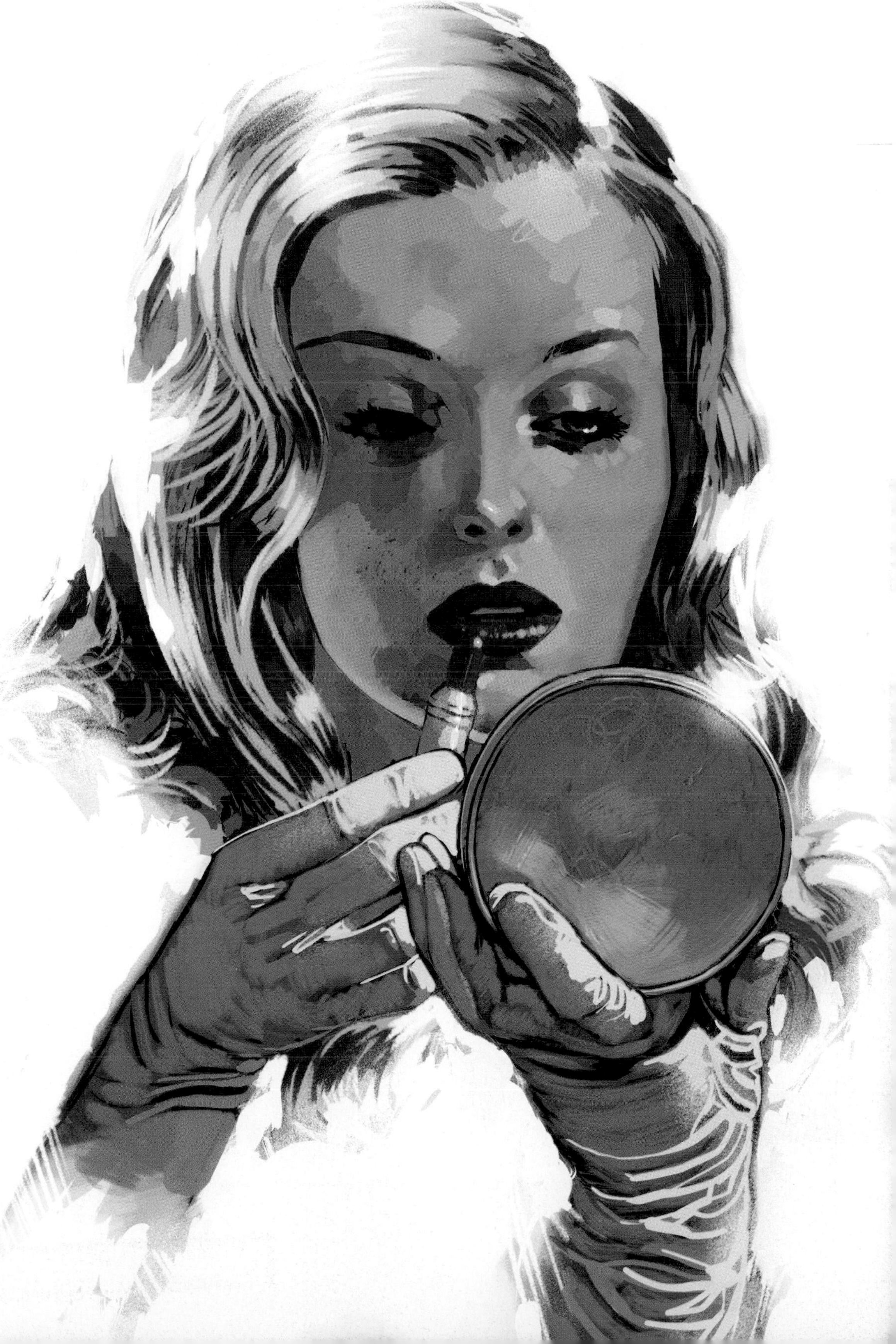

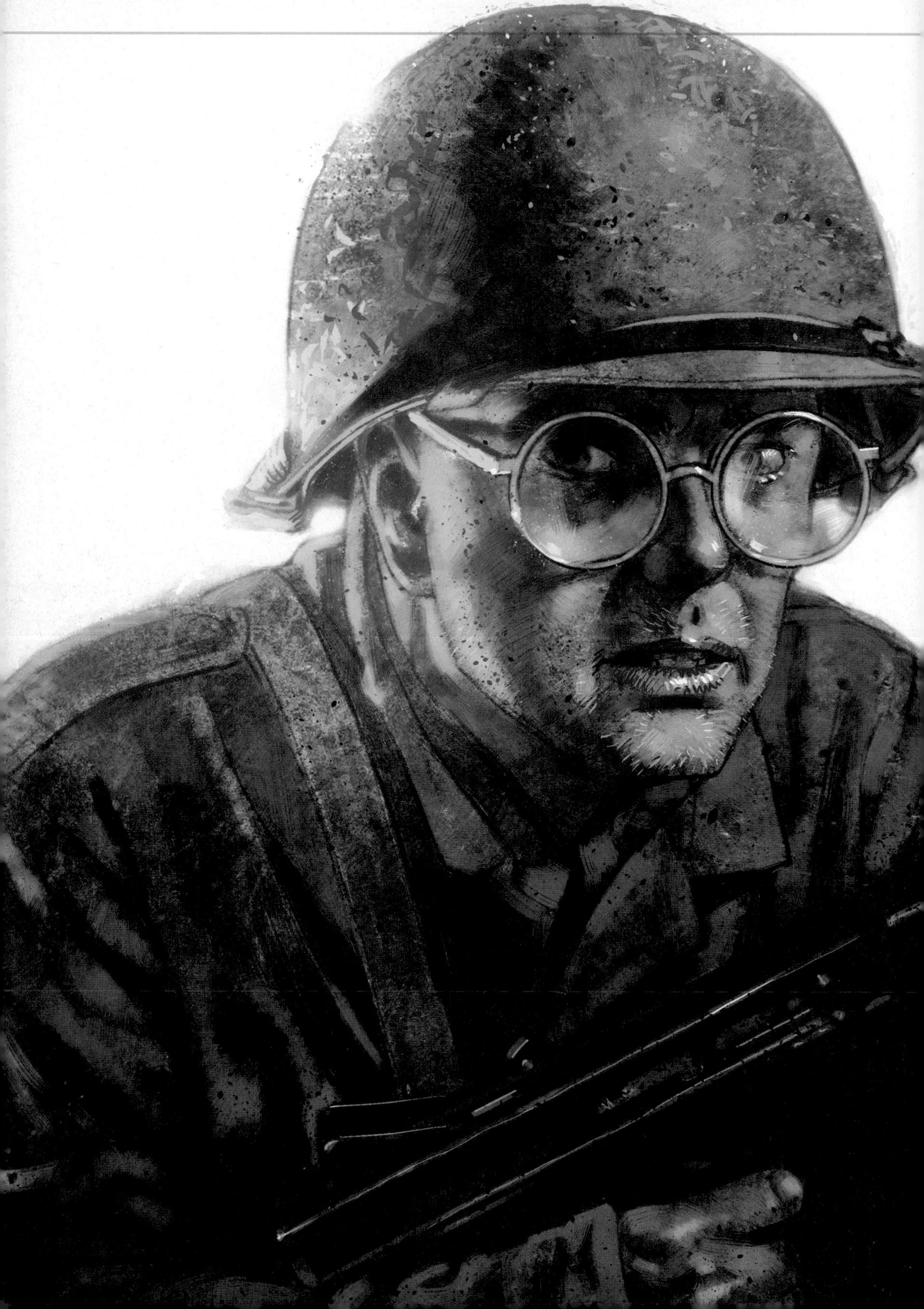